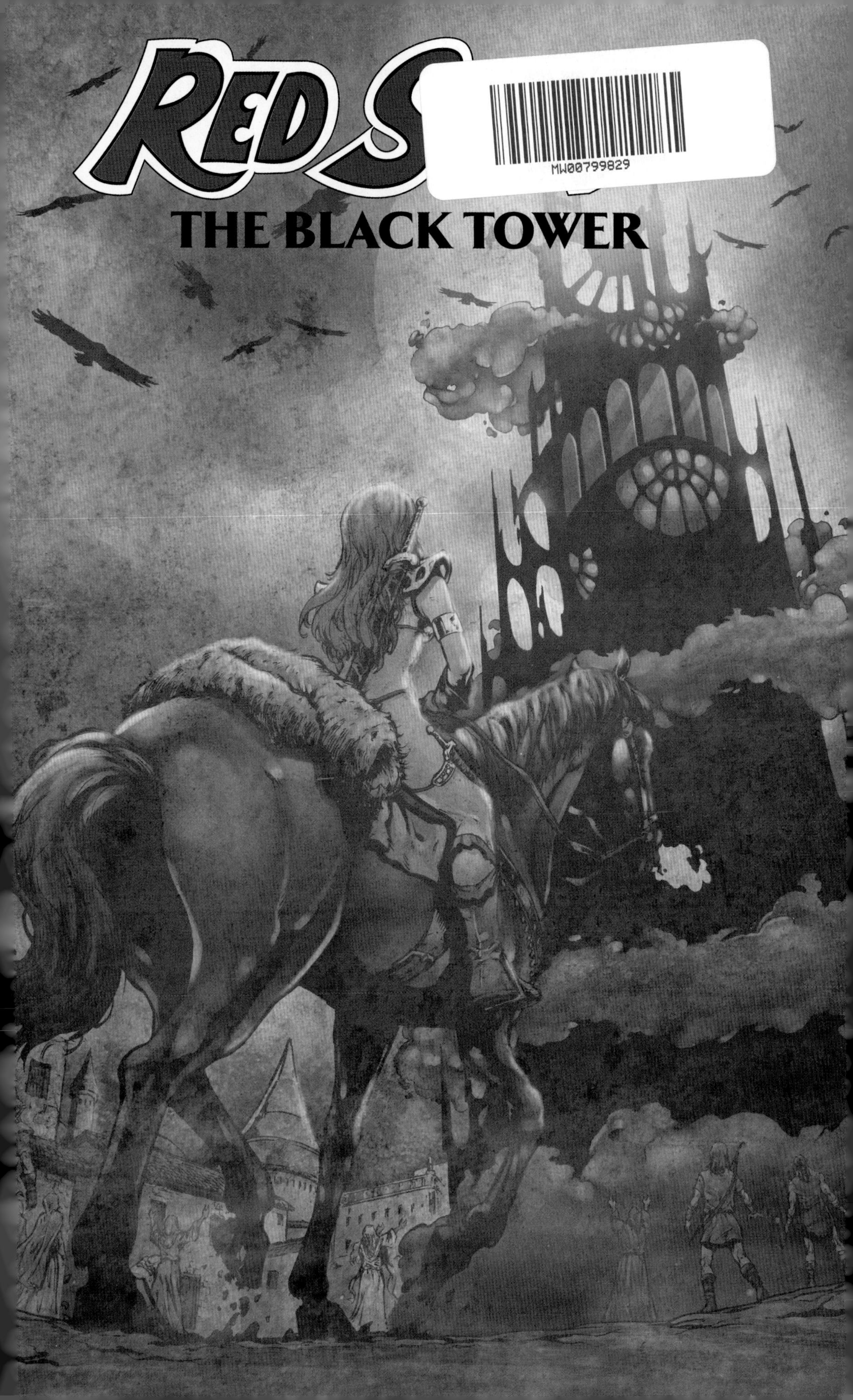
THE BLACK TOWER

RED SONJA

THE BLACK TOWER

written by FRANK TIERI

art by CEZAR RAZEK

colors by SALVATORE AIALA STUDIOS

letters by SIMON BOWLAND

main cover art by AMANDA CONNER

main cover colors by PAUL MOUNTS

collection design by GEOFF HARKINS

edited by JOSEPH RYBANDT
based on the heroine created by ROBERT E. HOWARD
executive editor - Red Sonja LUKE LIEBERMAN
in memory of ARTHUR LIEBERMAN

DYNAMITE

Nick Barrucci, CEO / Publisher
Juan Collado, President / COO
Joe Rybandt, Senior Editor

Jason Ullmeyer, Design Director
Katie Hidalgo, Graphic Designer
Geoff Harkins, Graphic Designer
Chris Caniano, Digital Associate
Rachel Kilbury, Digital Assistant

Rich Young, Director Business Development
Keith Davidsen, Marketing Manager
Kevin Pearl, Sales Associate

Visit us online at **www.DYNAMITE.com**
Follow us on Twitter **@dynamitecomics**
Like us on Facebook **/Dynamitecomics**
Watch us on YouTube **/Dynamitecomics**

First Printing
ISBN-10: 1-60690-792-1
ISBN-13: 978-1-60690-792-4
10 9 8 7 6 5 4 3 2 1

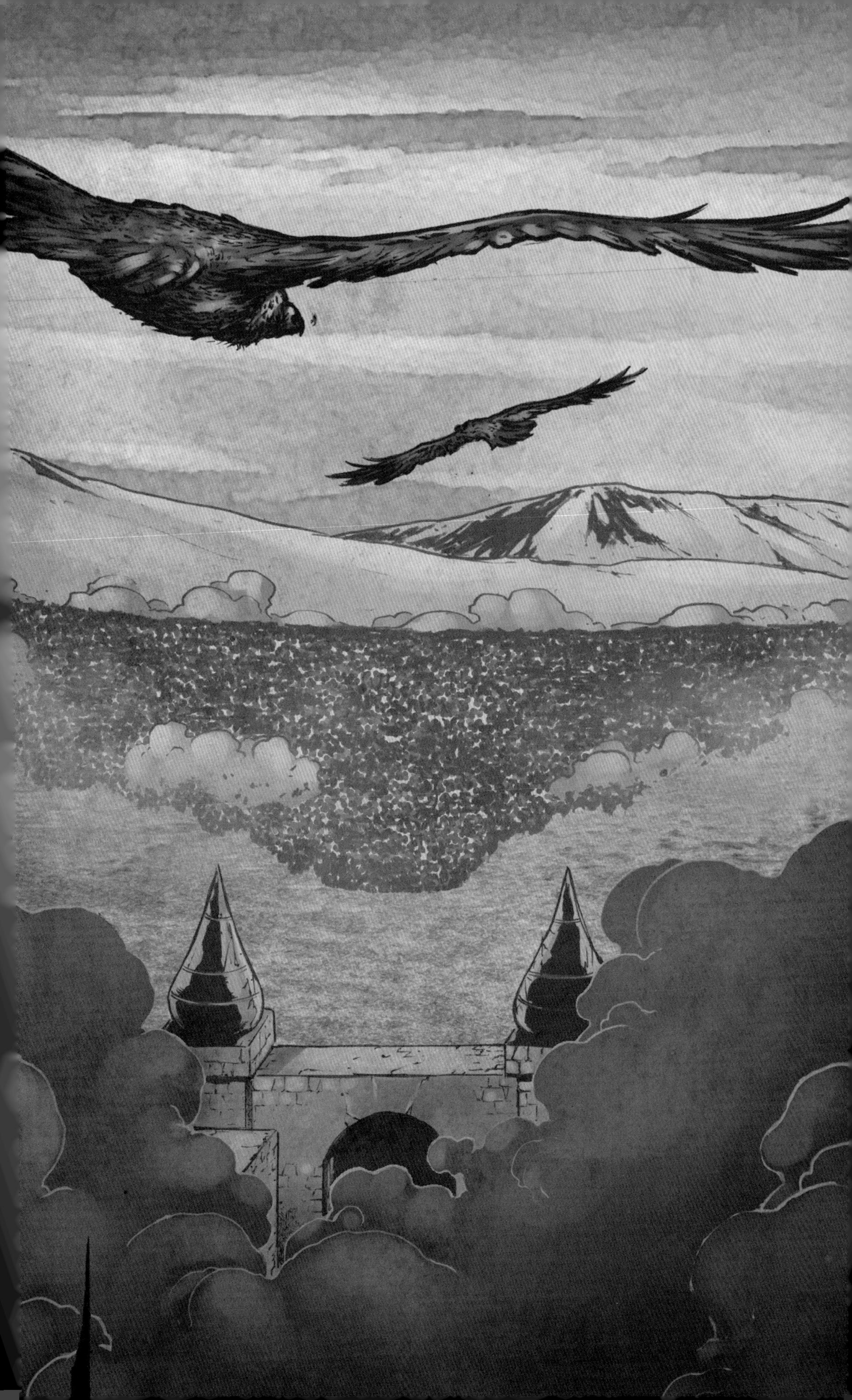

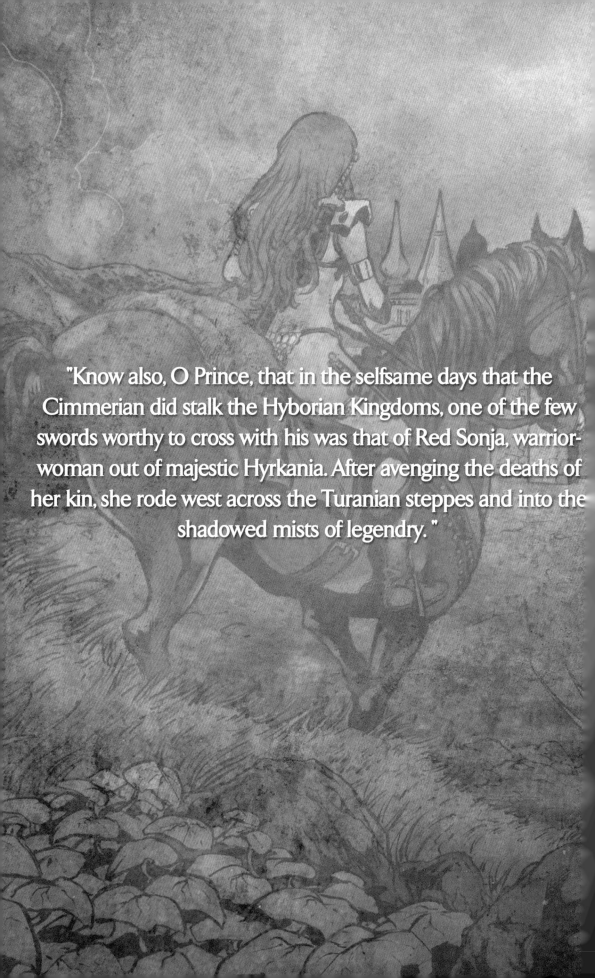

"Know also, O Prince, that in the selfsame days that the Cimmerian did stalk the Hyborian Kingdoms, one of the few swords worthy to cross with his was that of Red Sonja, warrior-woman out of majestic Hyrkania. After avenging the deaths of her kin, she rode west across the Turanian steppes and into the shadowed mists of legendry."

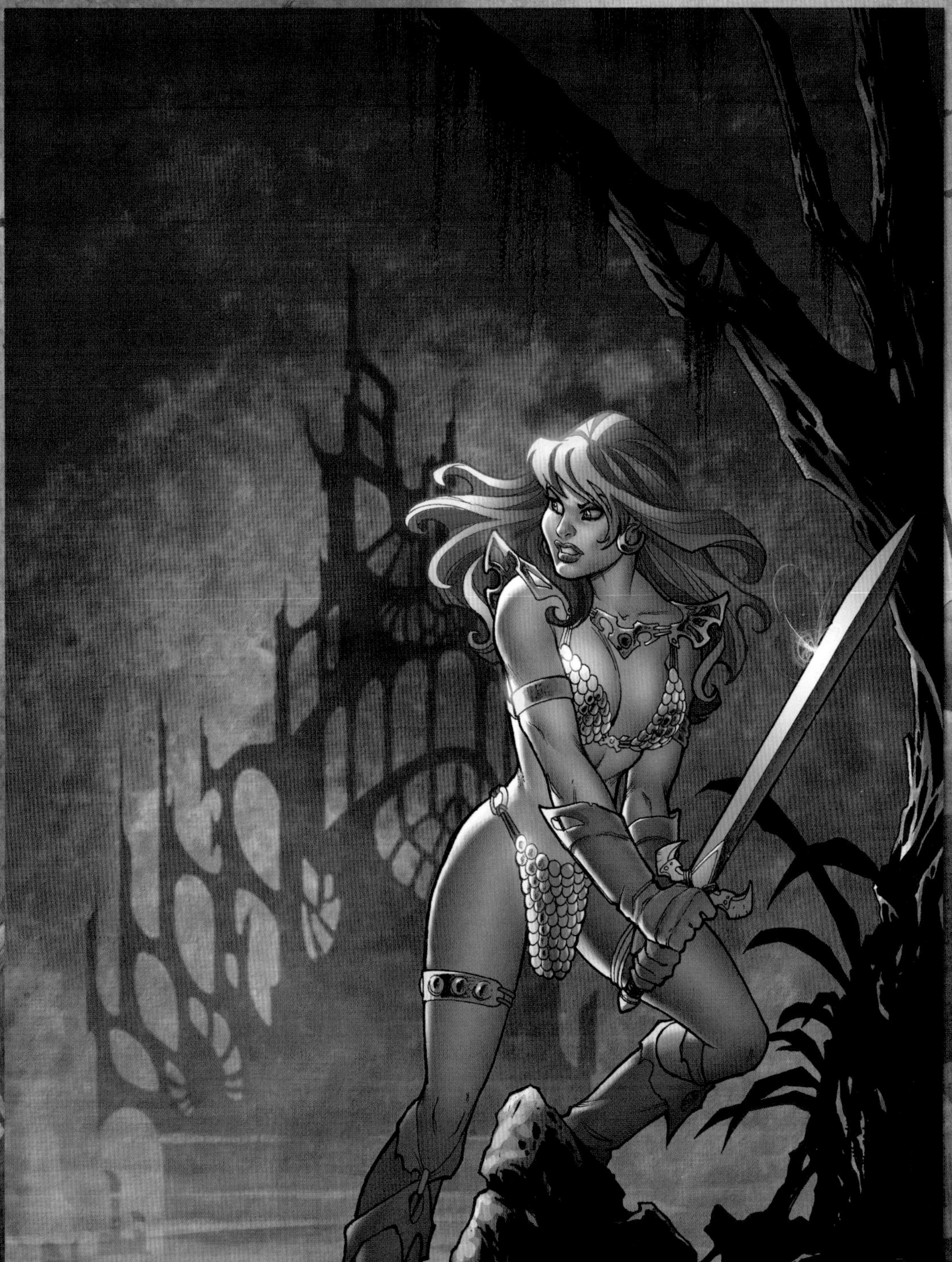
CONNER

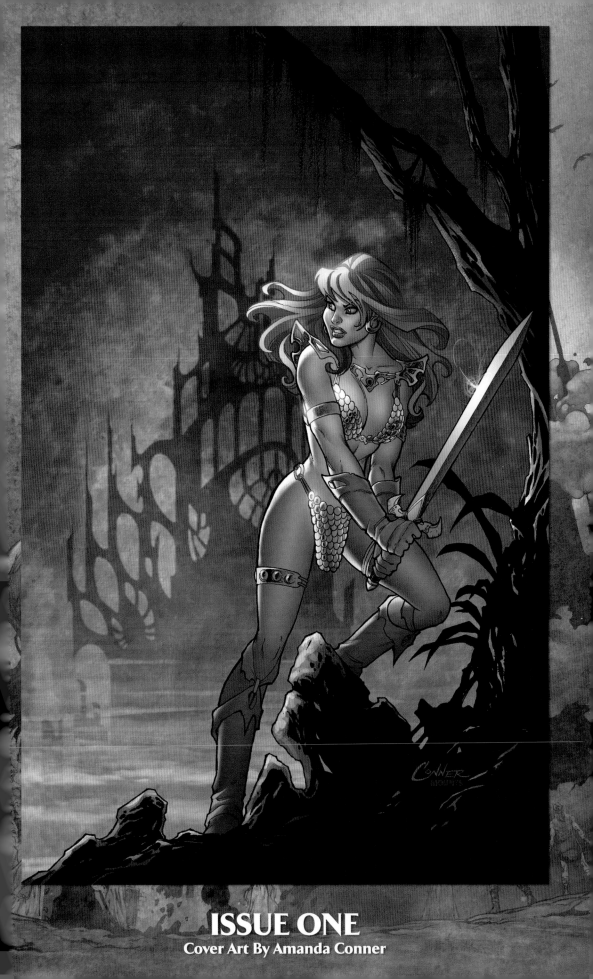

ISSUE ONE
Cover Art By Amanda Conner

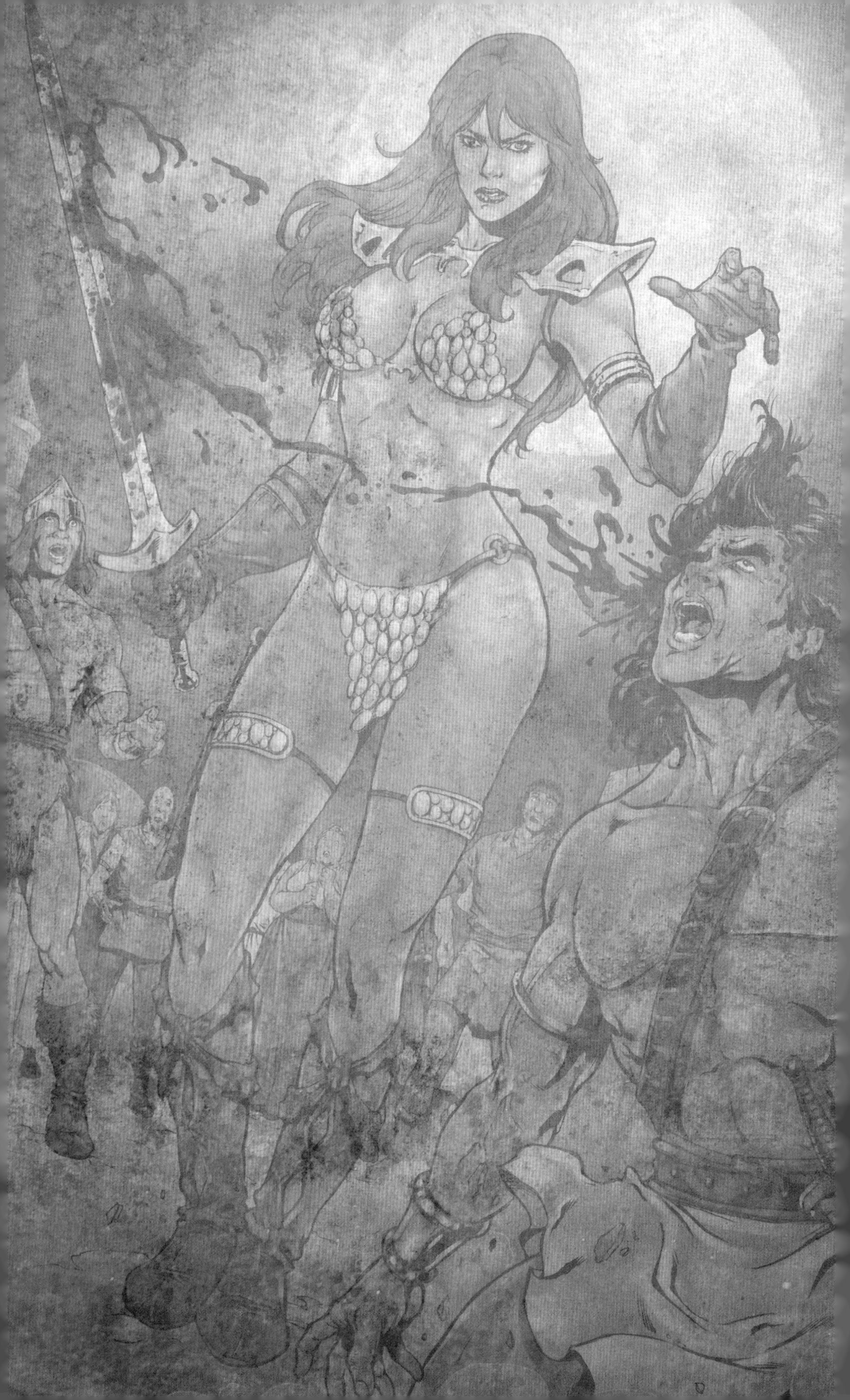

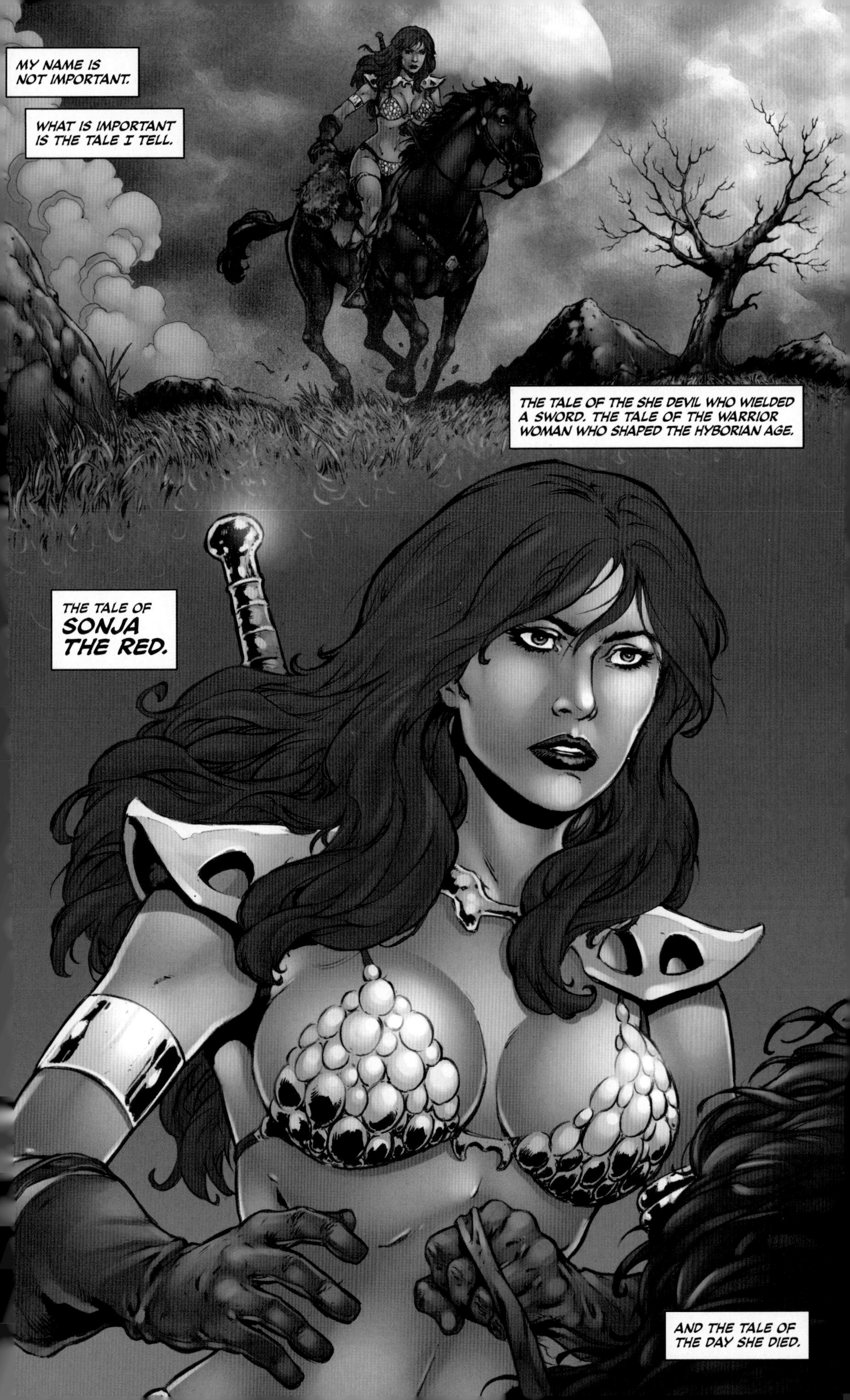
MY NAME IS NOT IMPORTANT.
WHAT IS IMPORTANT IS THE TALE I TELL.
THE TALE OF THE SHE DEVIL WHO WIELDED A SWORD. THE TALE OF THE WARRIOR WOMAN WHO SHAPED THE HYBORIAN AGE.
THE TALE OF SONJA THE RED.
AND THE TALE OF THE DAY SHE DIED.

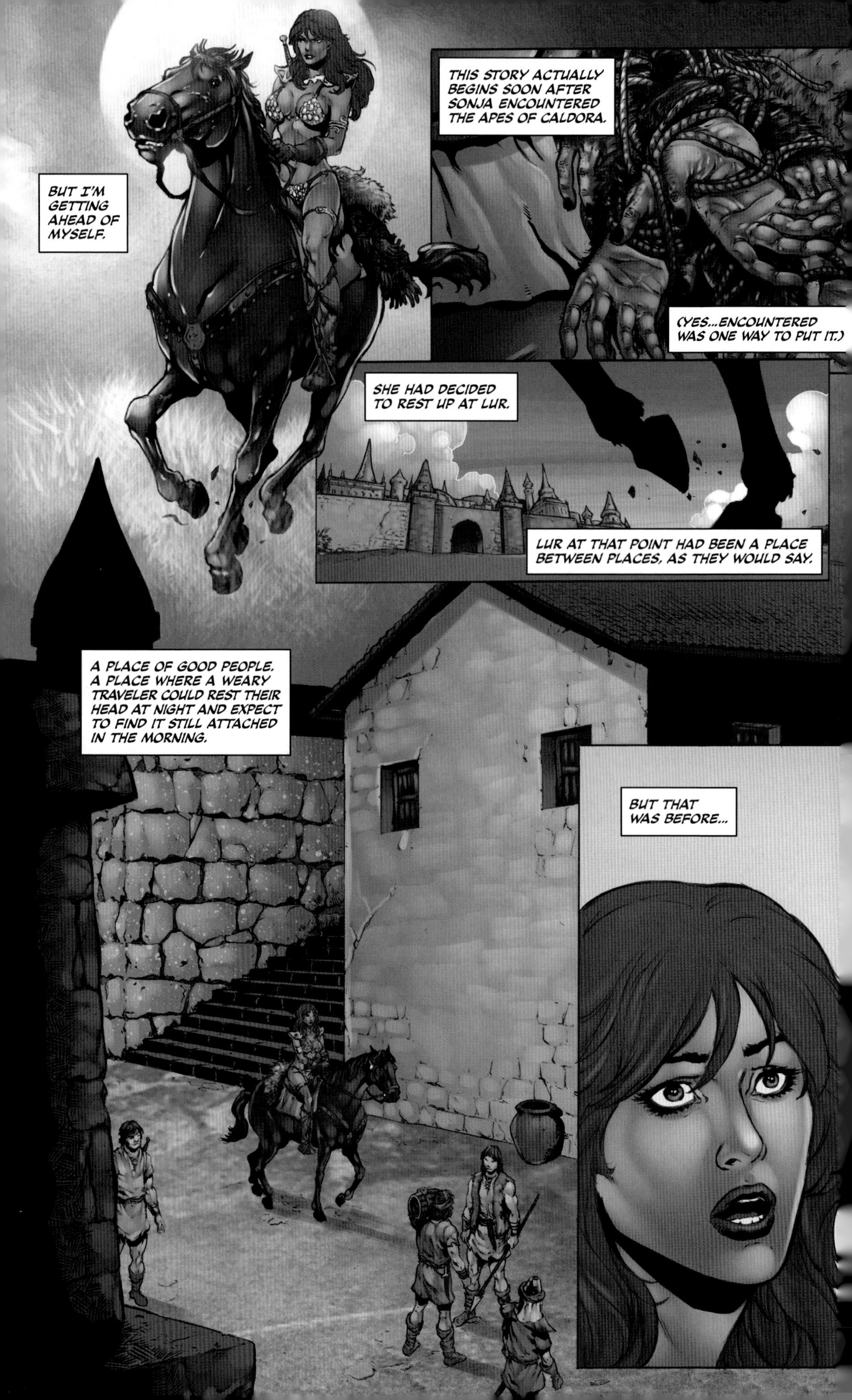
THIS STORY ACTUALLY BEGINS SOON AFTER SONJA ENCOUNTERED THE APES OF CALDORA.
(YES...ENCOUNTERED WAS ONE WAY TO PUT IT.)
BUT I'M GETTING AHEAD OF MYSELF.
SHE HAD DECIDED TO REST UP AT LUR.
LUR AT THAT POINT HAD BEEN A PLACE BETWEEN PLACES, AS THEY WOULD SAY.
A PLACE OF GOOD PEOPLE. A PLACE WHERE A WEARY TRAVELER COULD REST THEIR HEAD AT NIGHT AND EXPECT TO FIND IT STILL ATTACHED IN THE MORNING.
BUT THAT WAS BEFORE...

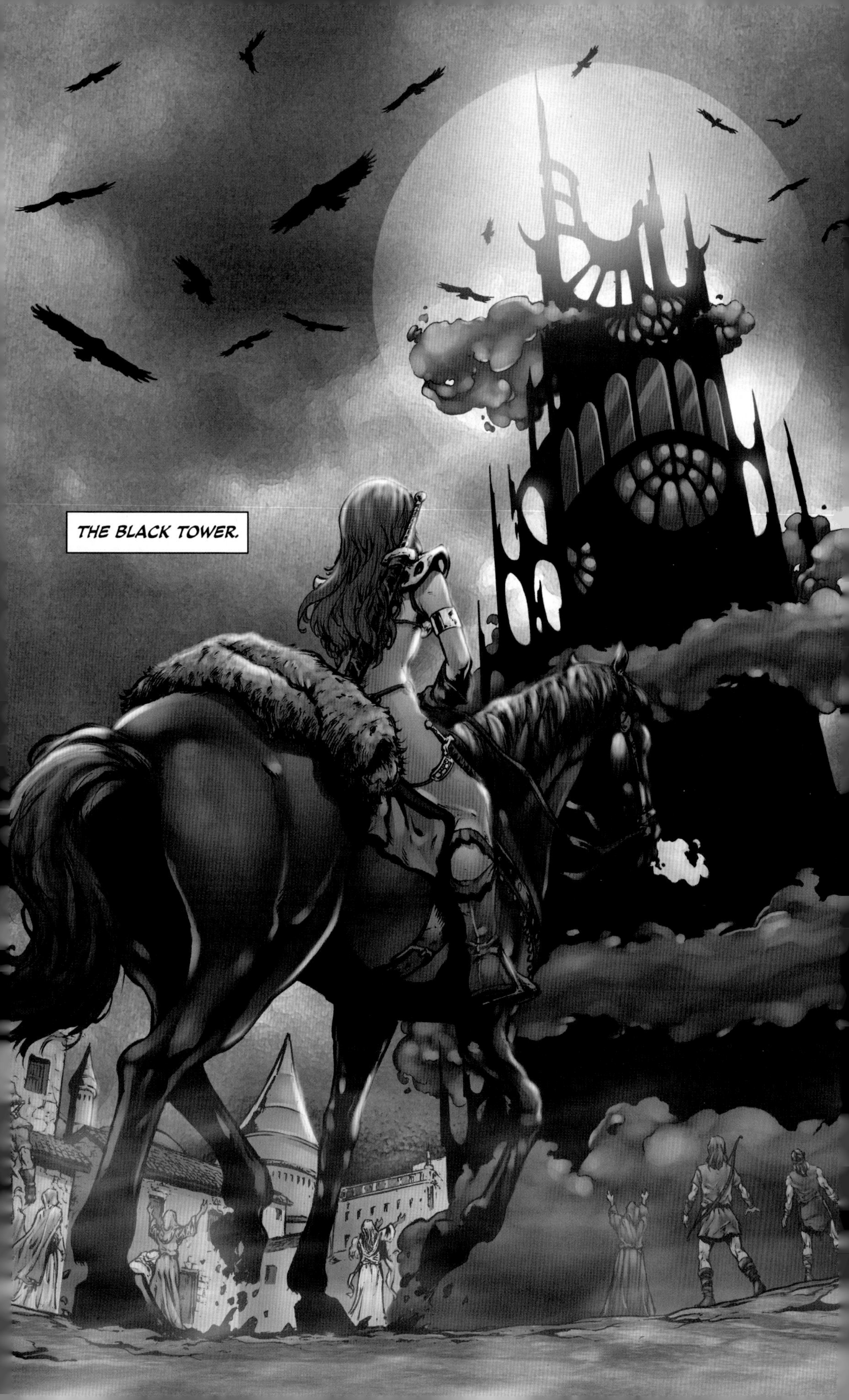
THE BLACK TOWER.

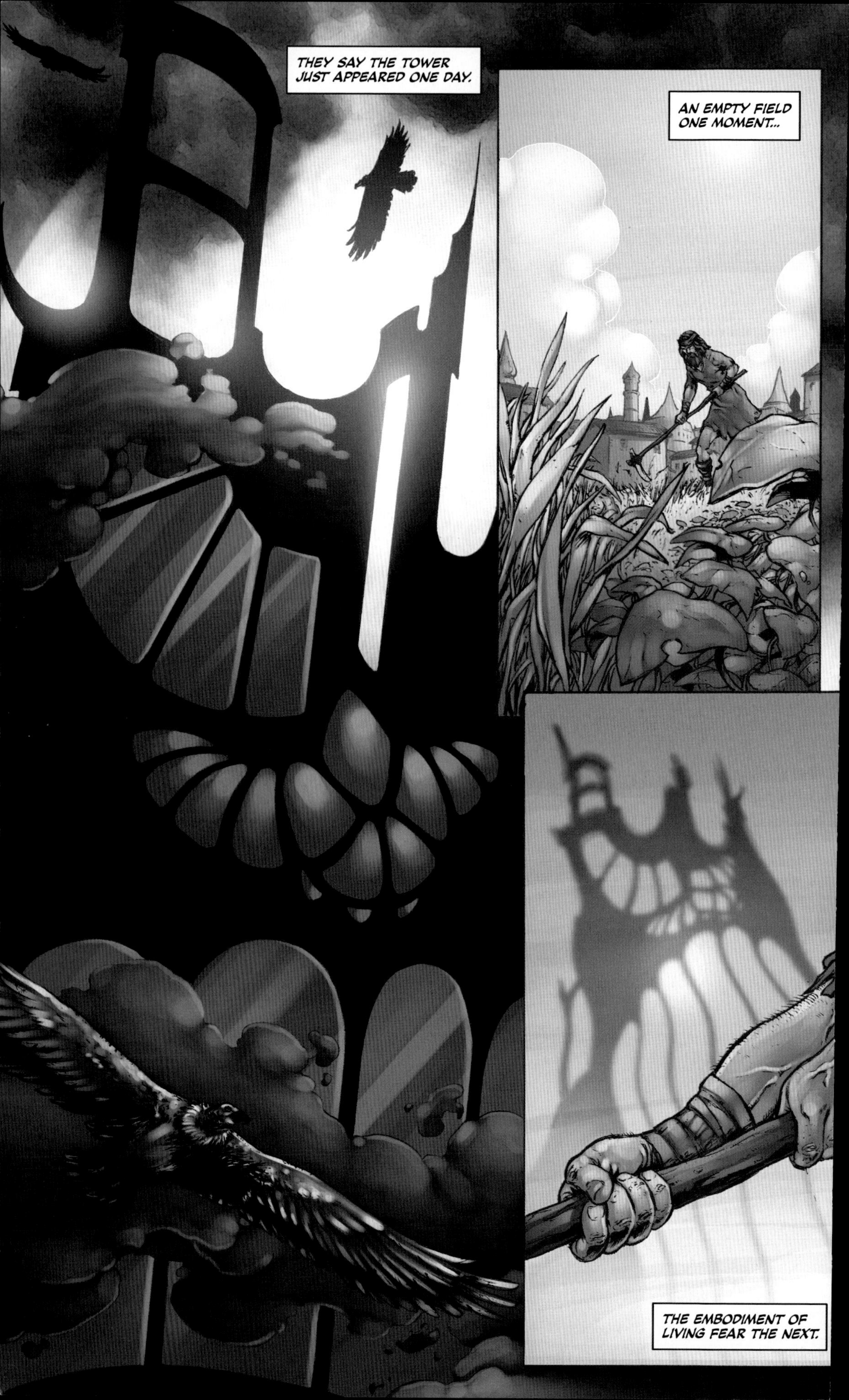
THEY SAY THE TOWER JUST APPEARED ONE DAY.
AN EMPTY FIELD ONE MOMENT...
THE EMBODIMENT OF LIVING FEAR THE NEXT.

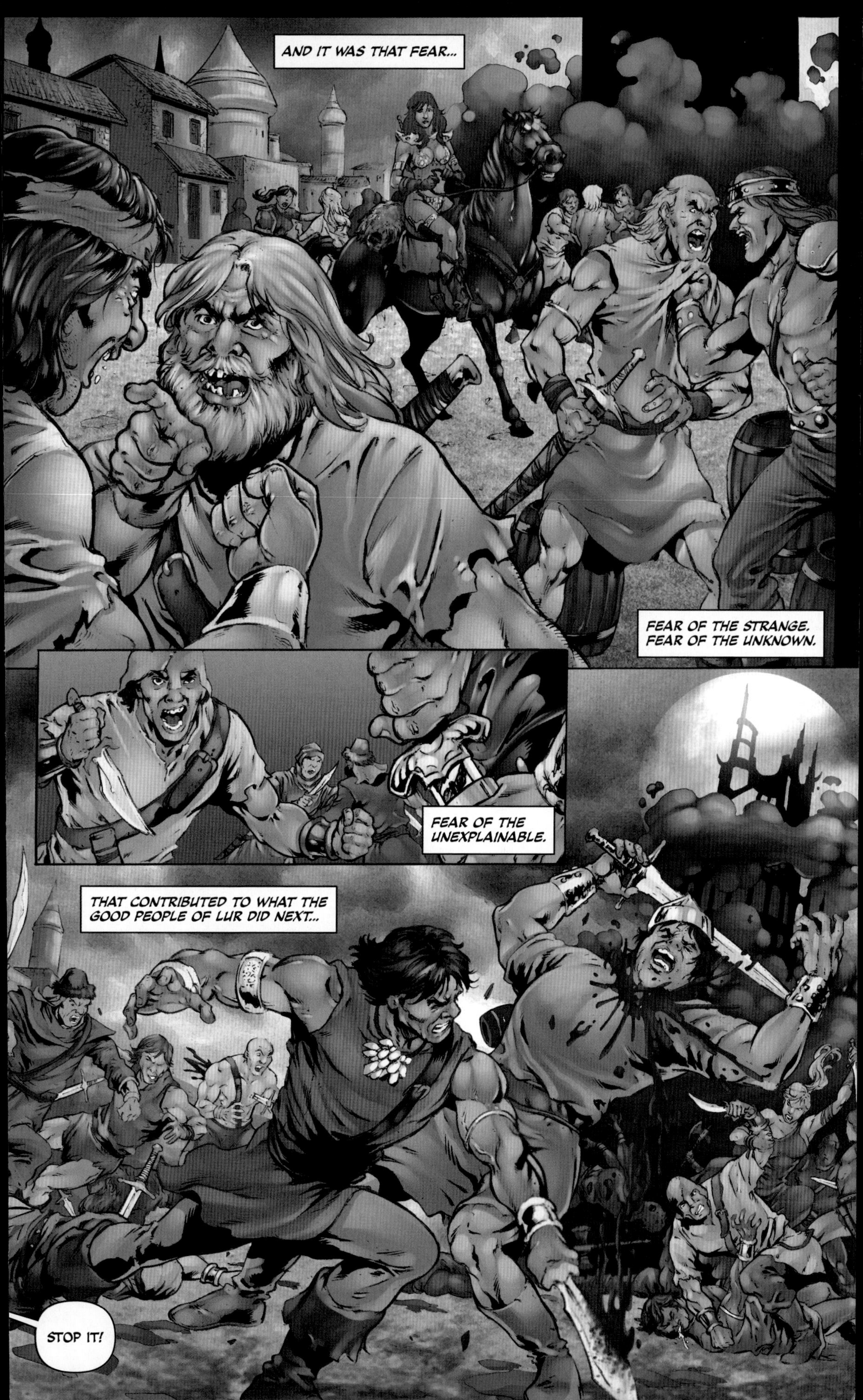
AND IT WAS THAT FEAR...
FEAR OF THE STRANGE. FEAR OF THE UNKNOWN.
FEAR OF THE UNEXPLAINABLE.
THAT CONTRIBUTED TO WHAT THE GOOD PEOPLE OF LUR DID NEXT...
STOP IT!

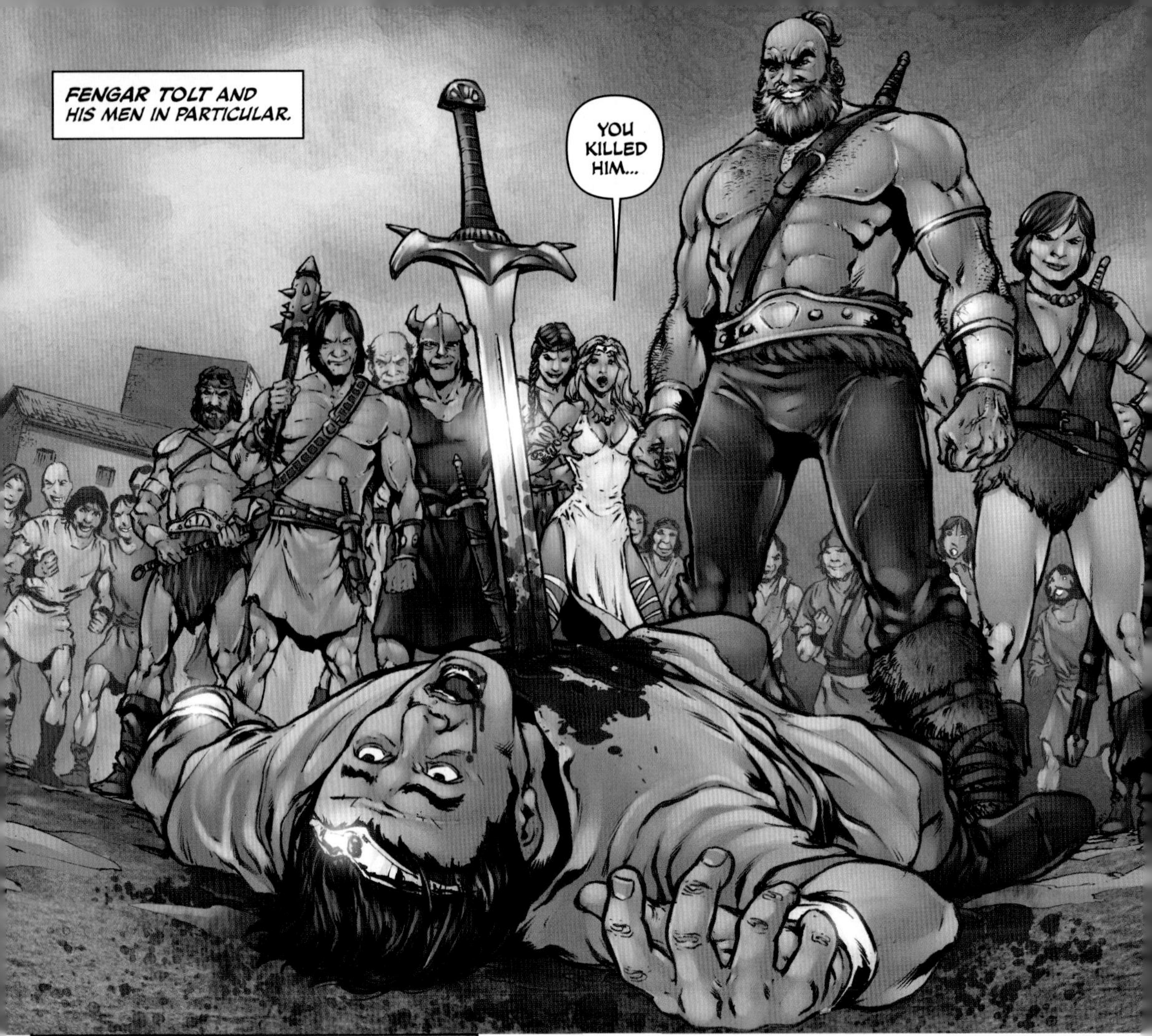
FENGAR TOLT AND HIS MEN IN PARTICULAR.
YOU KILLED HIM...

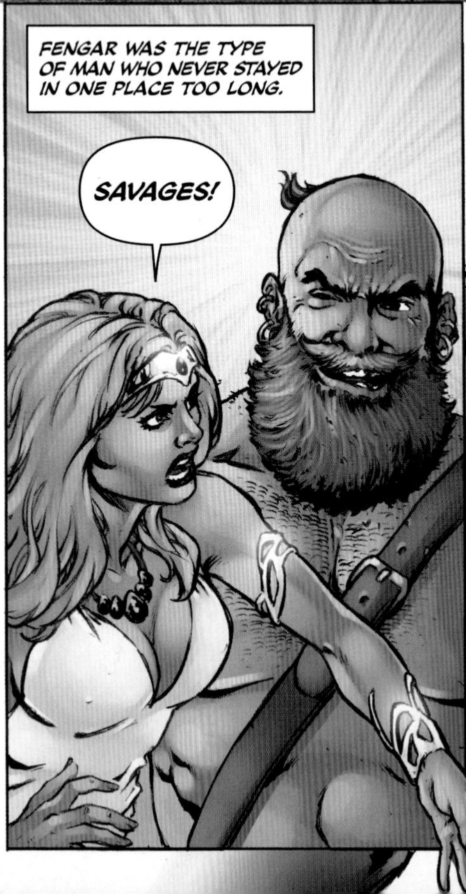
FENGAR WAS THE TYPE OF MAN WHO NEVER STAYED IN ONE PLACE TOO LONG.
SAVAGES!

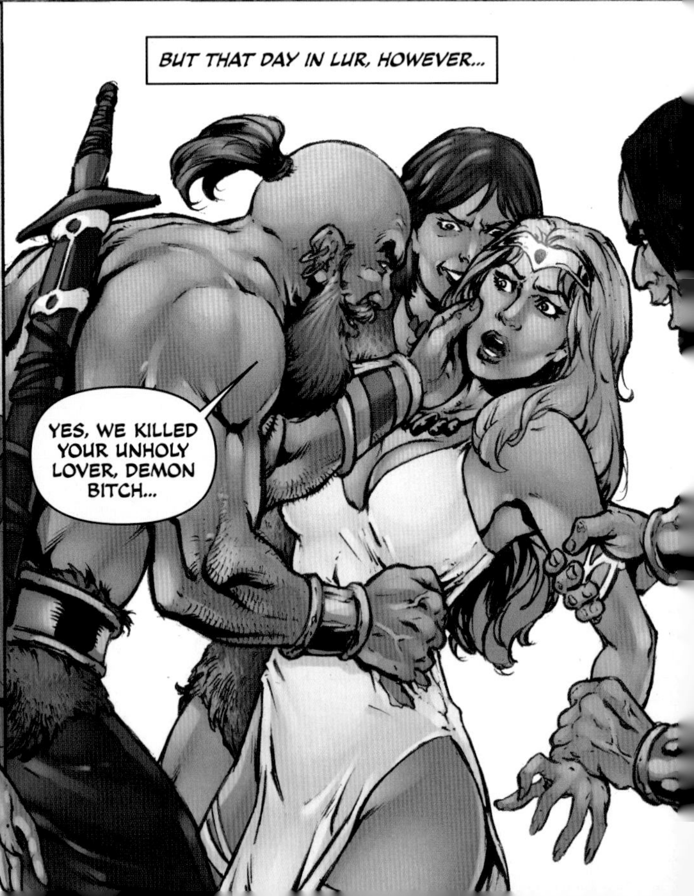
BUT THAT DAY IN LUR, HOWEVER...
YES, WE KILLED YOUR UNHOLY LOVER, DEMON BITCH...

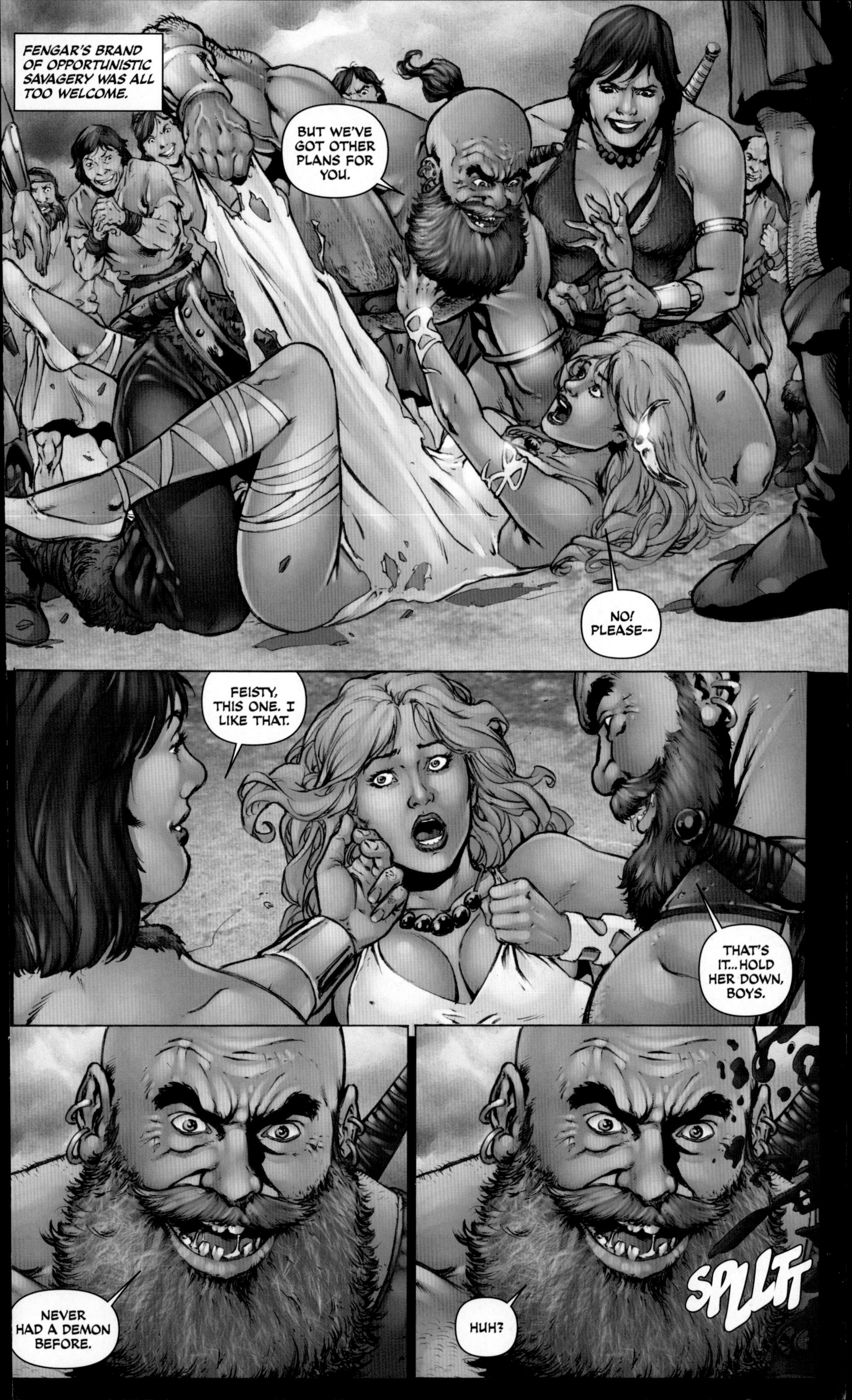
FENGAR'S BRAND OF OPPORTUNISTIC SAVAGERY WAS ALL TOO WELCOME.
BUT WE'VE GOT OTHER PLANS FOR YOU.
NO! PLEASE--
FEISTY, THIS ONE. I LIKE THAT.
THAT'S IT... HOLD HER DOWN, BOYS.
NEVER HAD A DEMON BEFORE.
HUH?
SPLLTT

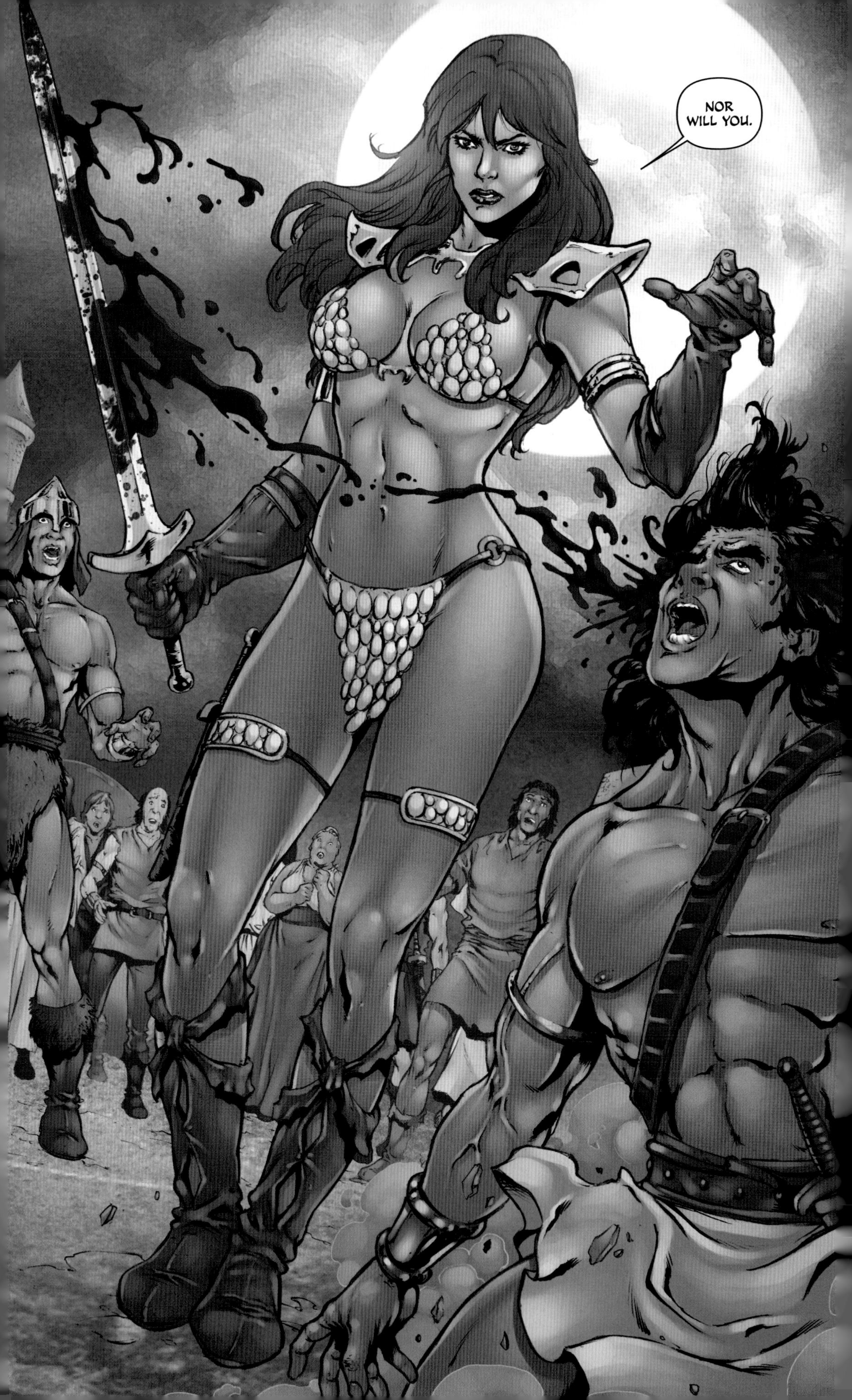
NOR WILL YOU.

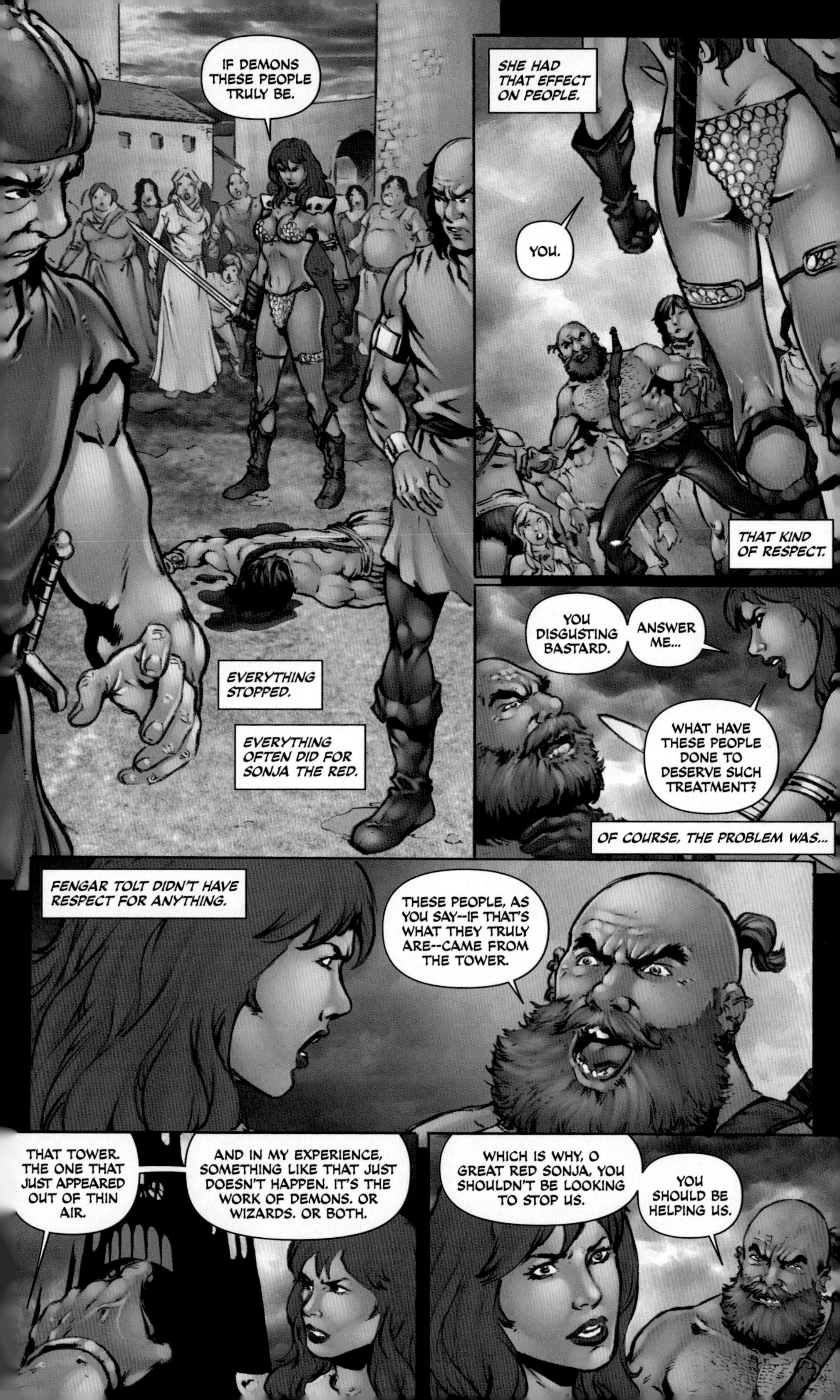
IF DEMONS THESE PEOPLE TRULY BE.
EVERYTHING STOPPED.
EVERYTHING OFTEN DID FOR SONJA THE RED.
SHE HAD THAT EFFECT ON PEOPLE.
YOU.
THAT KIND OF RESPECT.
ANSWER ME...
YOU DISGUSTING BASTARD.
WHAT HAVE THESE PEOPLE DONE TO DESERVE SUCH TREATMENT?
OF COURSE, THE PROBLEM WAS...
FENGAR TOLT DIDN'T HAVE RESPECT FOR ANYTHING.
THESE PEOPLE, AS YOU SAY--IF THAT'S WHAT THEY TRULY ARE--CAME FROM THE TOWER.
THAT TOWER. THE ONE THAT JUST APPEARED OUT OF THIN AIR.
AND IN MY EXPERIENCE, SOMETHING LIKE THAT JUST DOESN'T HAPPEN. IT'S THE WORK OF DEMONS. OR WIZARDS. OR BOTH.
WHICH IS WHY, O GREAT RED SONJA, YOU SHOULDN'T BE LOOKING TO STOP US.
YOU SHOULD BE HELPING US.

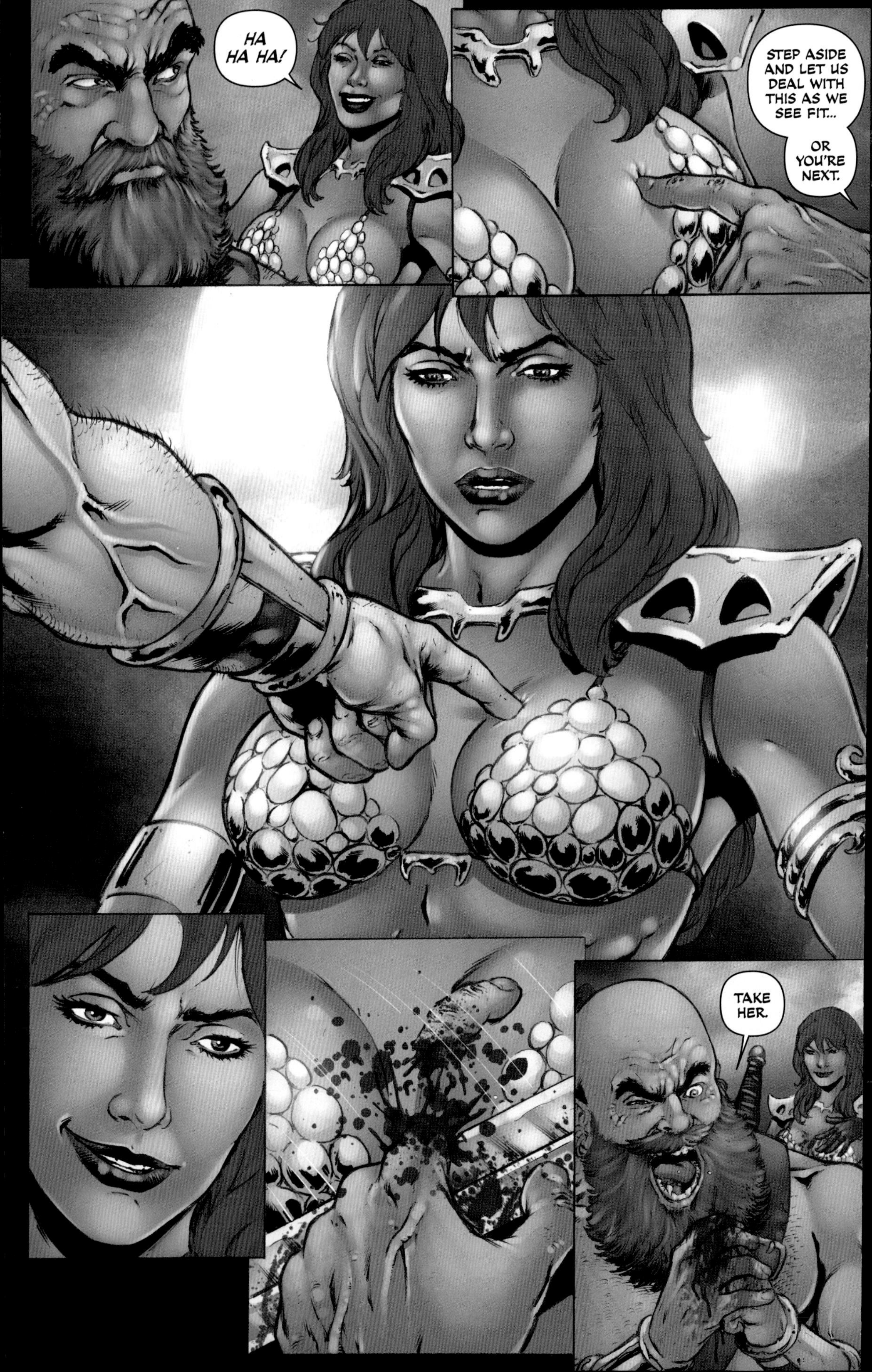
HA HA HA!
STEP ASIDE AND LET US DEAL WITH THIS AS WE SEE FIT...
OR YOU'RE NEXT.
TAKE HER.

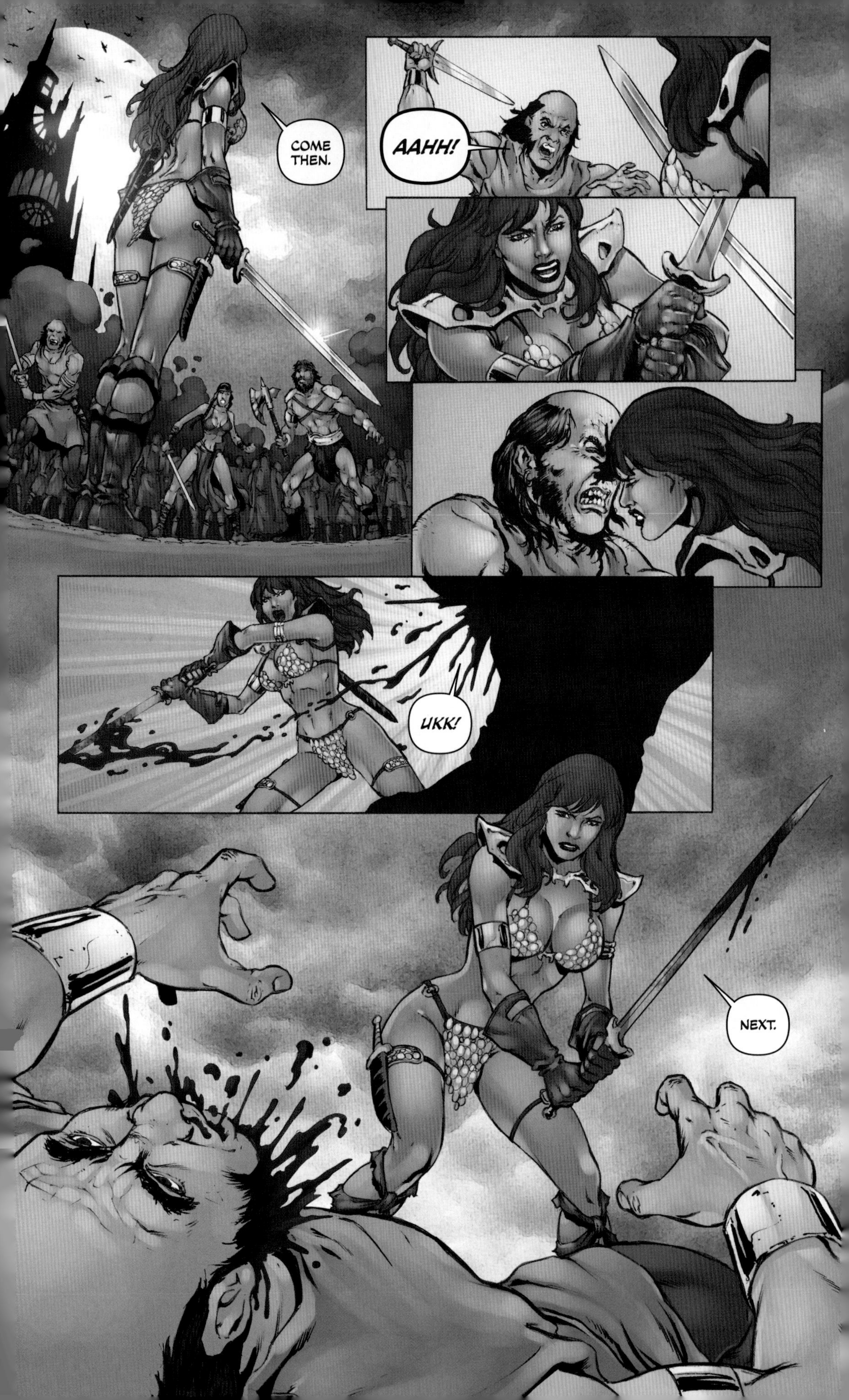
COME THEN.
AAHH!
UKK!
NEXT.

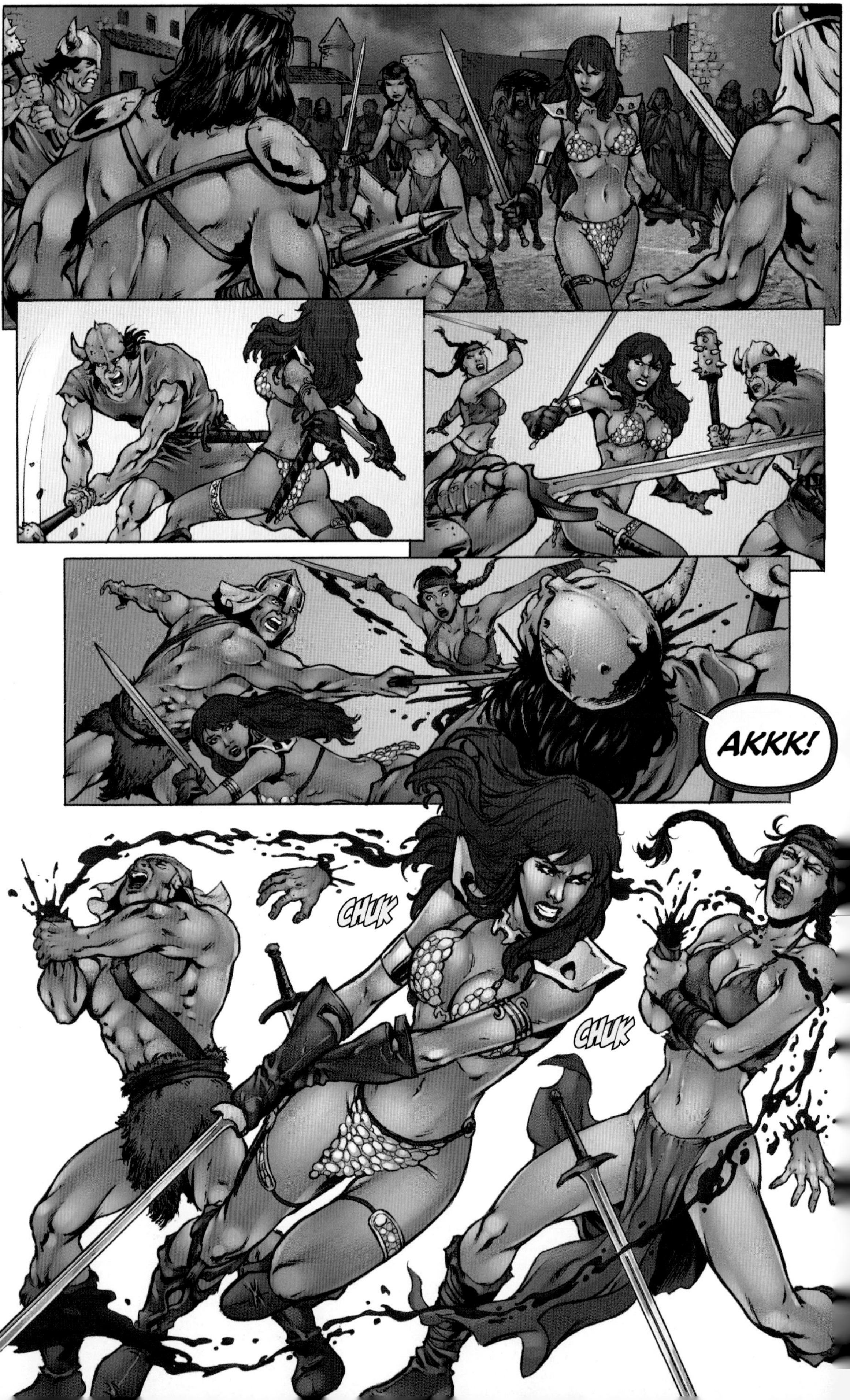
AKKK!
CHUK
CHUK

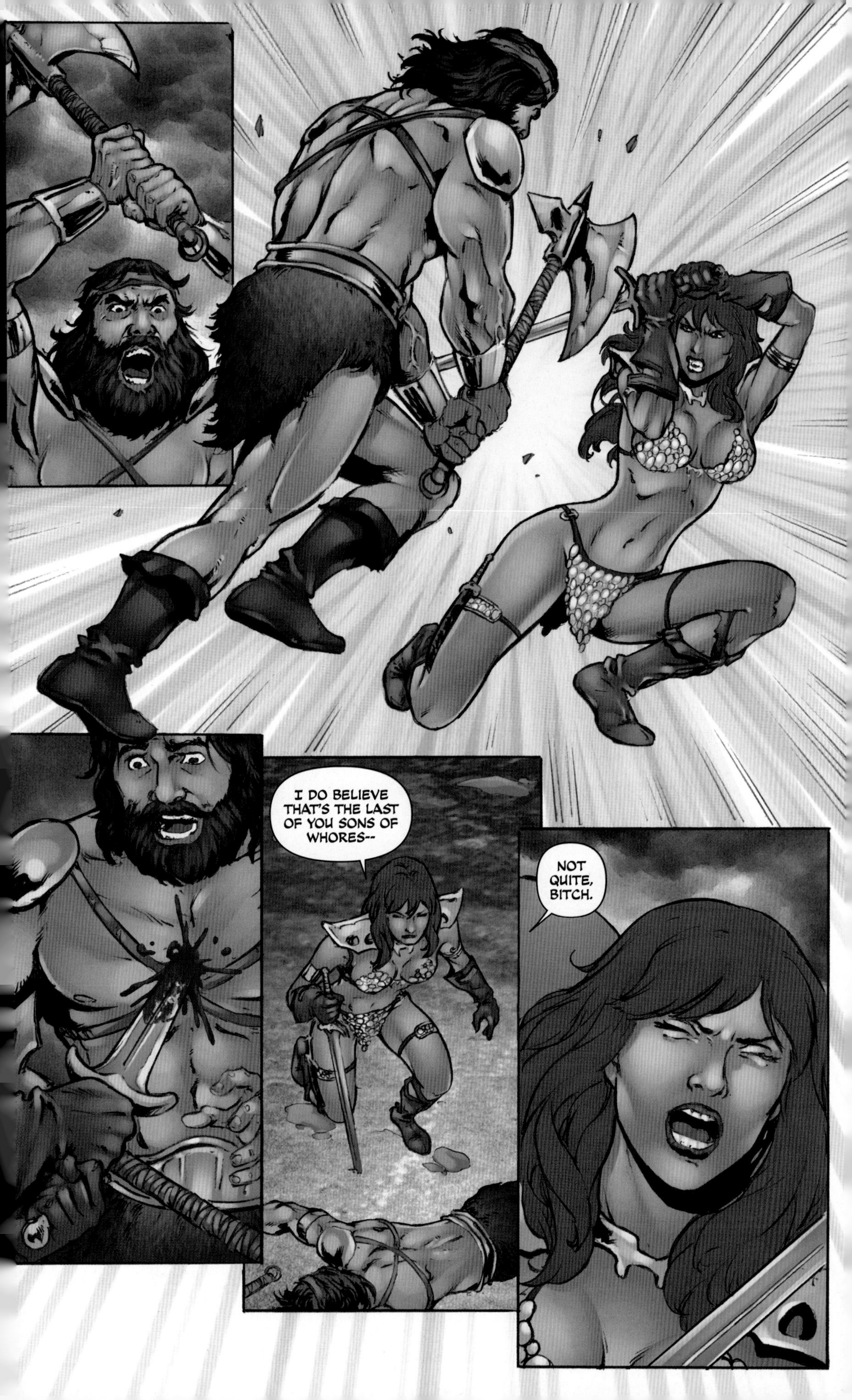
I DO BELIEVE THAT'S THE LAST OF YOU SONS OF WHORES--
NOT QUITE, BITCH.

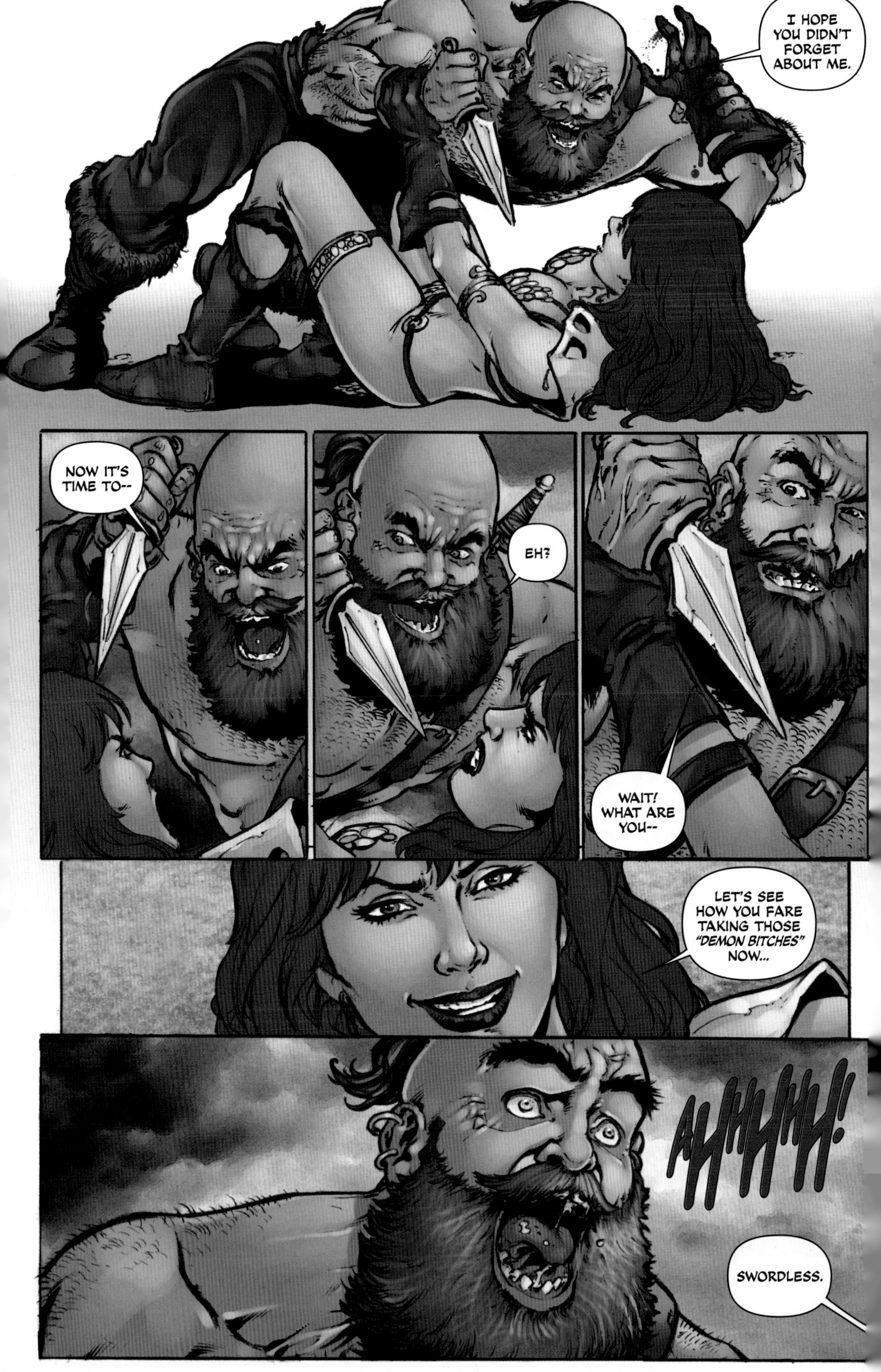
I HOPE YOU DIDN'T FORGET ABOUT ME.
NOW IT'S TIME TO--
EH?
WAIT! WHAT ARE YOU--
LET'S SEE HOW YOU FARE TAKING THOSE "DEMON BITCHES" NOW...
AHHHHH!
SWORDLESS.

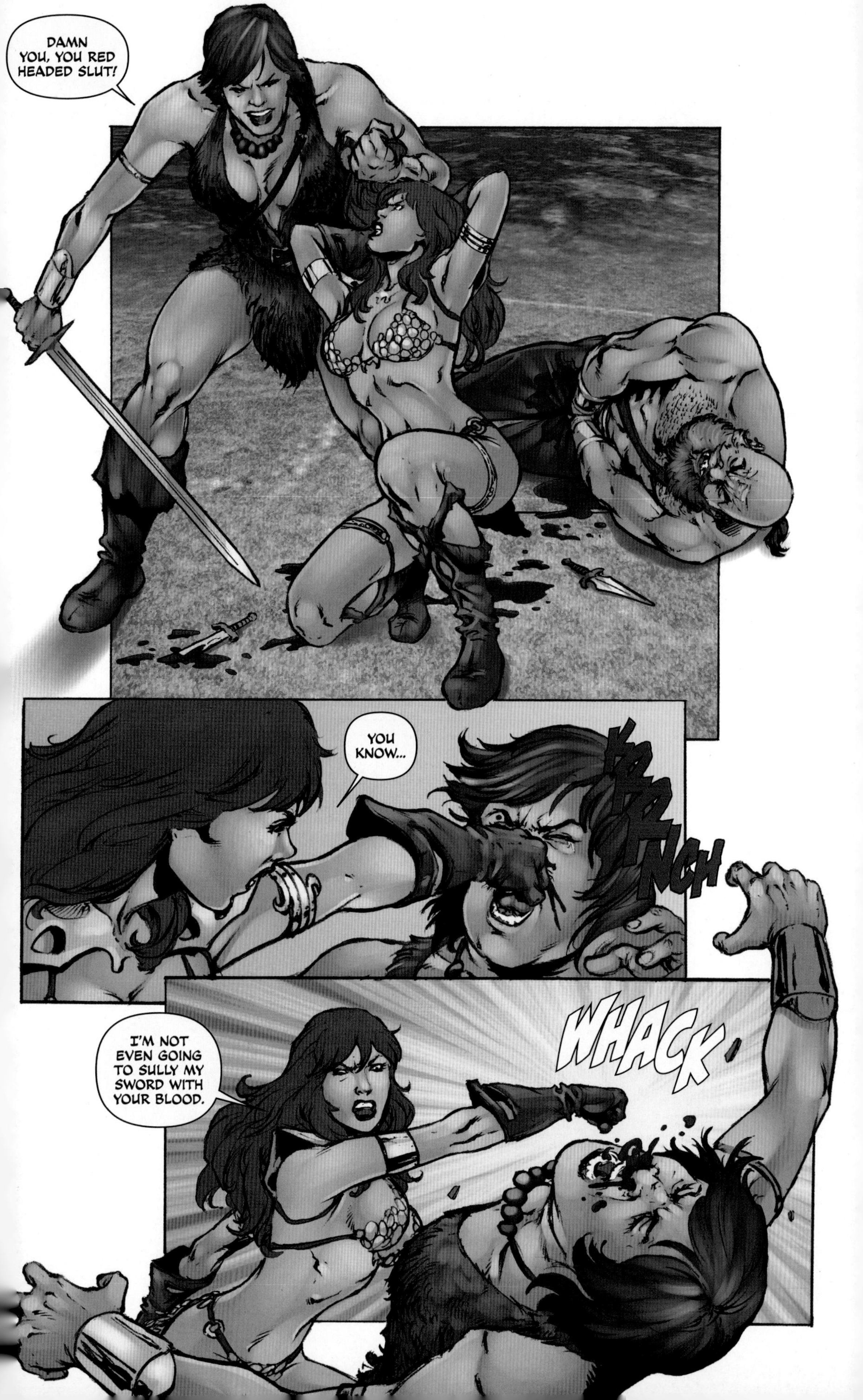
DAMN YOU, YOU RED HEADED SLUT!
YOU KNOW...
KRUNCH
I'M NOT EVEN GOING TO SULLY MY SWORD WITH YOUR BLOOD.
WHACK

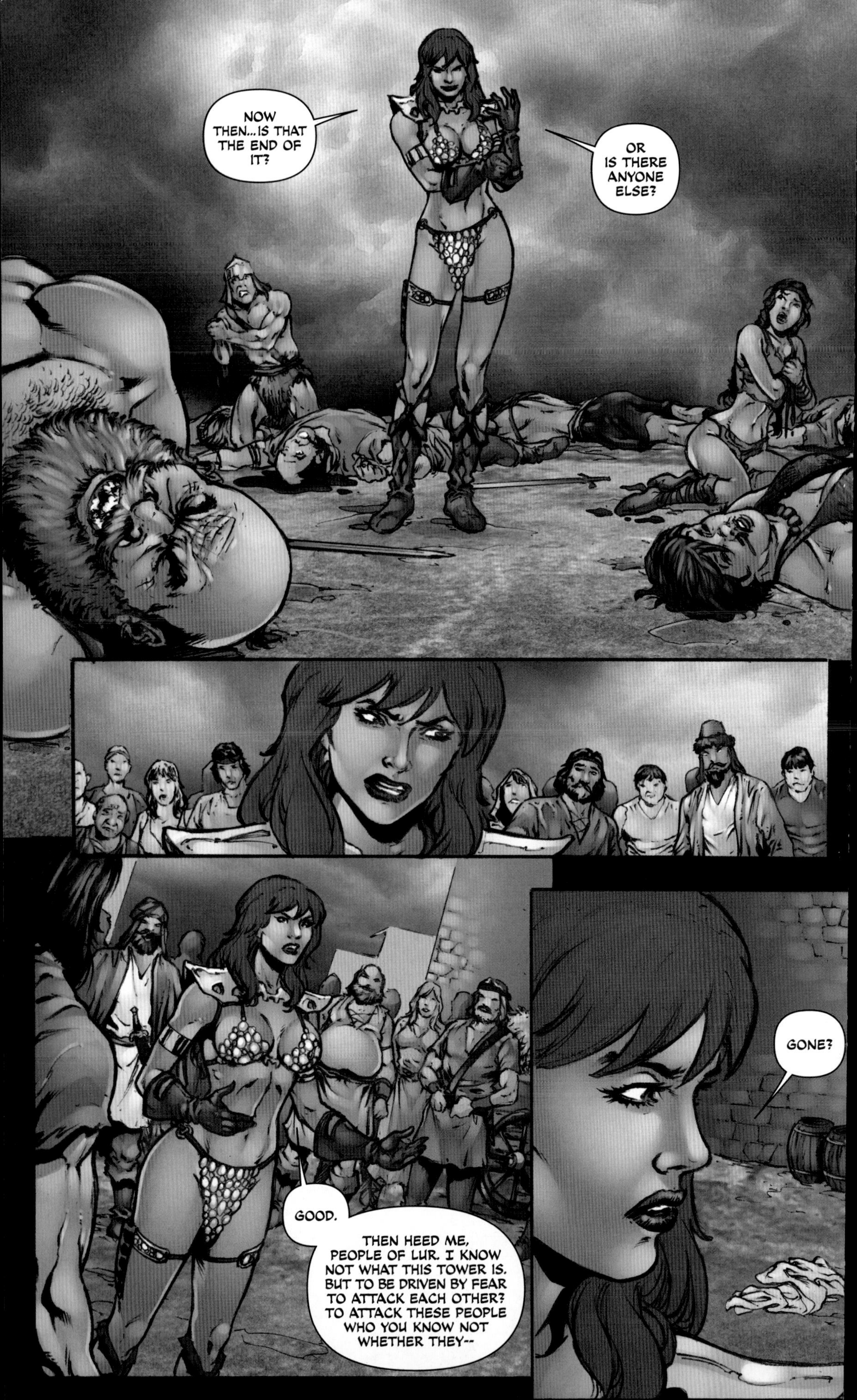
NOW THEN...IS THAT THE END OF IT?
OR IS THERE ANYONE ELSE?
GOOD.
THEN HEED ME, PEOPLE OF LUR. I KNOW NOT WHAT THIS TOWER IS. BUT TO BE DRIVEN BY FEAR TO ATTACK EACH OTHER? TO ATTACK THESE PEOPLE WHO YOU KNOW NOT WHETHER THEY--
GONE?

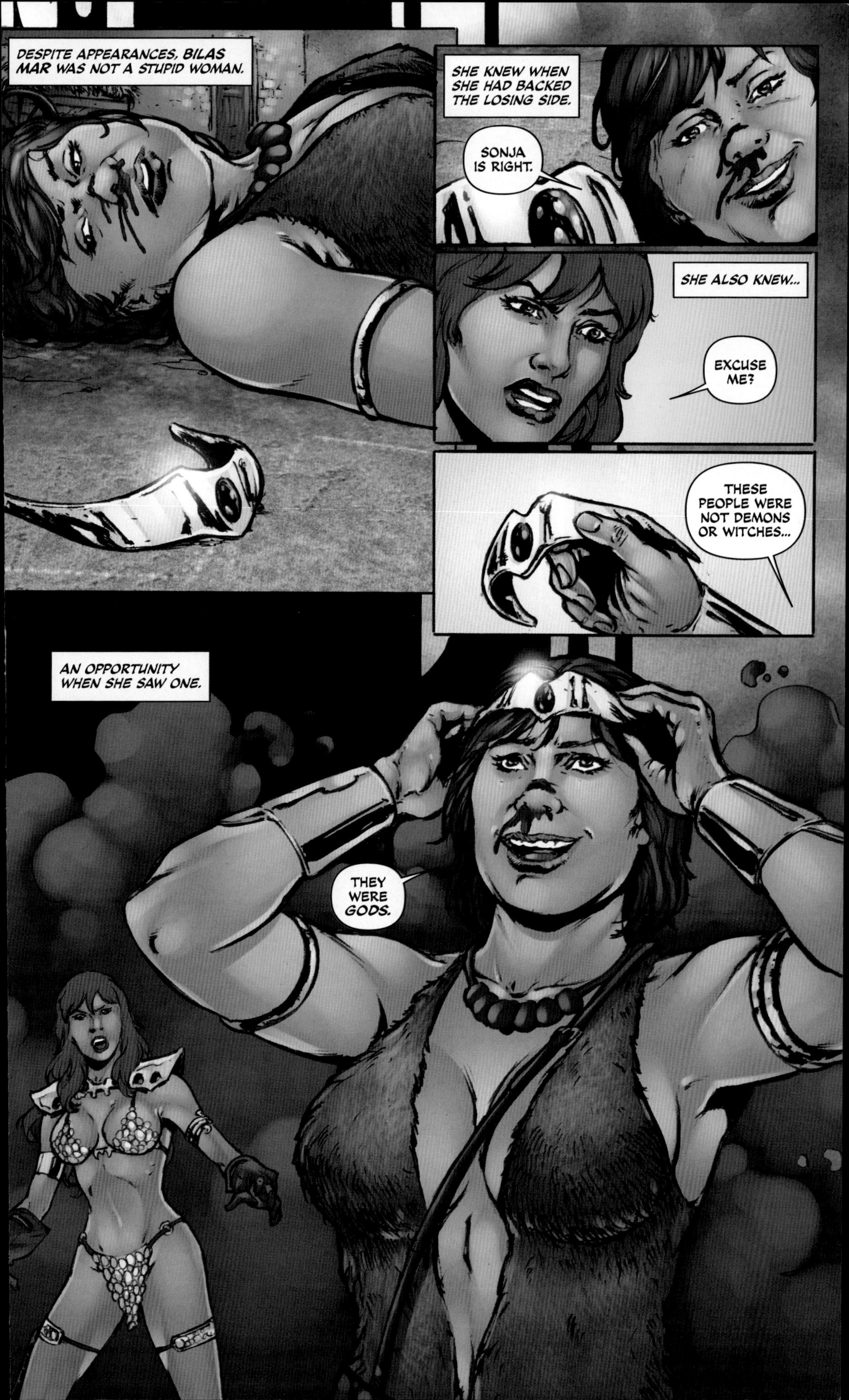
DESPITE APPEARANCES, BILAS MAR WAS NOT A STUPID WOMAN.
SHE KNEW WHEN SHE HAD BACKED THE LOSING SIDE.
SONJA IS RIGHT.
SHE ALSO KNEW...
EXCUSE ME?
THESE PEOPLE WERE NOT DEMONS OR WITCHES...
AN OPPORTUNITY WHEN SHE SAW ONE.
THEY WERE GODS.

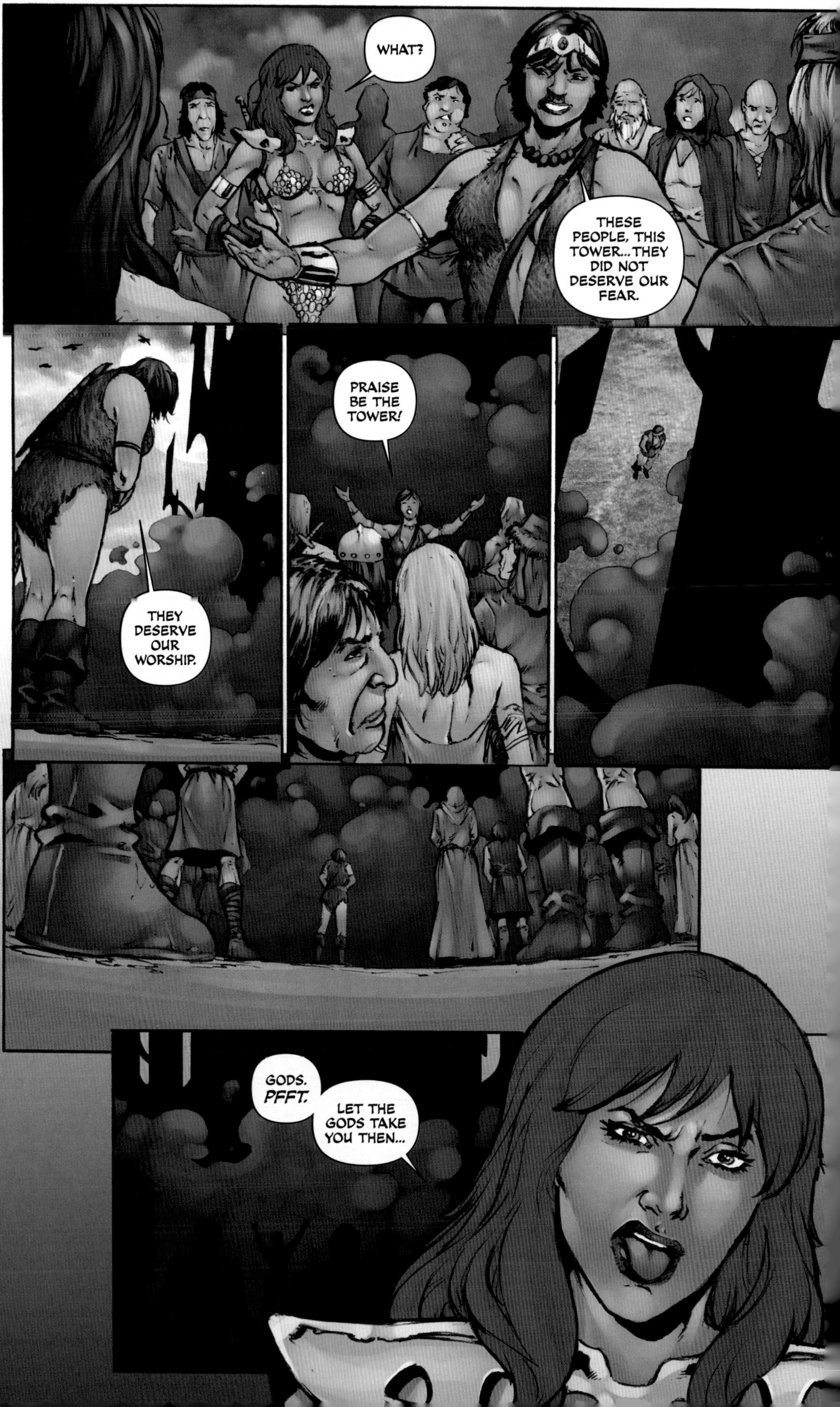
WHAT?
THESE PEOPLE, THIS TOWER...THEY DID NOT DESERVE OUR FEAR.
THEY DESERVE OUR WORSHIP.
PRAISE BE THE TOWER!
GODS. *PFFT.*
LET THE GODS TAKE YOU THEN...

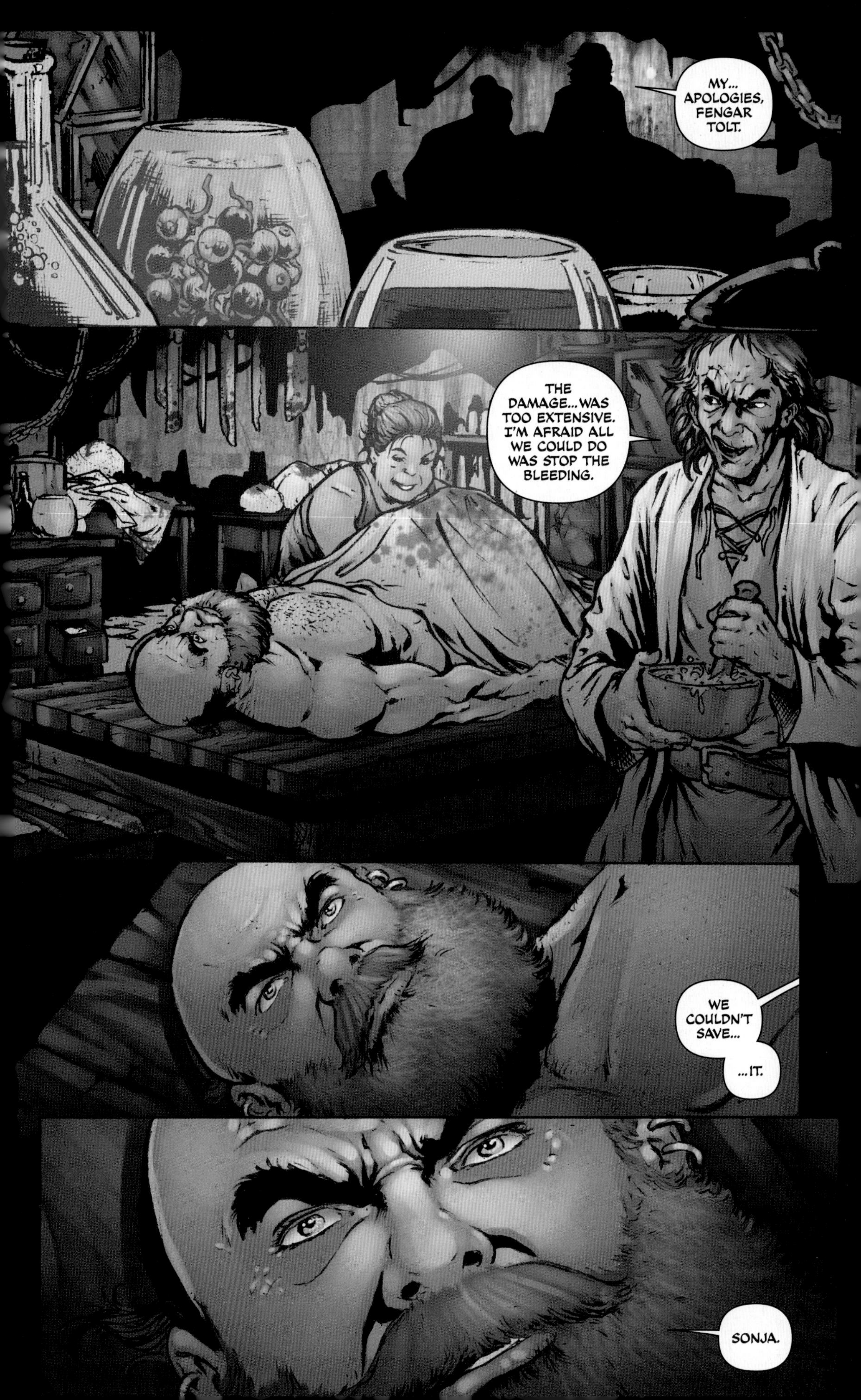
MY... APOLOGIES, FENGAR TOLT.
THE DAMAGE...WAS TOO EXTENSIVE. I'M AFRAID ALL WE COULD DO WAS STOP THE BLEEDING.
WE COULDN'T SAVE...
...IT.
SONJA.

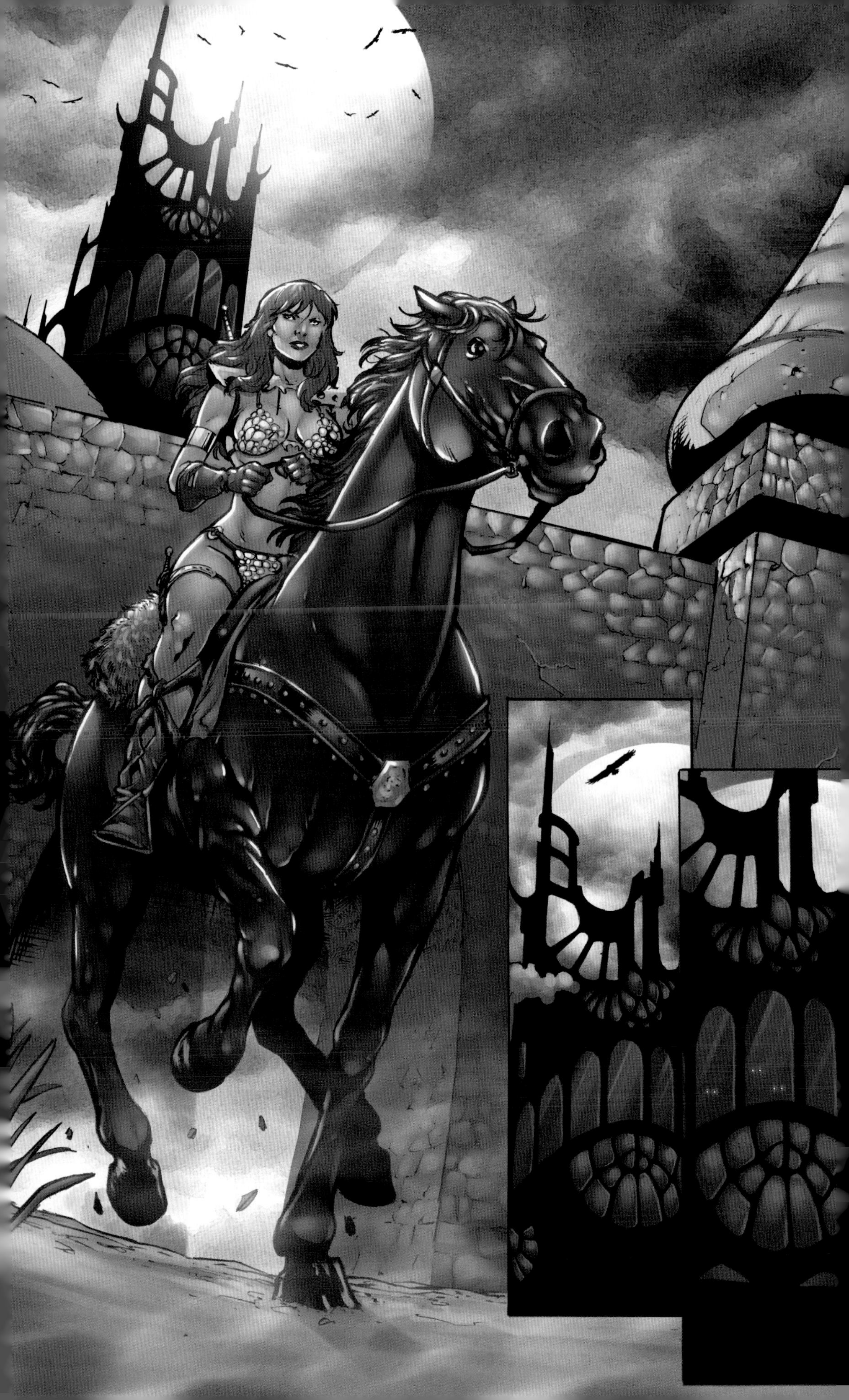

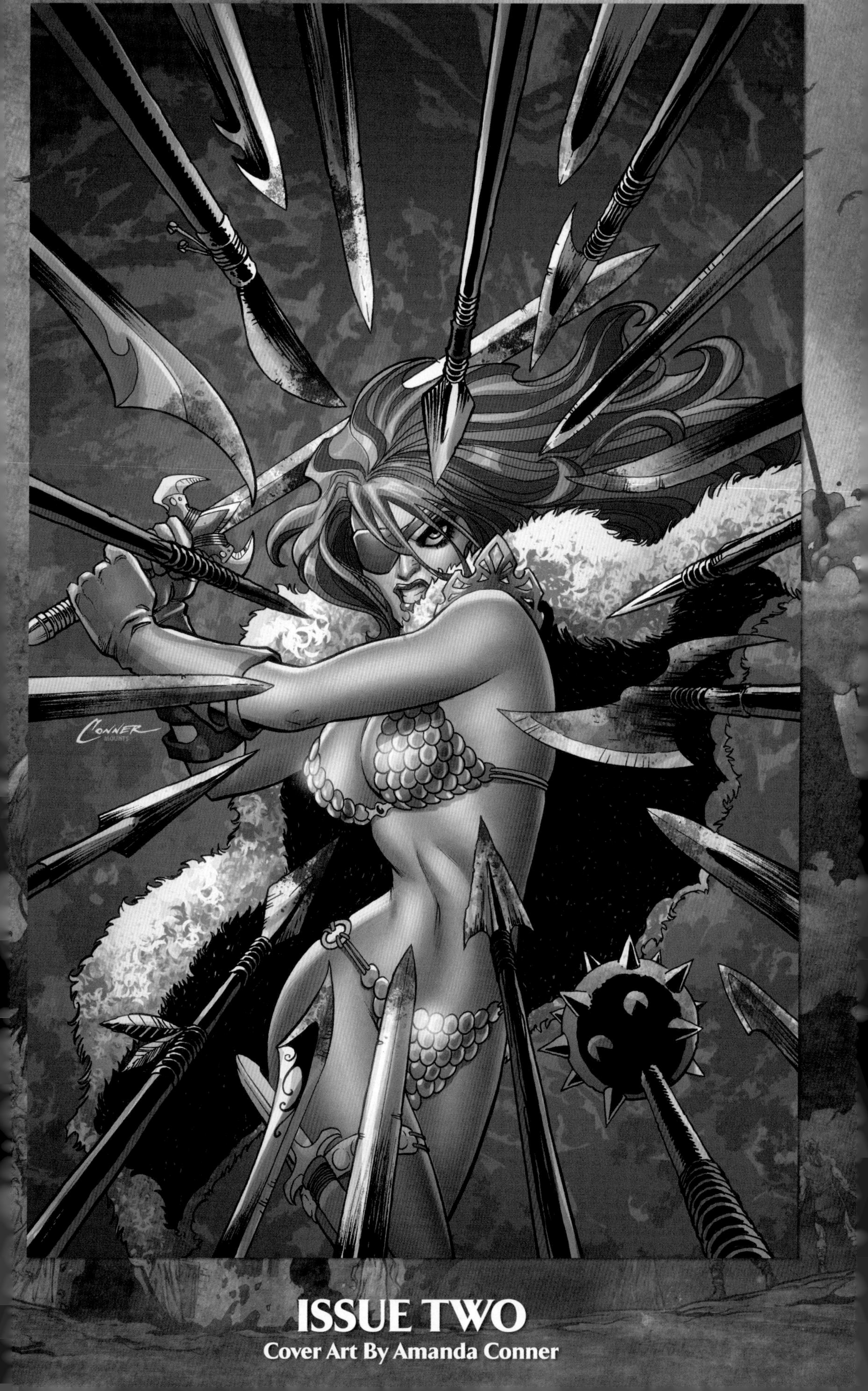
CONNER

ISSUE TWO

Cover Art By Amanda Conner

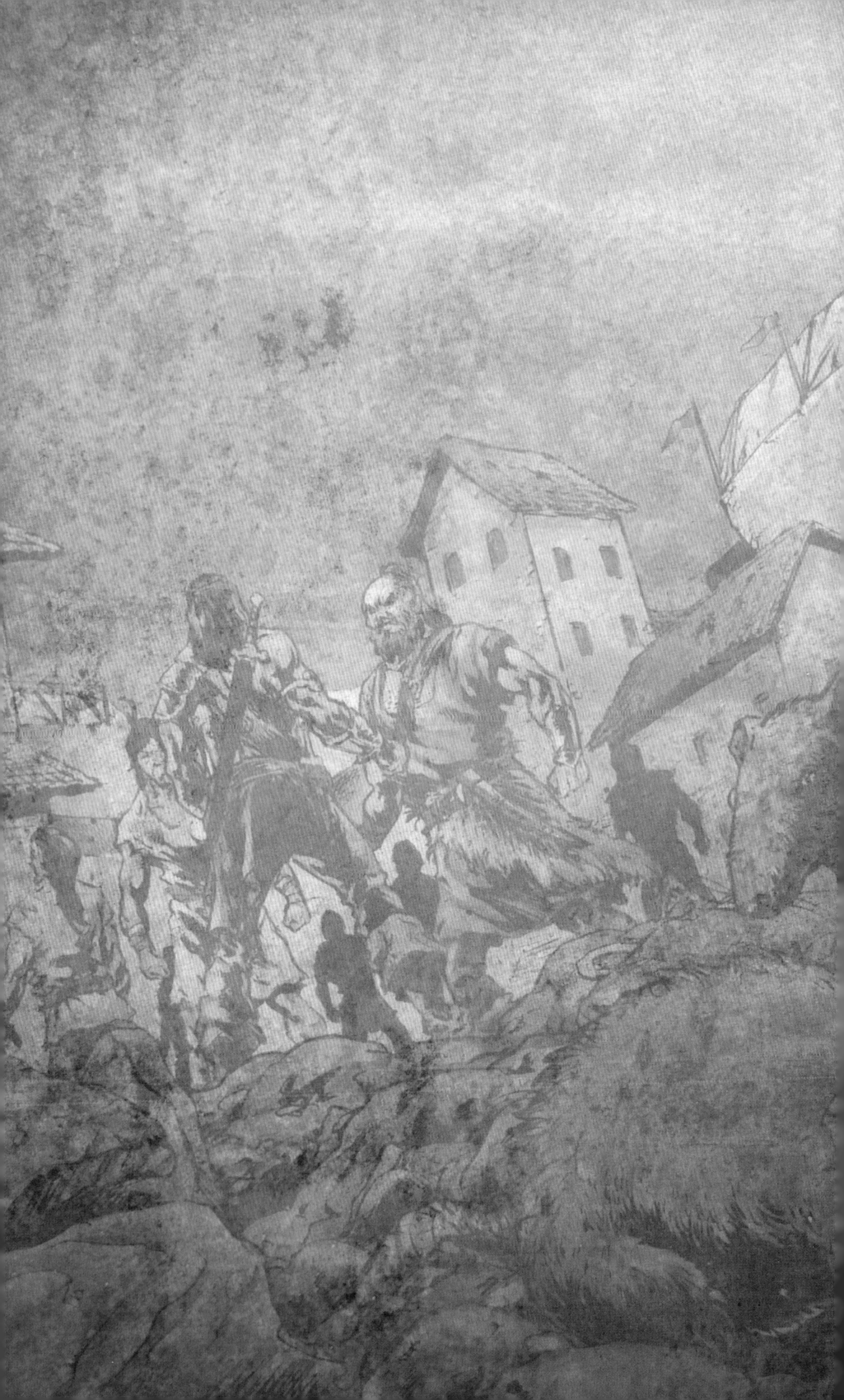

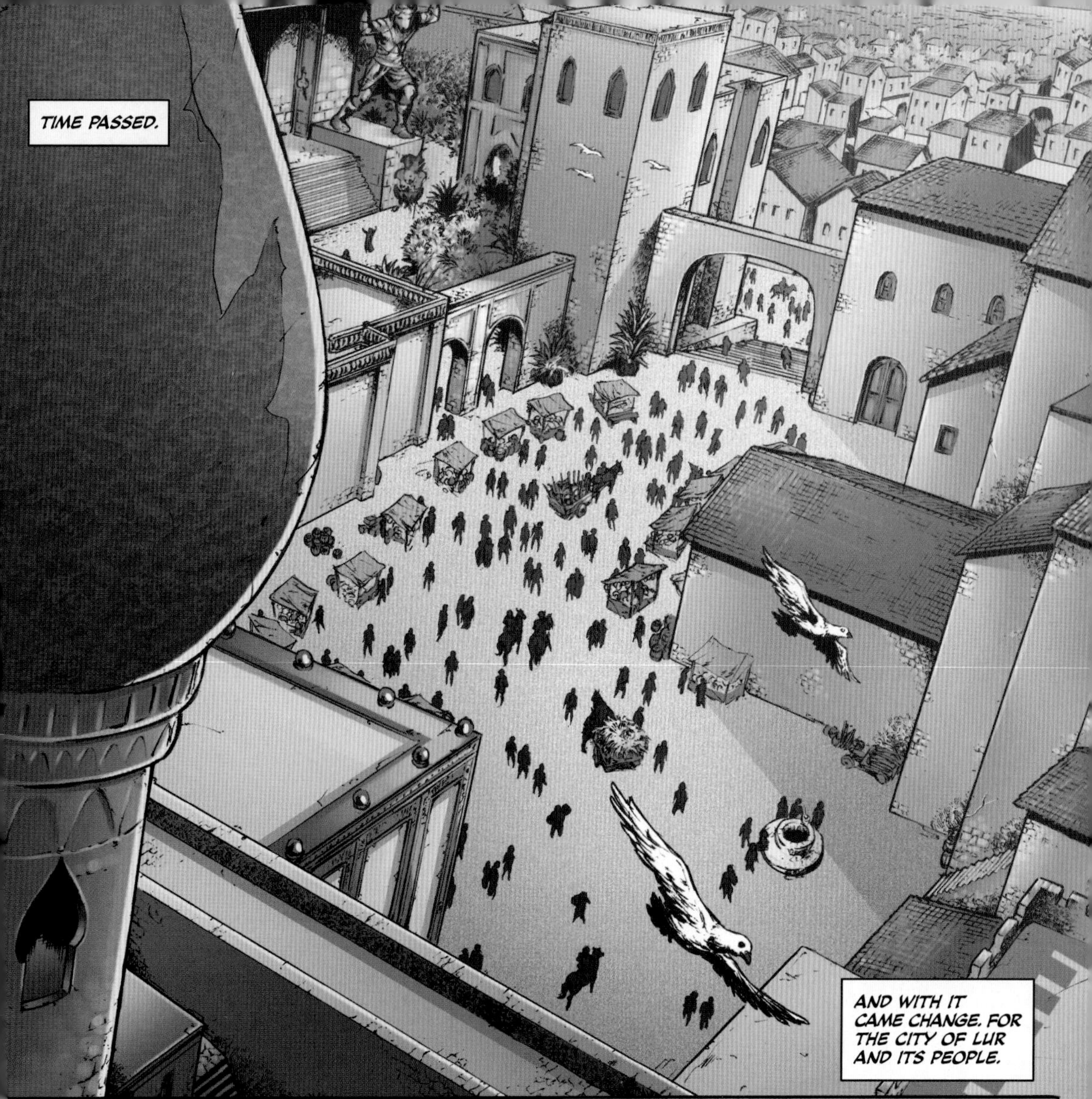
TIME PASSED.
AND WITH IT CAME CHANGE. FOR THE CITY OF LUR AND ITS PEOPLE.

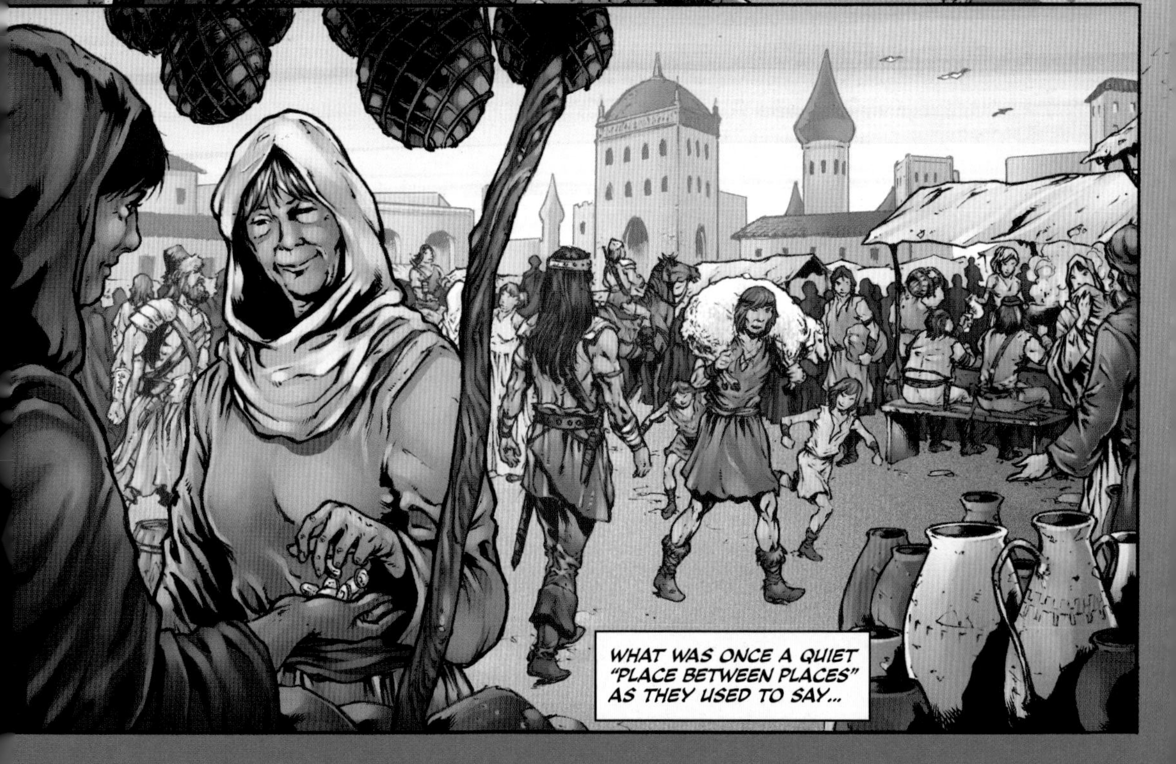
WHAT WAS ONCE A QUIET "PLACE BETWEEN PLACES" AS THEY USED TO SAY...

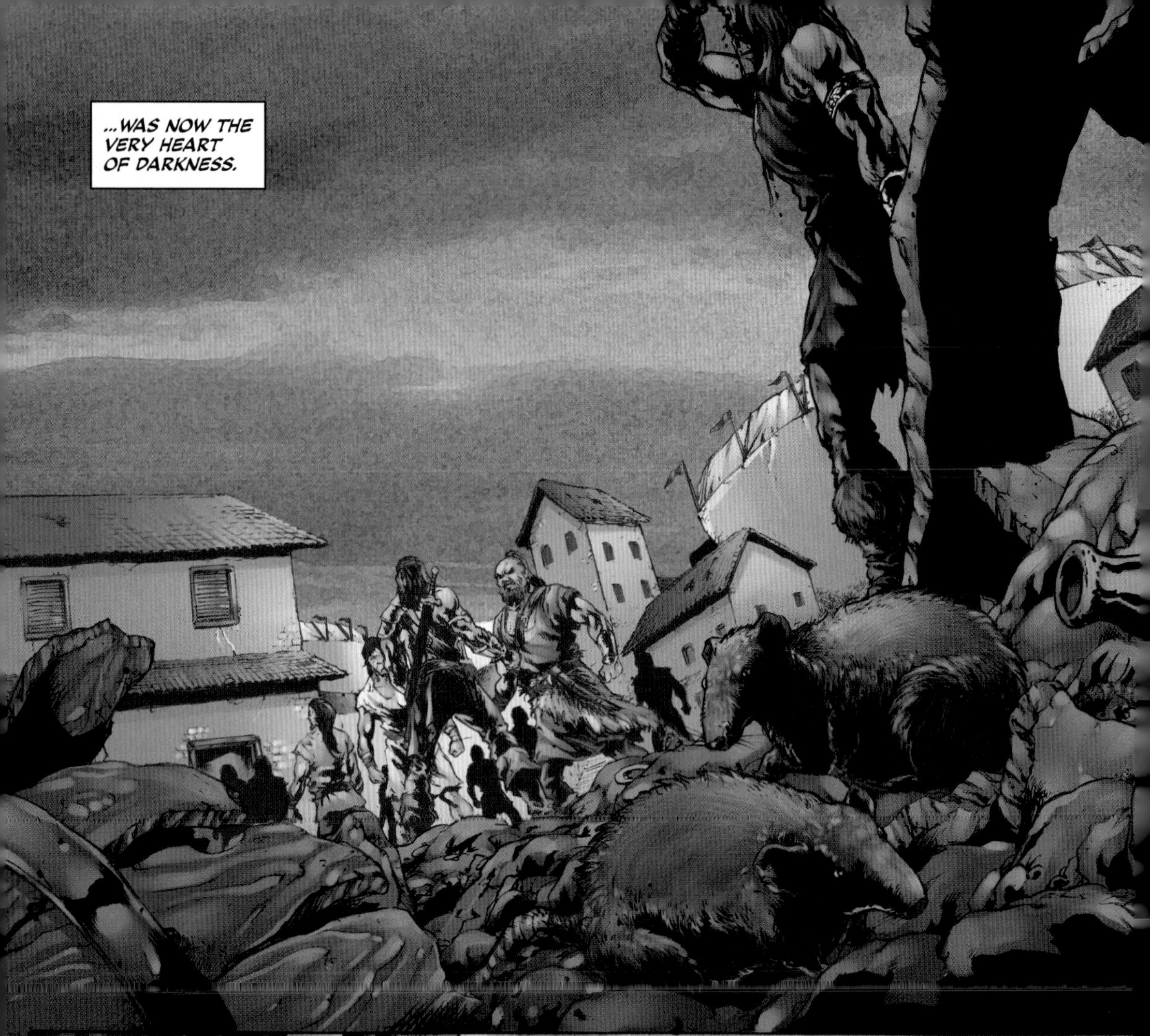
...WAS NOW THE VERY HEART OF DARKNESS.

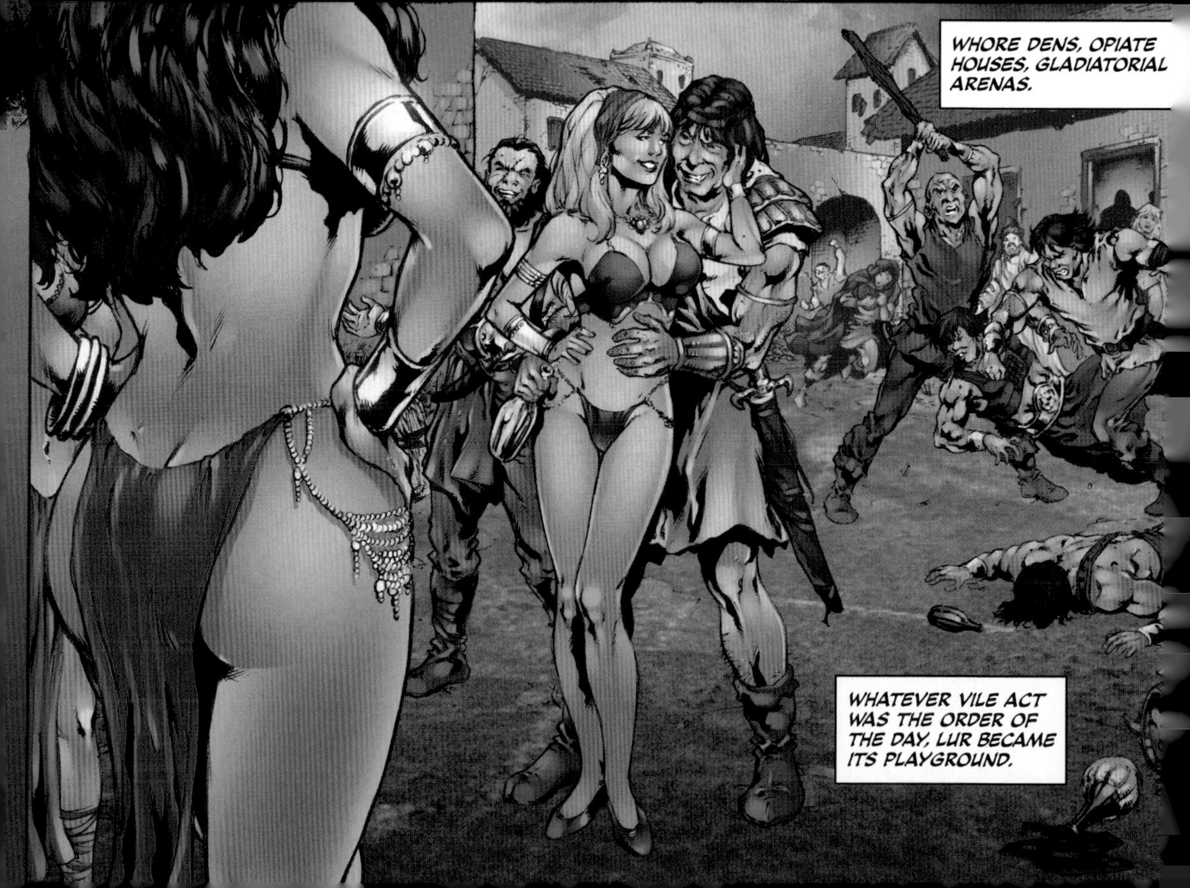
WHORE DENS, OPIATE HOUSES, GLADIATORIAL ARENAS.
WHATEVER VILE ACT WAS THE ORDER OF THE DAY, LUR BECAME ITS PLAYGROUND.

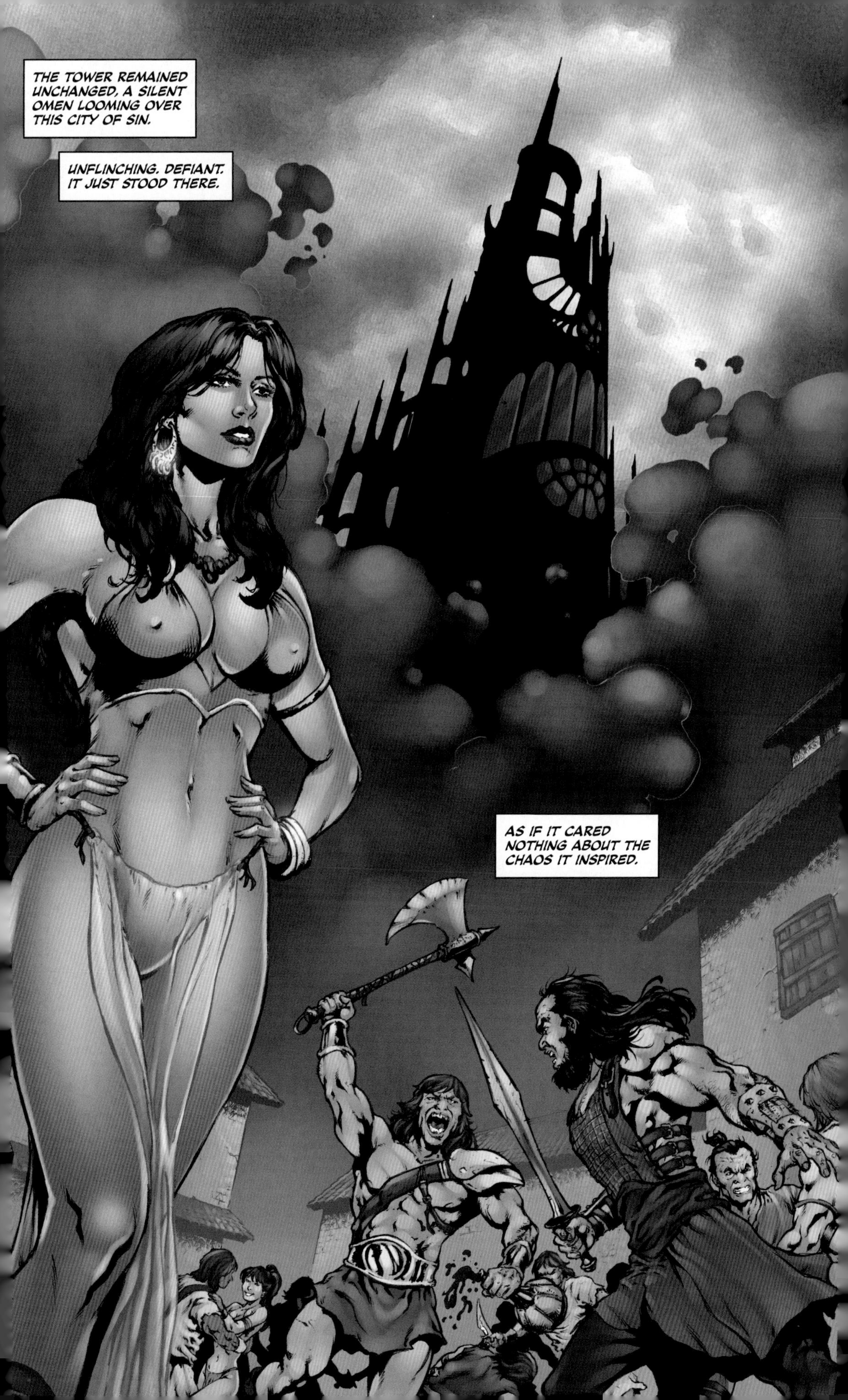
THE TOWER REMAINED UNCHANGED, A SILENT OMEN LOOMING OVER THIS CITY OF SIN.
UNFLINCHING. DEFIANT. IT JUST STOOD THERE.
AS IF IT CARED NOTHING ABOUT THE CHAOS IT INSPIRED.

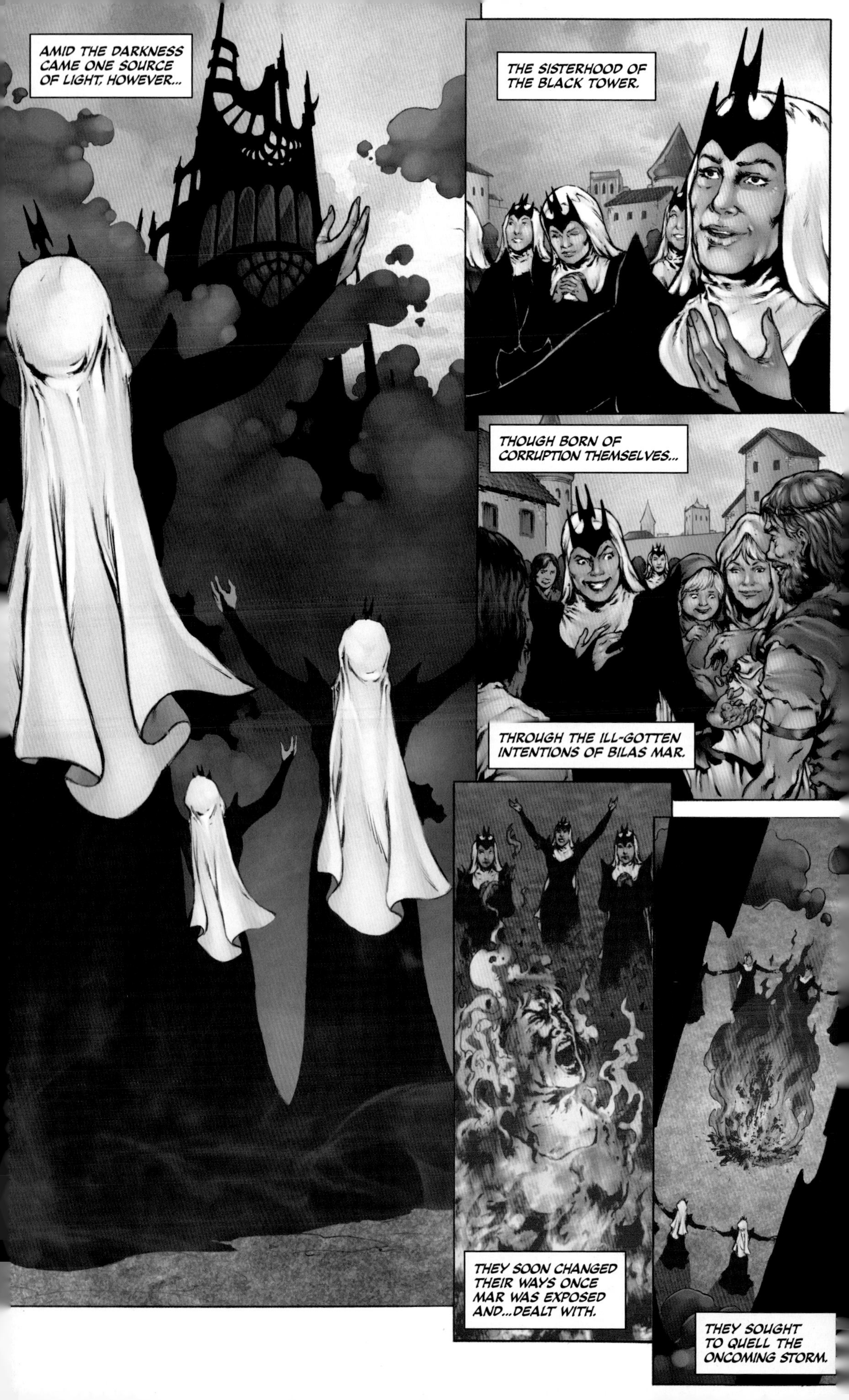
AMID THE DARKNESS CAME ONE SOURCE OF LIGHT, HOWEVER...
THE SISTERHOOD OF THE BLACK TOWER.
THOUGH BORN OF CORRUPTION THEMSELVES...
THROUGH THE ILL-GOTTEN INTENTIONS OF BILAS MAR.
THEY SOON CHANGED THEIR WAYS ONCE MAR WAS EXPOSED AND...DEALT WITH.
THEY SOUGHT TO QUELL THE ONCOMING STORM.

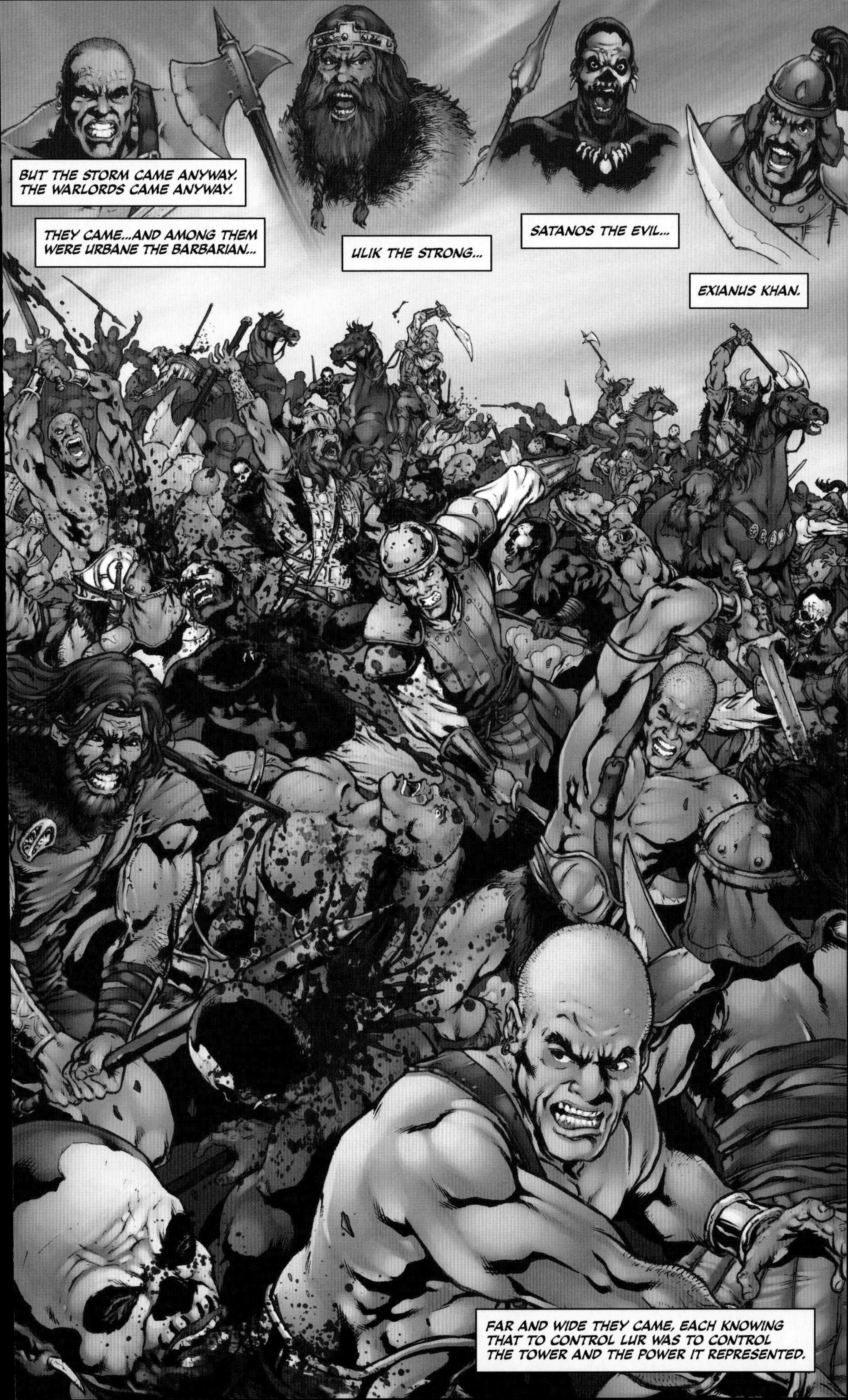
BUT THE STORM CAME ANYWAY. THE WARLORDS CAME ANYWAY.
THEY CAME...AND AMONG THEM WERE URBANE THE BARBARIAN...
ULIK THE STRONG...
SATANOS THE EVIL...
EXIANUS KHAN.
FAR AND WIDE THEY CAME, EACH KNOWING THAT TO CONTROL LUR WAS TO CONTROL THE TOWER AND THE POWER IT REPRESENTED.

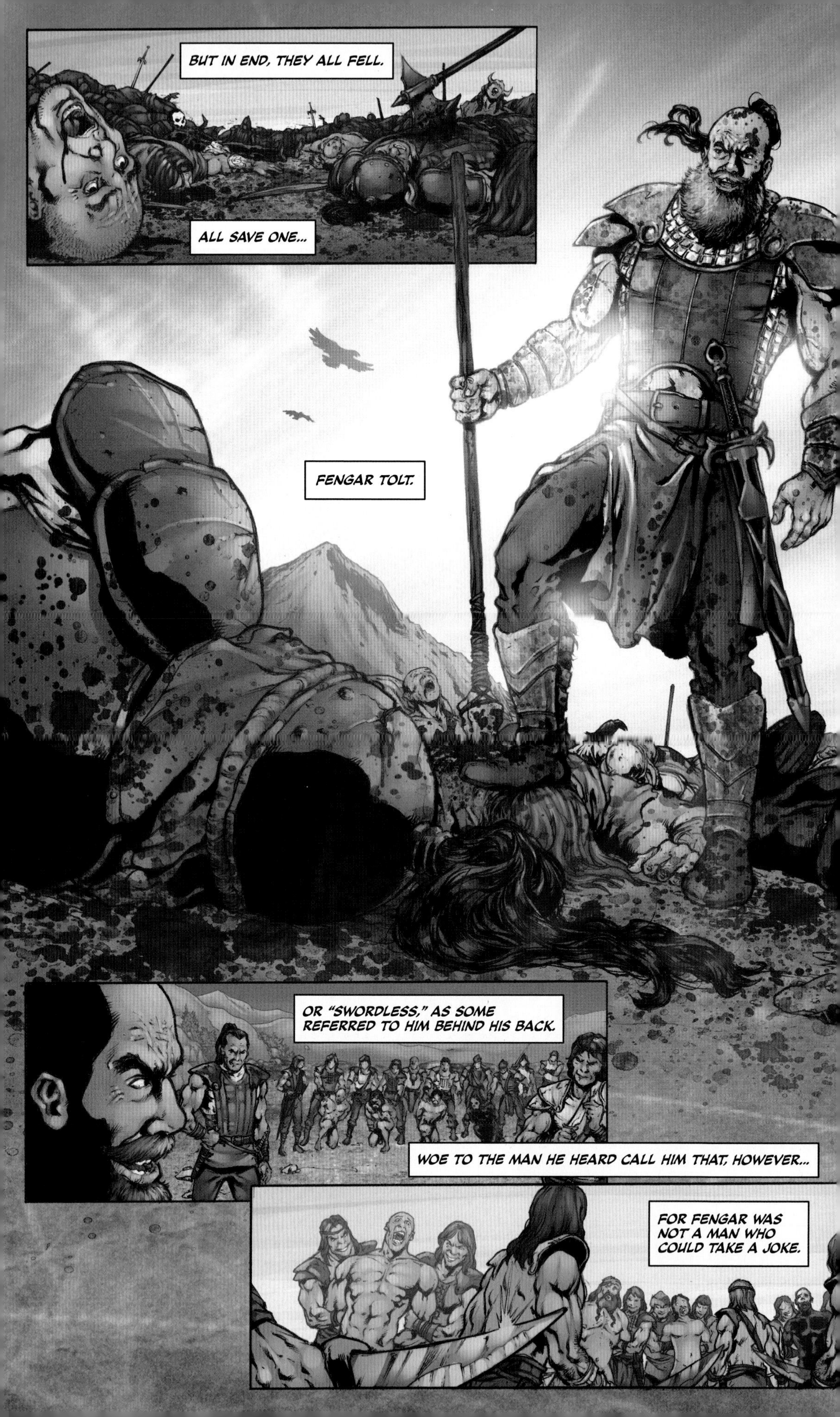
BUT IN END, THEY ALL FELL.
ALL SAVE ONE...
FENGAR TOLT.
OR "SWORDLESS," AS SOME REFERRED TO HIM BEHIND HIS BACK.
WOE TO THE MAN HE HEARD CALL HIM THAT, HOWEVER...
FOR FENGAR WAS NOT A MAN WHO COULD TAKE A JOKE.

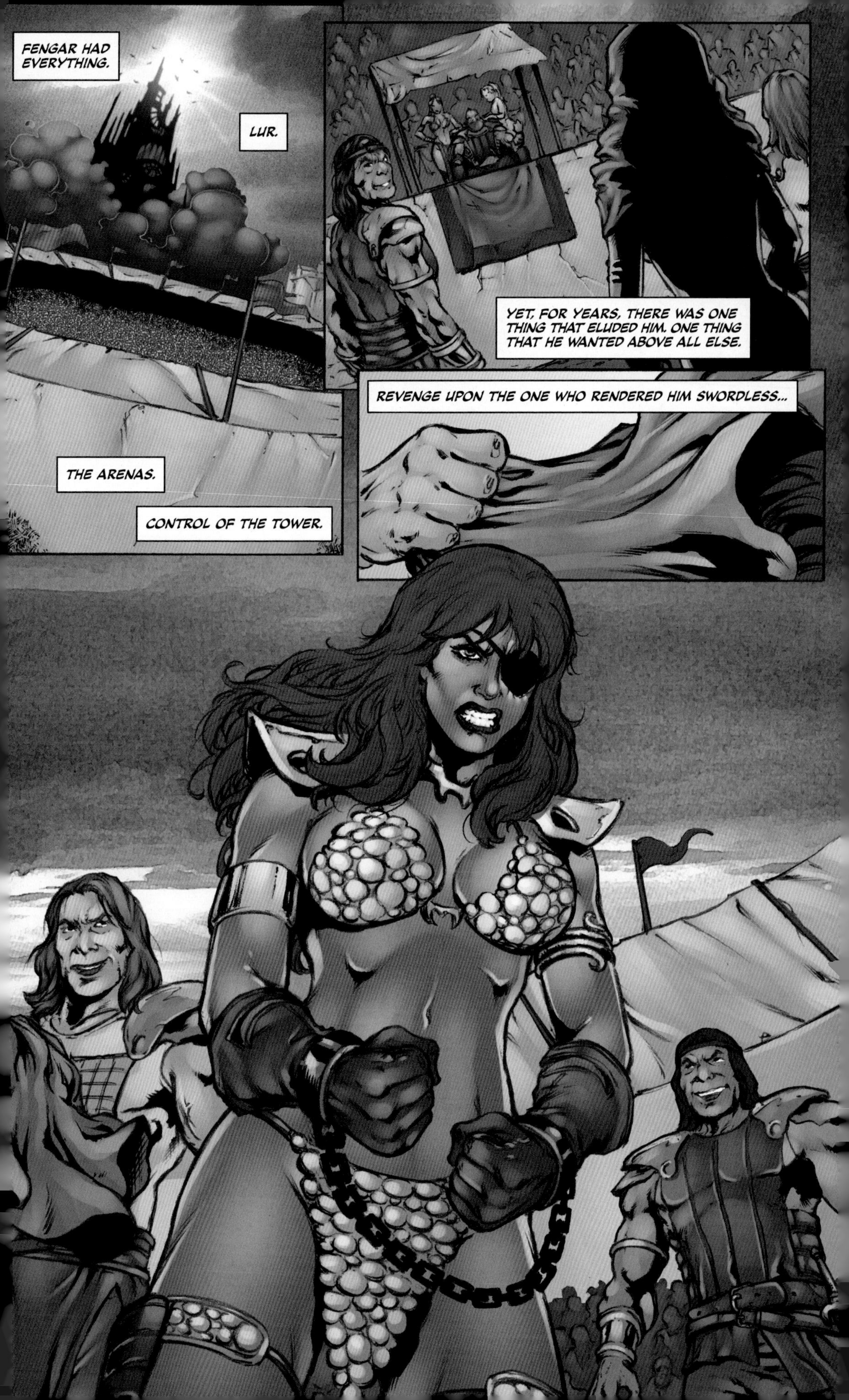
FENGAR HAD EVERYTHING.
LUR.
THE ARENAS.
CONTROL OF THE TOWER.
YET, FOR YEARS, THERE WAS ONE THING THAT ELUDED HIM. ONE THING THAT HE WANTED ABOVE ALL ELSE.
REVENGE UPON THE ONE WHO RENDERED HIM SWORDLESS...

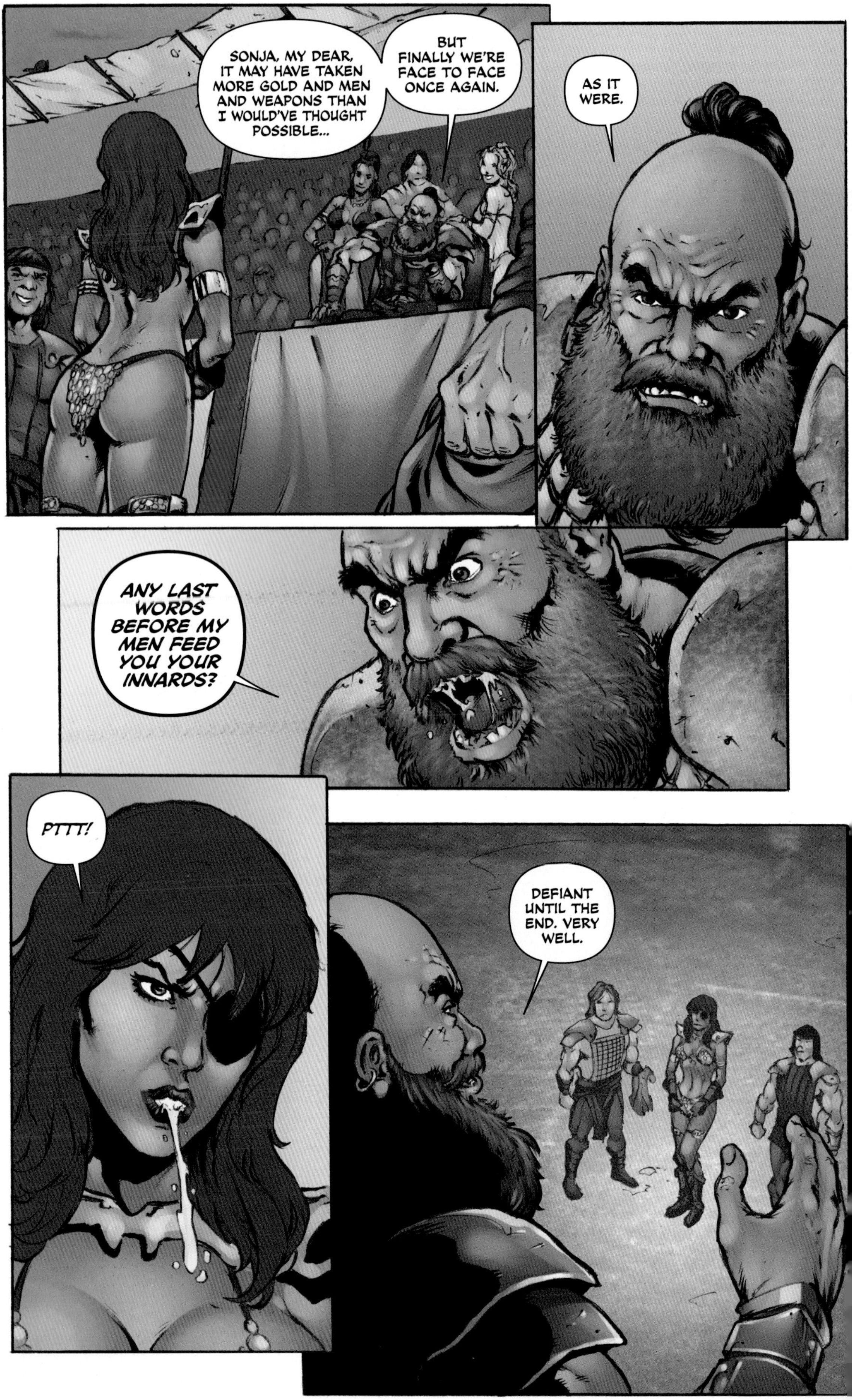
SONJA, MY DEAR, IT MAY HAVE TAKEN MORE GOLD AND MEN AND WEAPONS THAN I WOULD'VE THOUGHT POSSIBLE...
BUT FINALLY WE'RE FACE TO FACE ONCE AGAIN.
AS IT WERE.
ANY LAST WORDS BEFORE MY MEN FEED YOU YOUR INNARDS?
PTTT!
DEFIANT UNTIL THE END. VERY WELL.

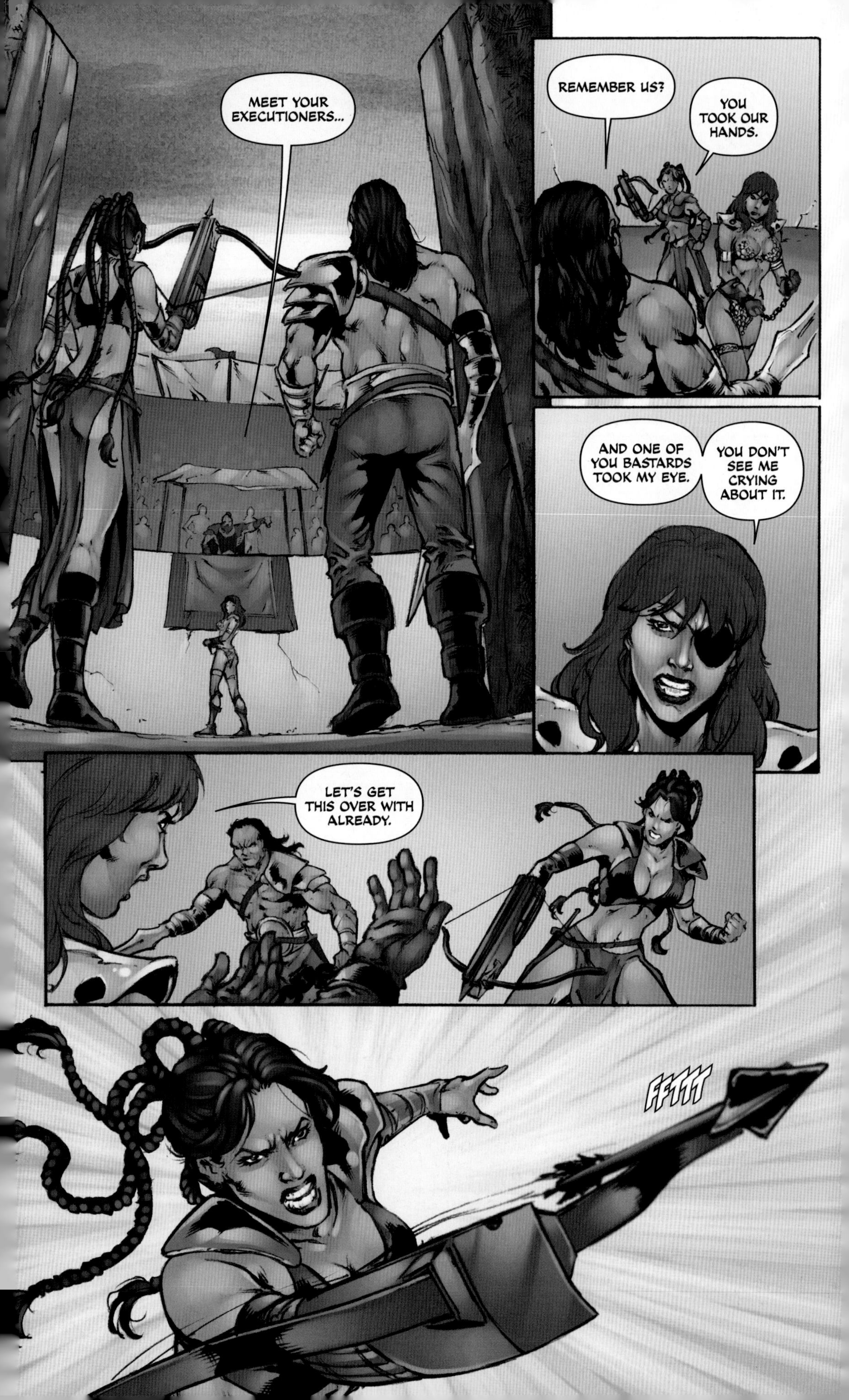
MEET YOUR EXECUTIONERS...
REMEMBER US?
YOU TOOK OUR HANDS.
AND ONE OF YOU BASTARDS TOOK MY EYE.
YOU DON'T SEE ME CRYING ABOUT IT.
LET'S GET THIS OVER WITH ALREADY.
FFTTT

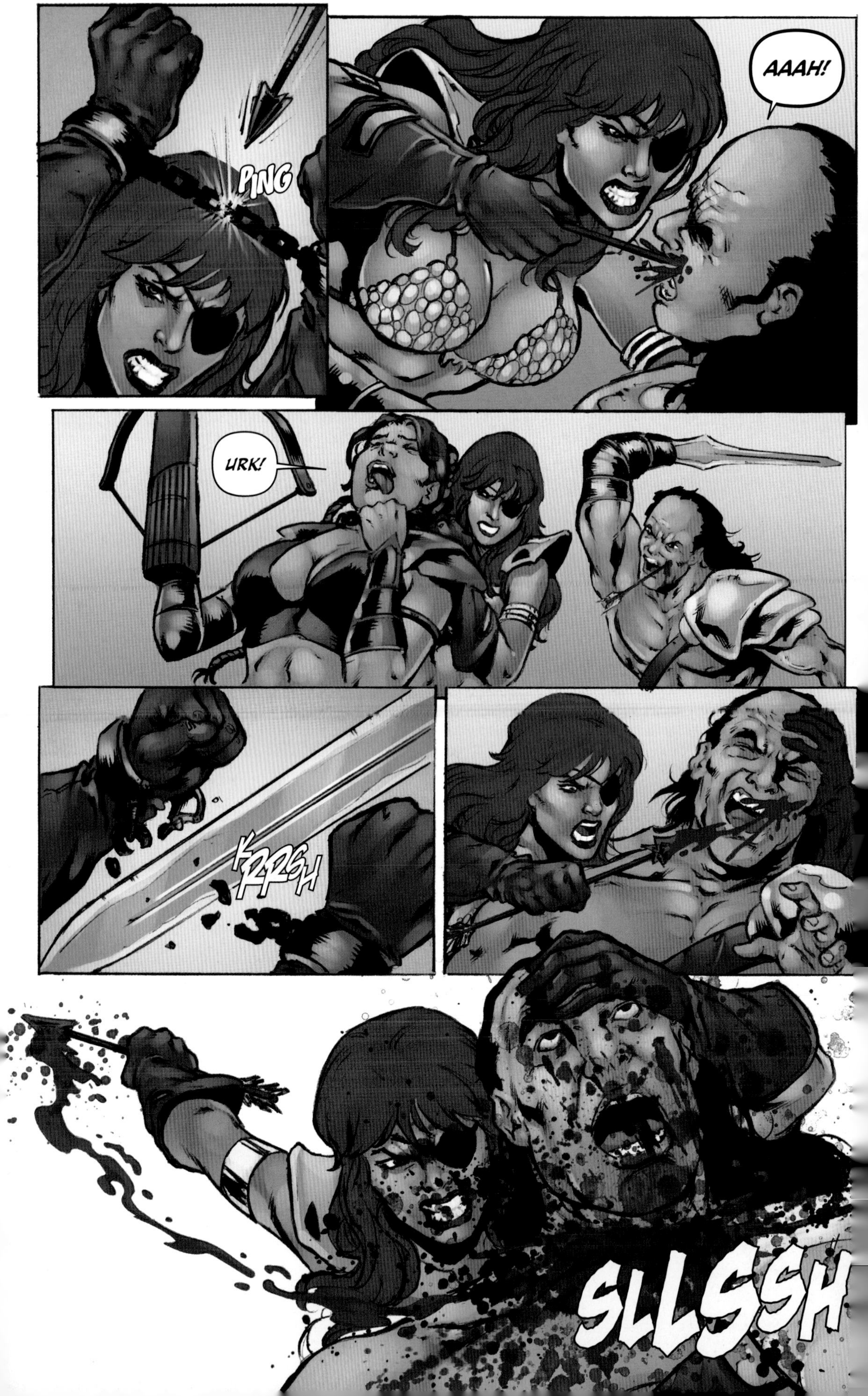
PING
AAAH!
URK!
KRRSH
SLLSSH

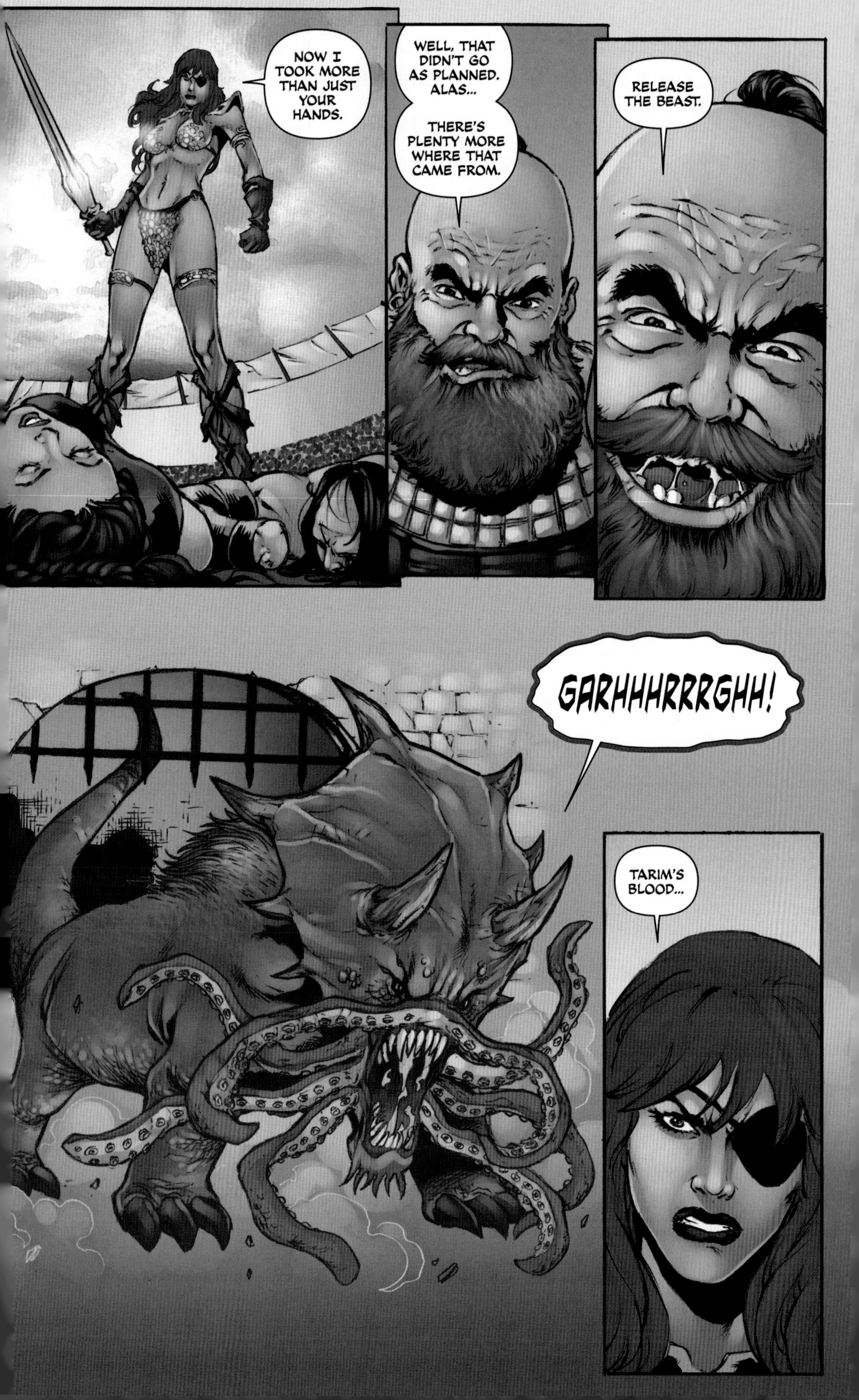
NOW I TOOK MORE THAN JUST YOUR HANDS.
WELL, THAT DIDN'T GO AS PLANNED. ALAS...
THERE'S PLENTY MORE WHERE THAT CAME FROM.
RELEASE THE BEAST.
GARHHHRRRGHH!
TARIM'S BLOOD...

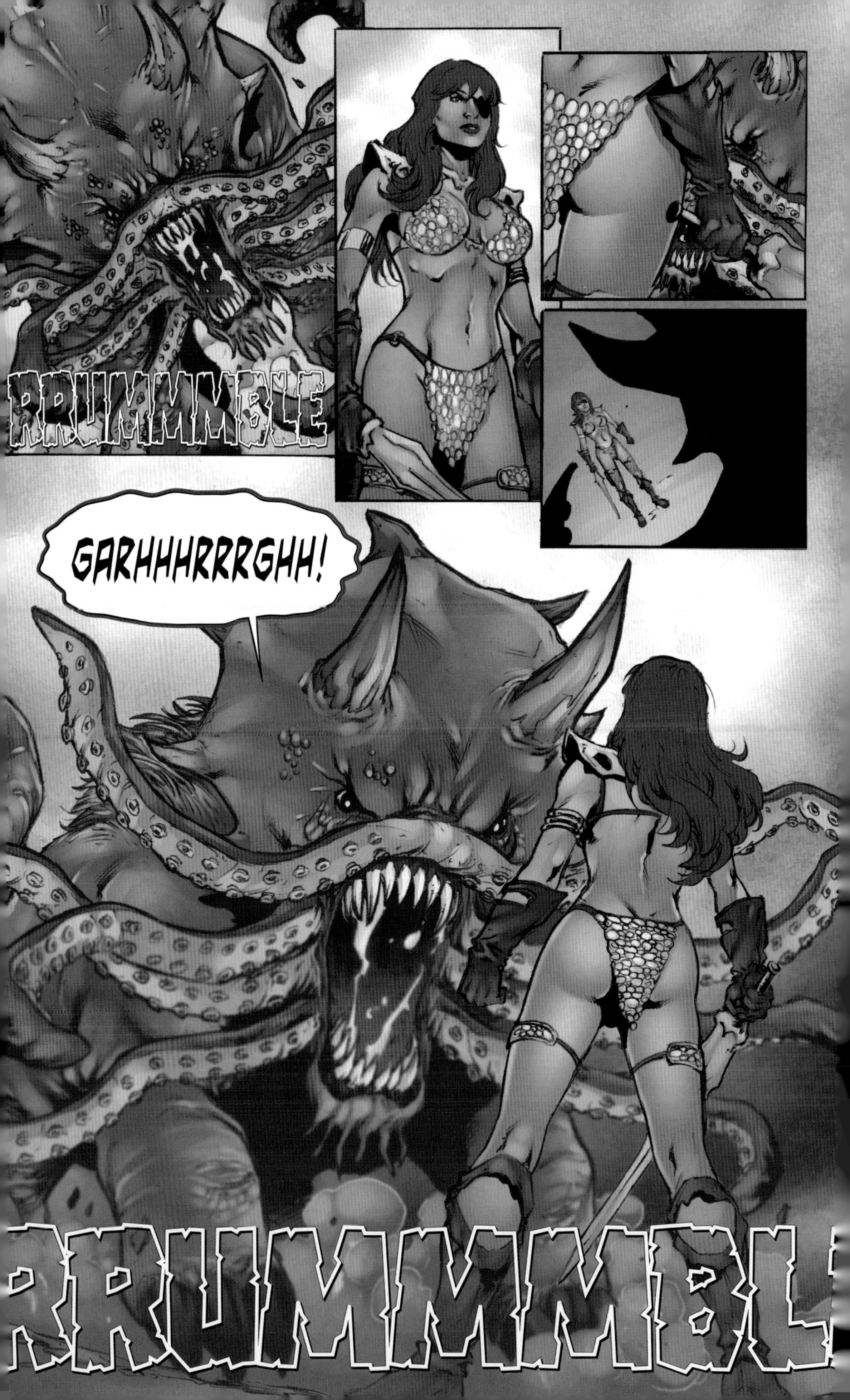
RRUMMMBLE
GARHHHRRRGHH!
RRUMMMBL

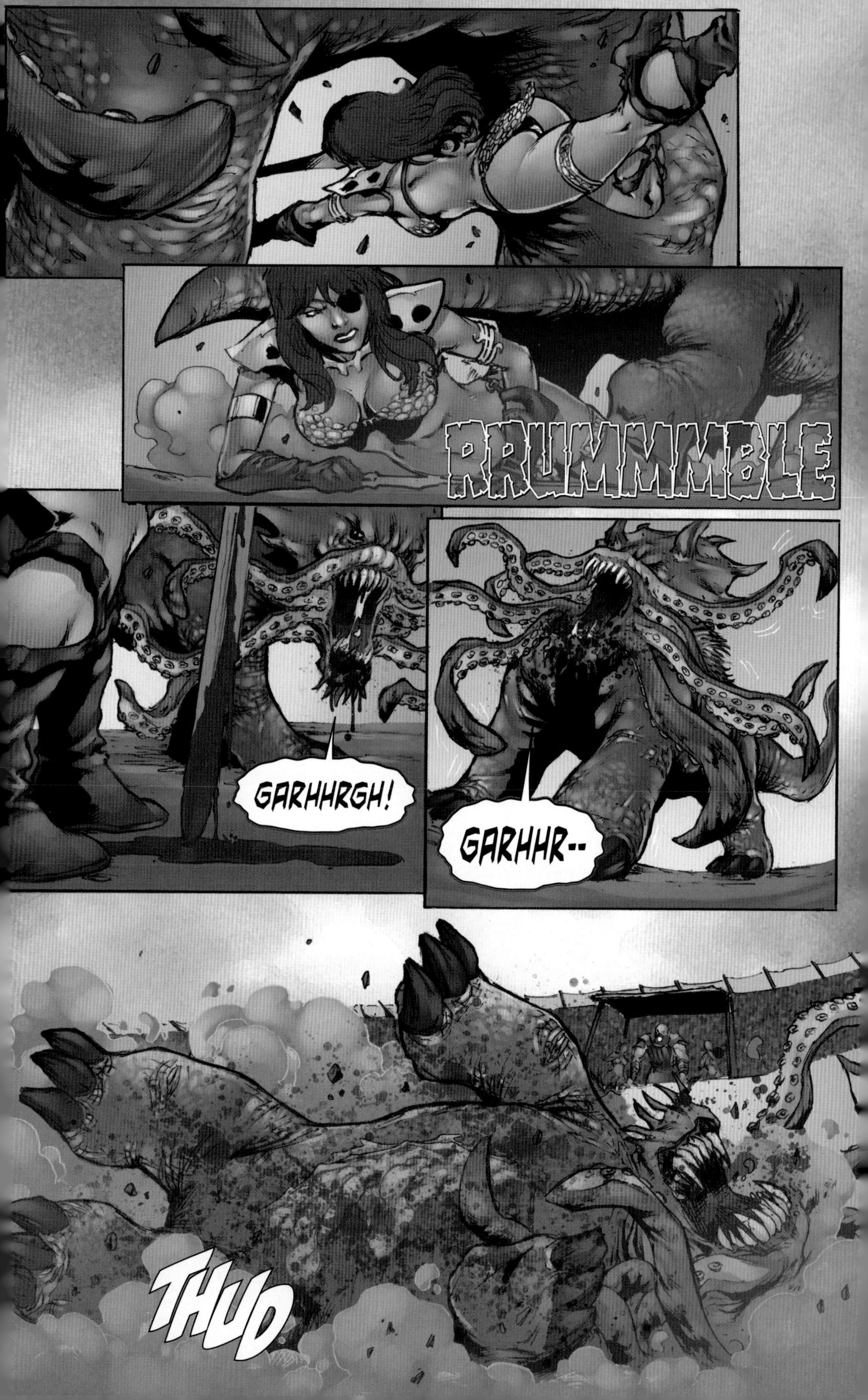
RRUMMMBLE
GARHHRGH!
GARHHR--
THUD

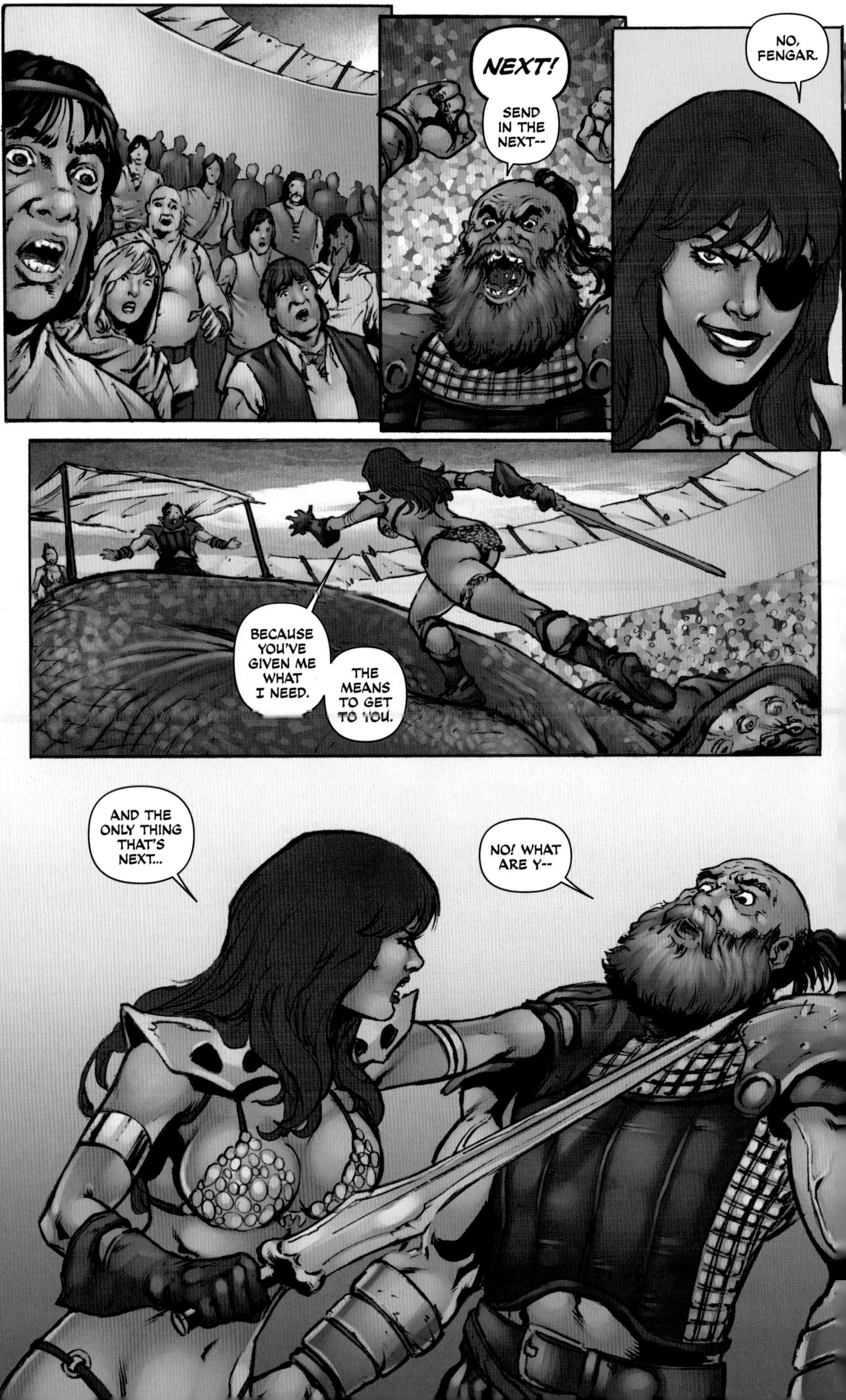
NEXT!
SEND IN THE NEXT--
NO, FENGAR.
BECAUSE YOU'VE GIVEN ME WHAT I NEED.
THE MEANS TO GET TO YOU.
AND THE ONLY THING THAT'S NEXT...
NO! WHAT ARE Y--

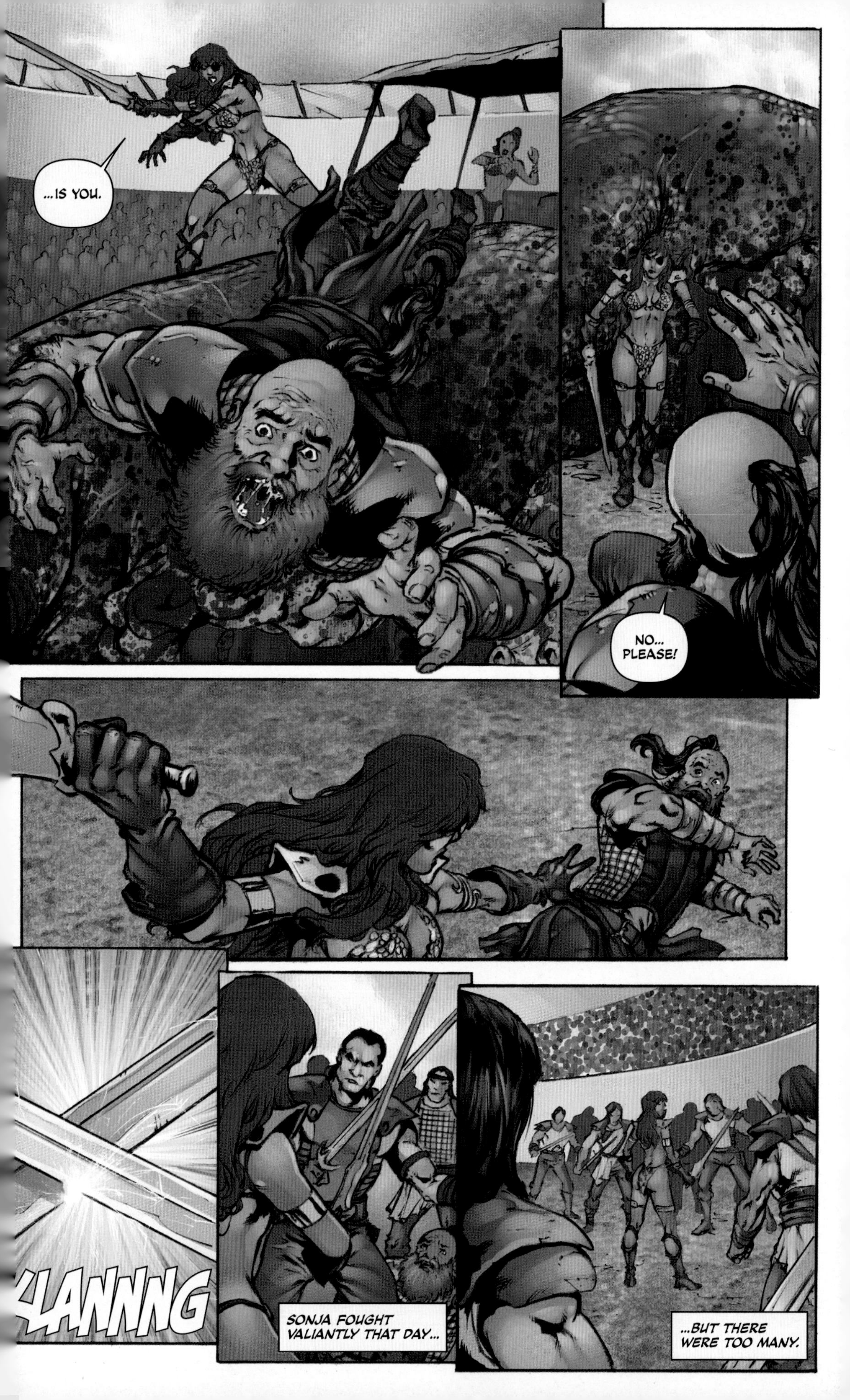
...IS YOU.
NO... PLEASE!
LANNNG
SONJA FOUGHT VALIANTLY THAT DAY...
...BUT THERE WERE TOO MANY.

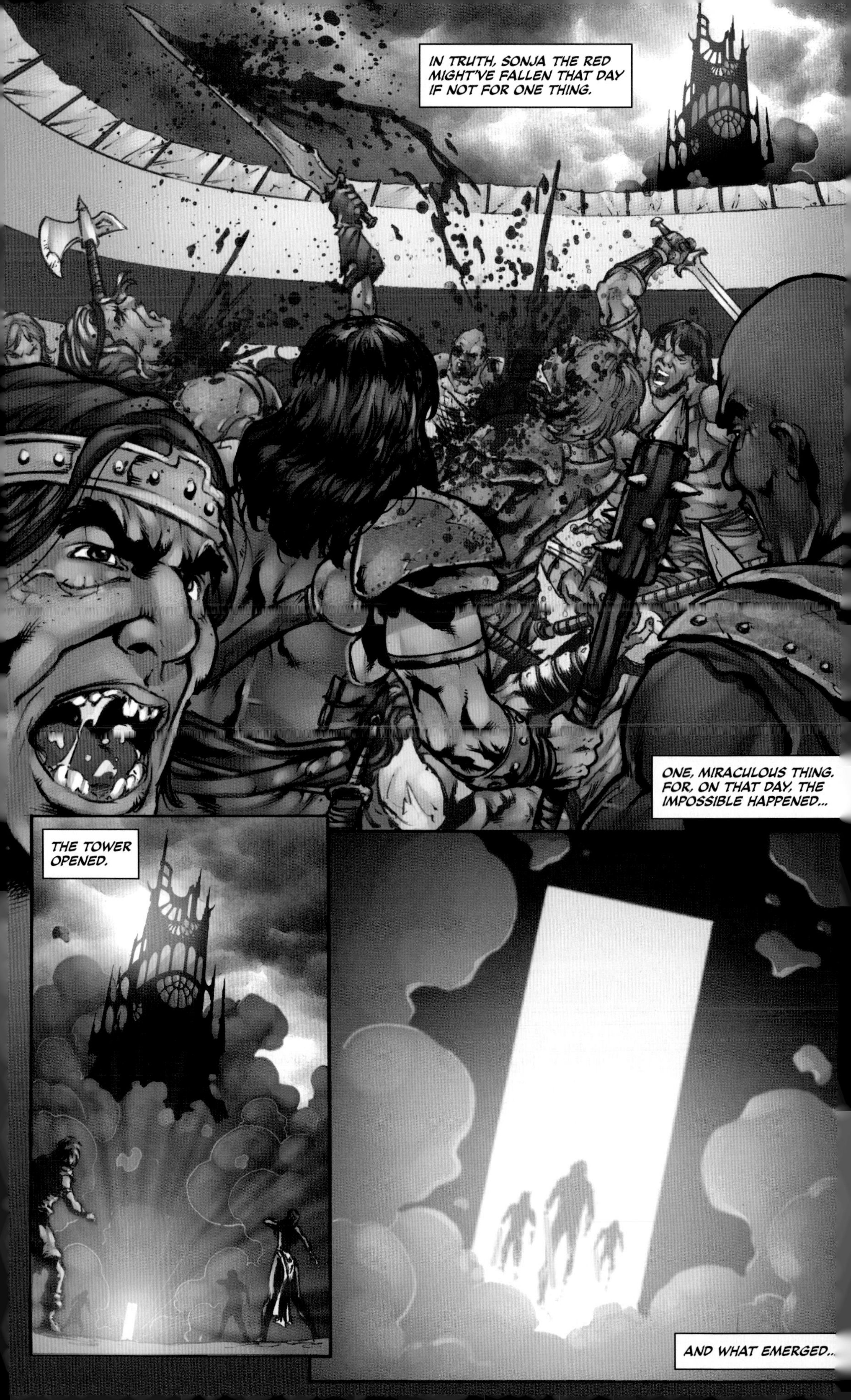
IN TRUTH, SONJA THE RED MIGHT'VE FALLEN THAT DAY IF NOT FOR ONE THING.
ONE, MIRACULOUS THING. FOR, ON THAT DAY, THE IMPOSSIBLE HAPPENED...
THE TOWER OPENED.
AND WHAT EMERGED...

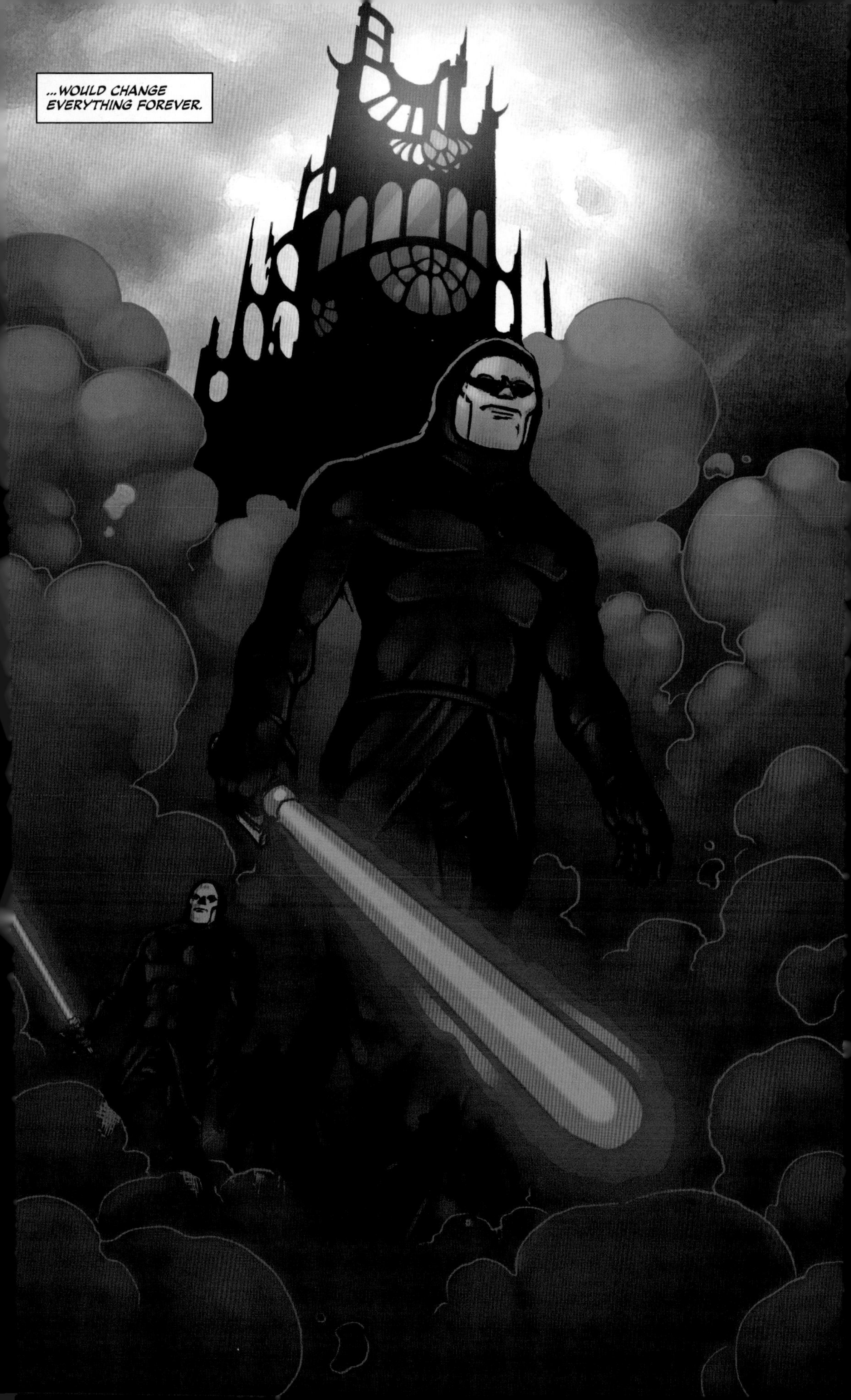
...WOULD CHANGE EVERYTHING FOREVER.

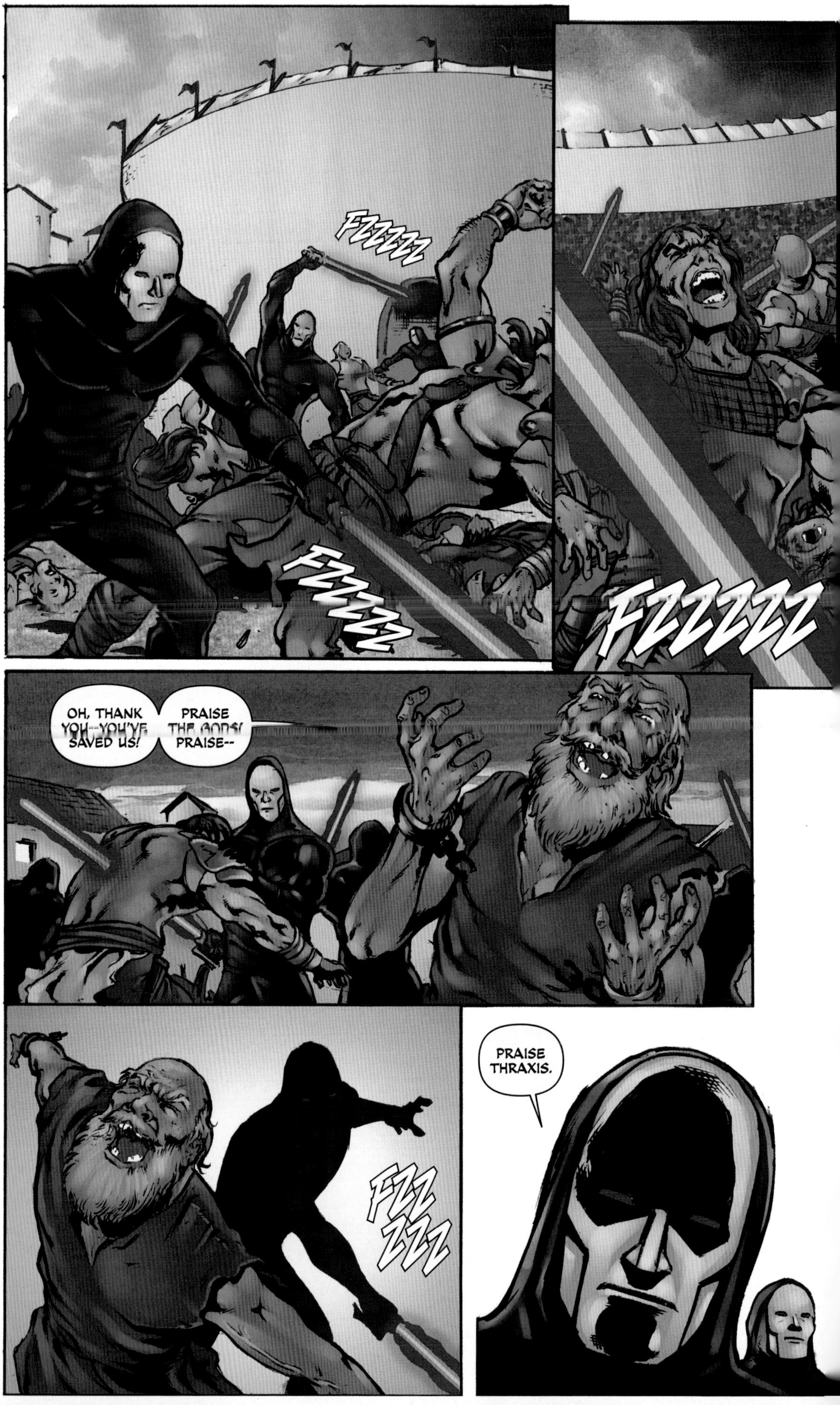
FZZZZZ
FZZZZZ
FZZZZZ
OH, THANK YOU--YOU'VE SAVED US!
PRAISE THE GODS! PRAISE--
FZZ ZZZ
PRAISE THRAXIS.

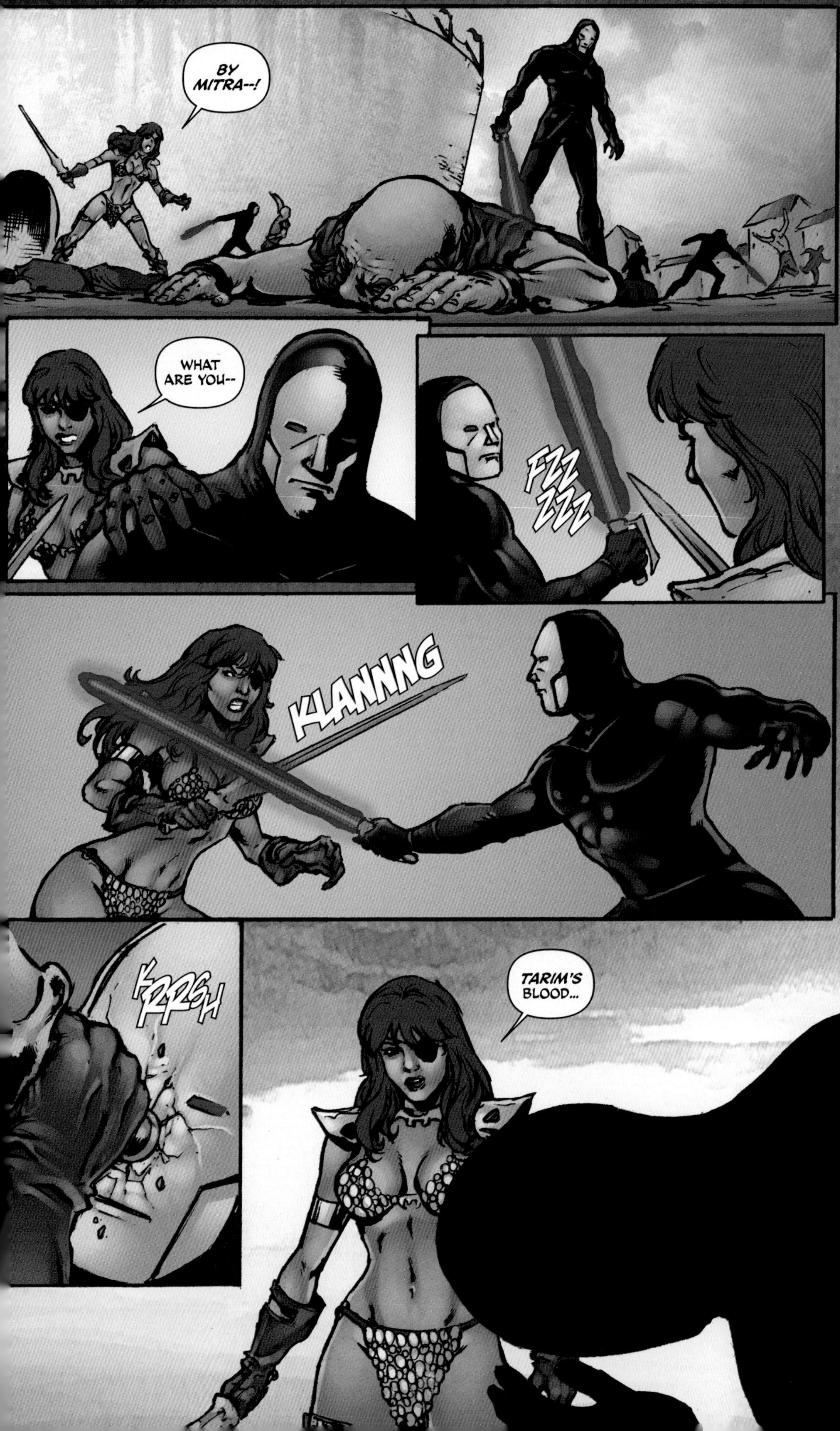

BY MITRA--!
WHAT ARE YOU--
FZZ ZZZ
KLANNNG
KRRSH
TARIM'S BLOOD...

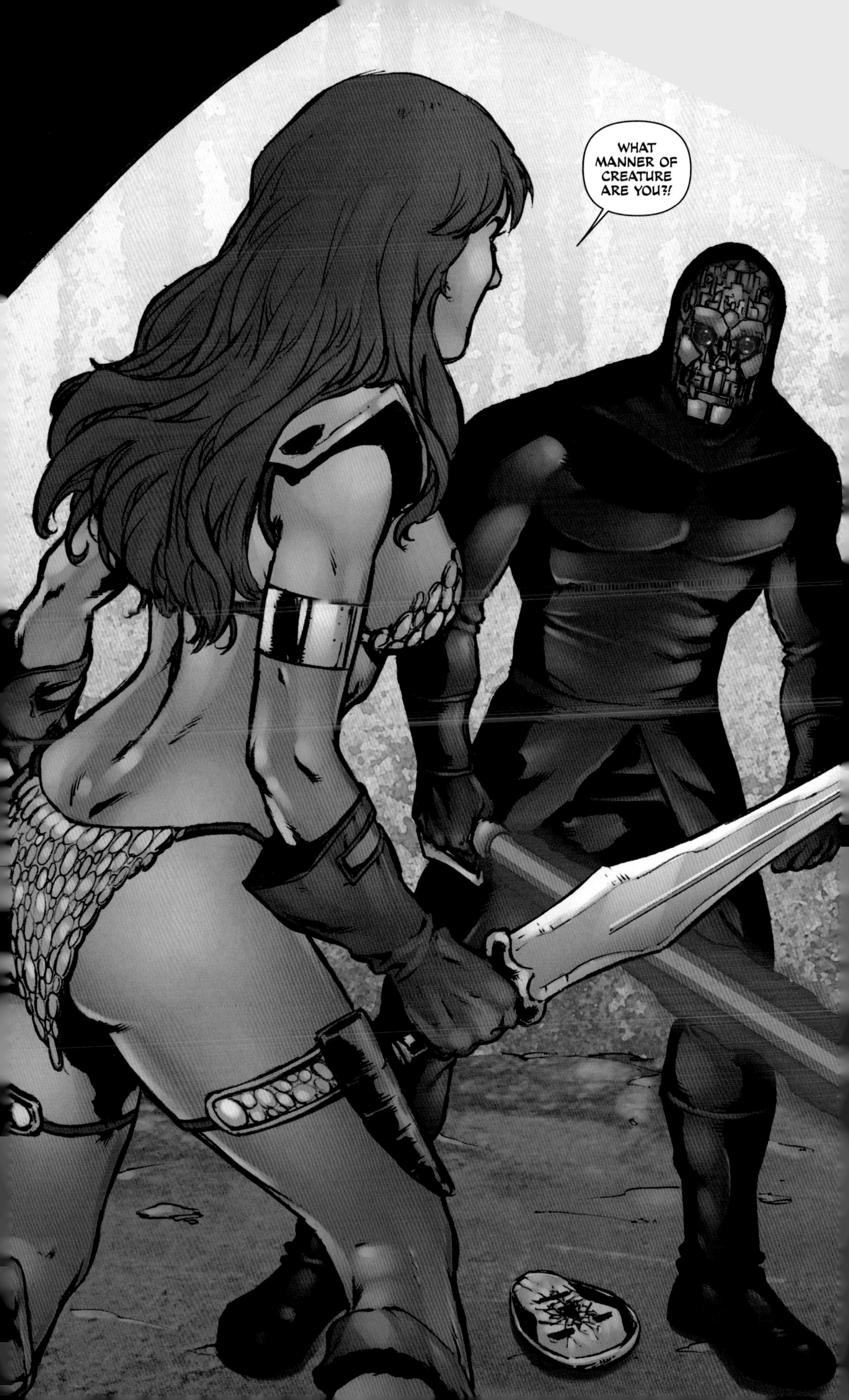
WHAT MANNER OF CREATURE ARE YOU?!

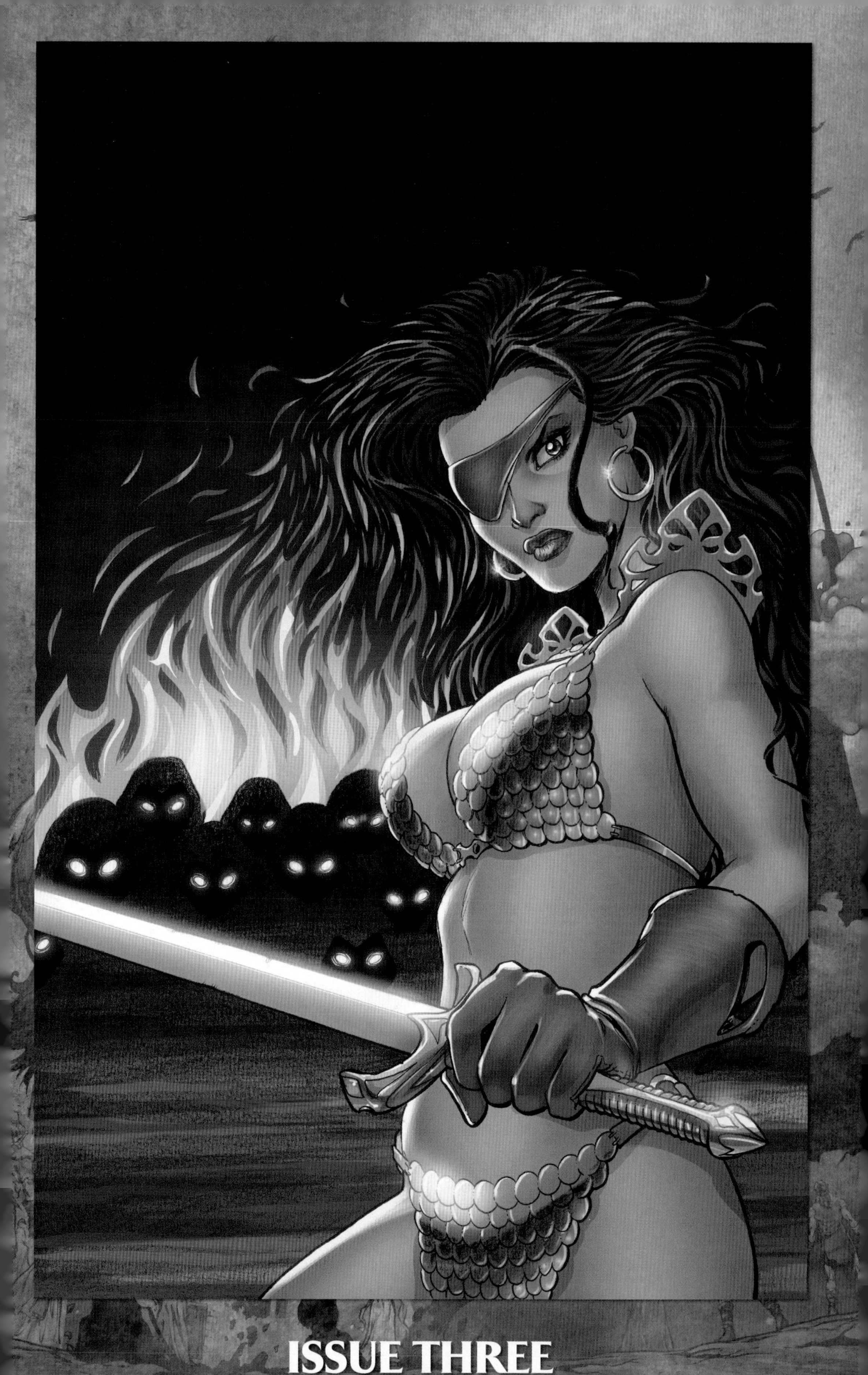

ISSUE THREE
Cover Art By Amanda Conner

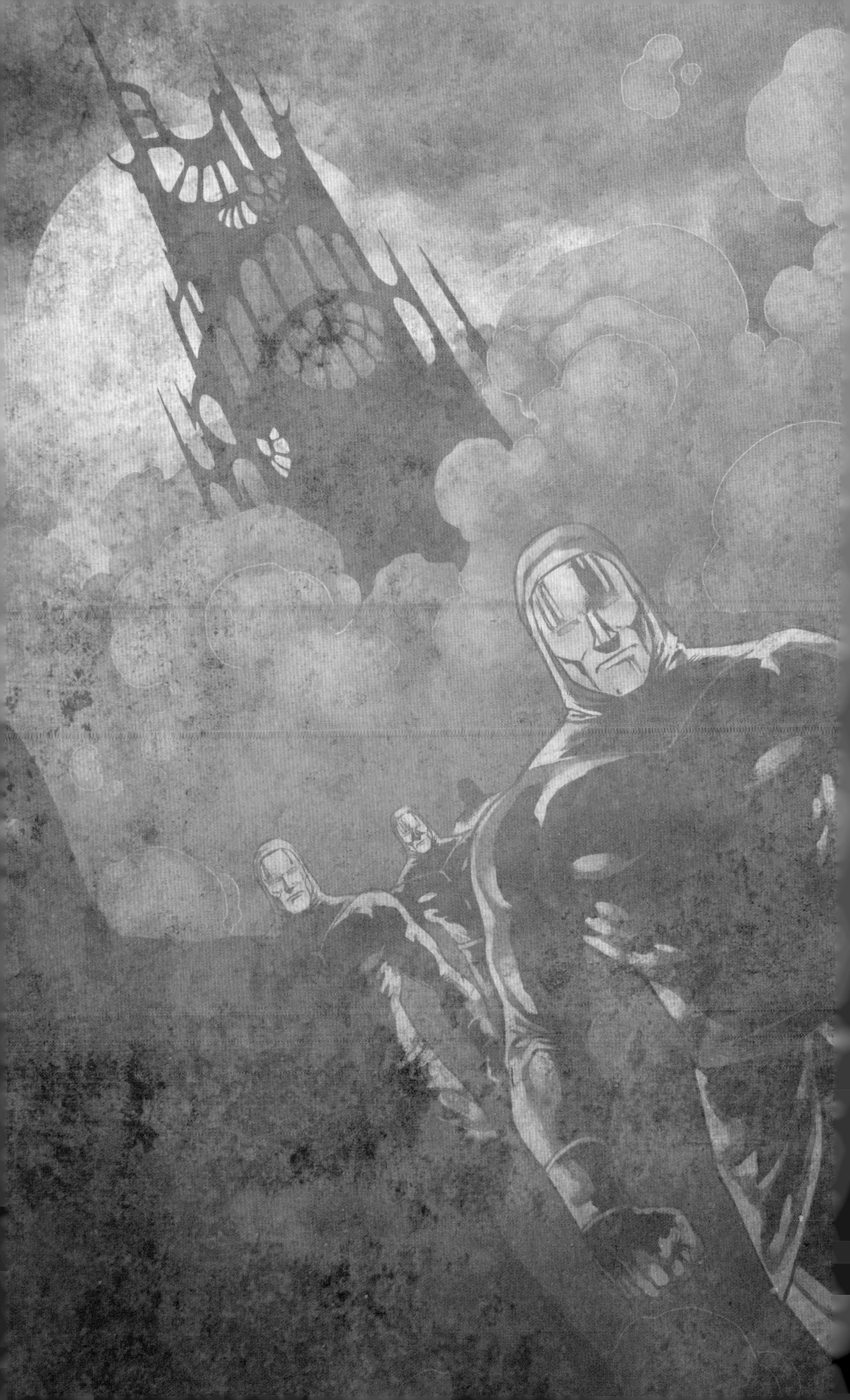

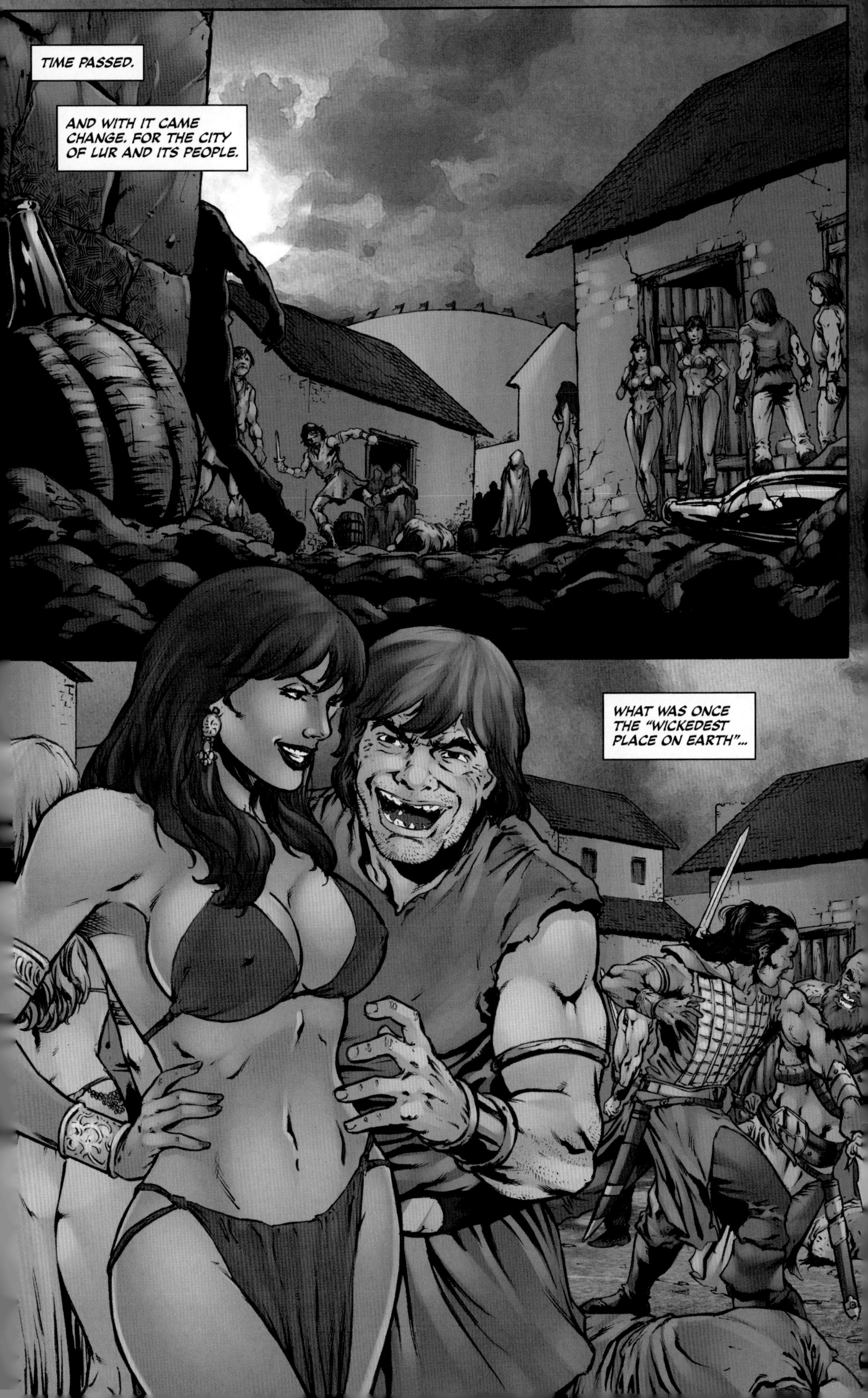
TIME PASSED.
AND WITH IT CAME CHANGE. FOR THE CITY OF LUR AND ITS PEOPLE.
WHAT WAS ONCE THE "WICKEDEST PLACE ON EARTH"...

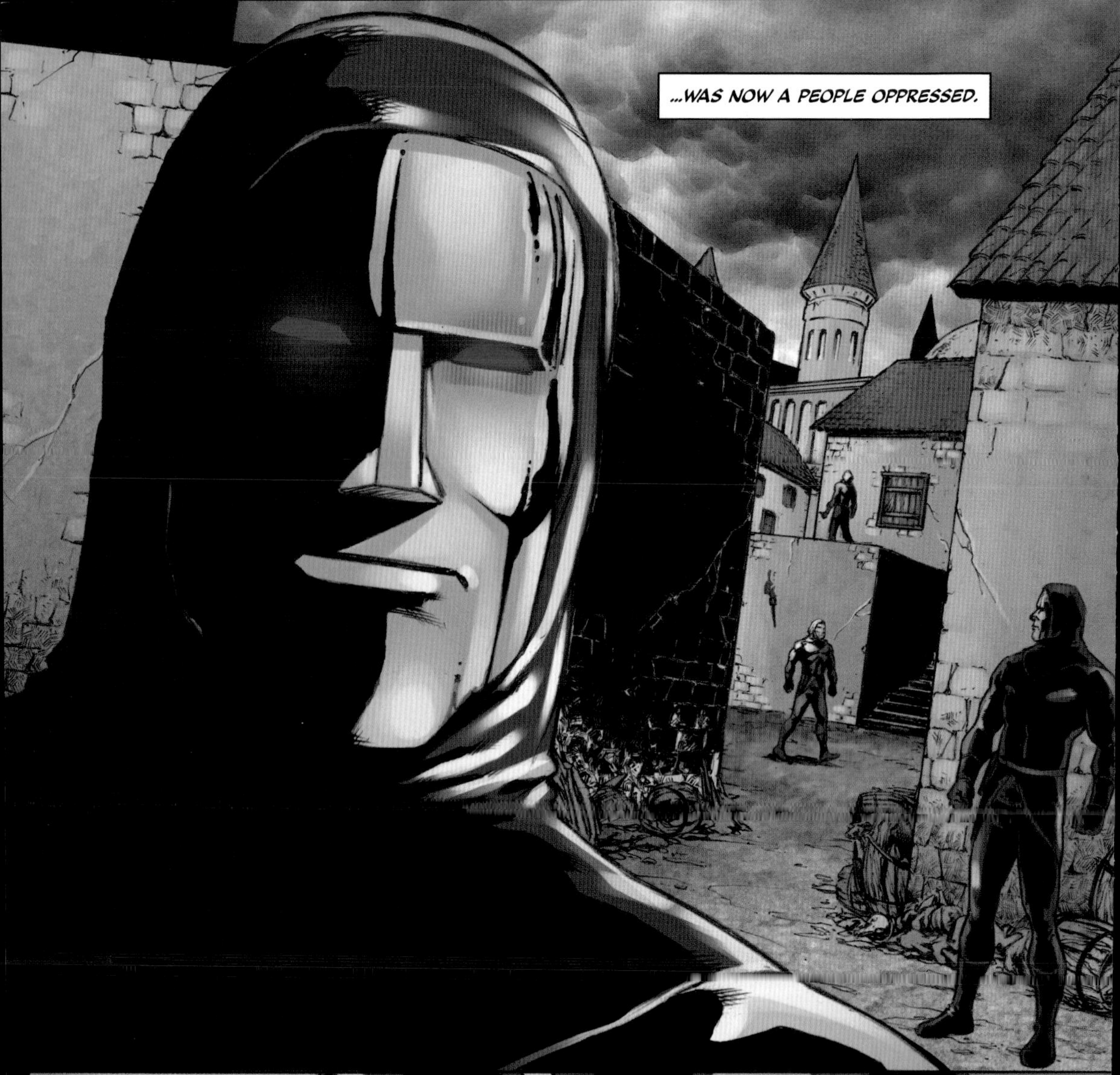
...WAS NOW A PEOPLE OPPRESSED.

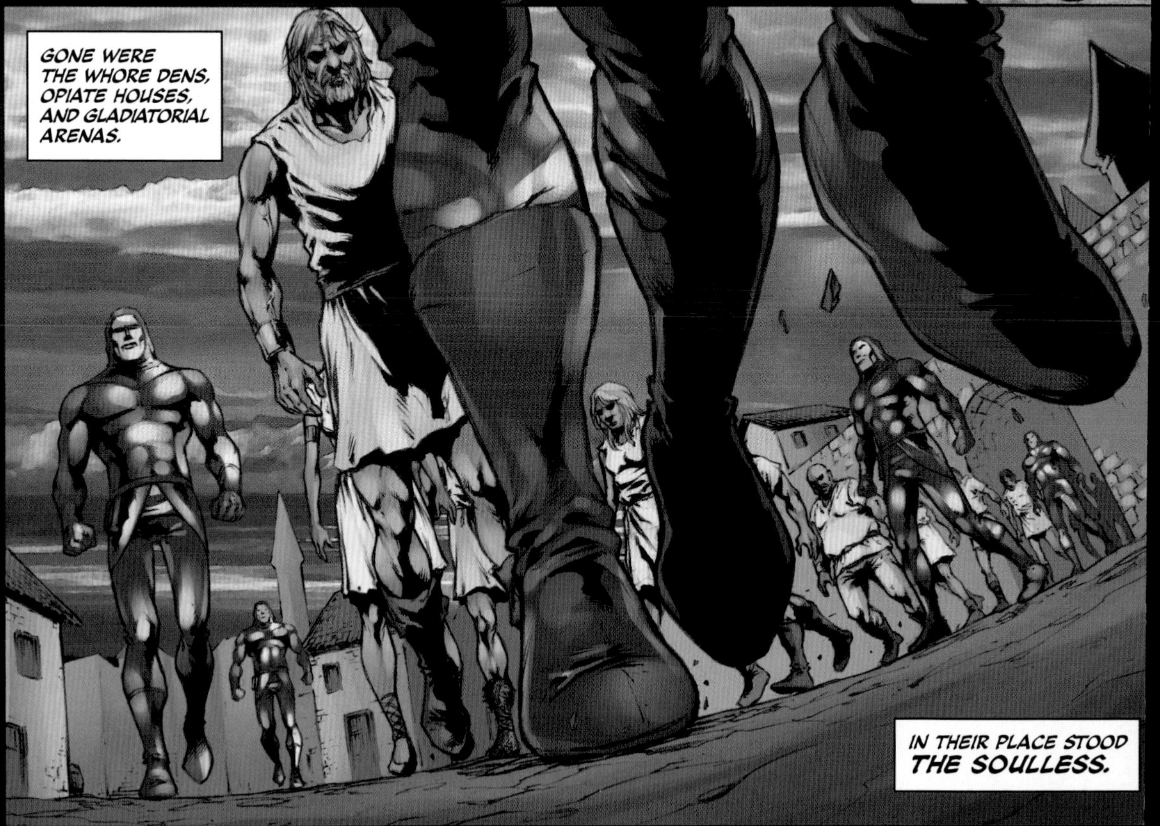
GONE WERE THE WHORE DENS, OPIATE HOUSES, AND GLADIATORIAL ARENAS.
IN THEIR PLACE STOOD THE SOULLESS.

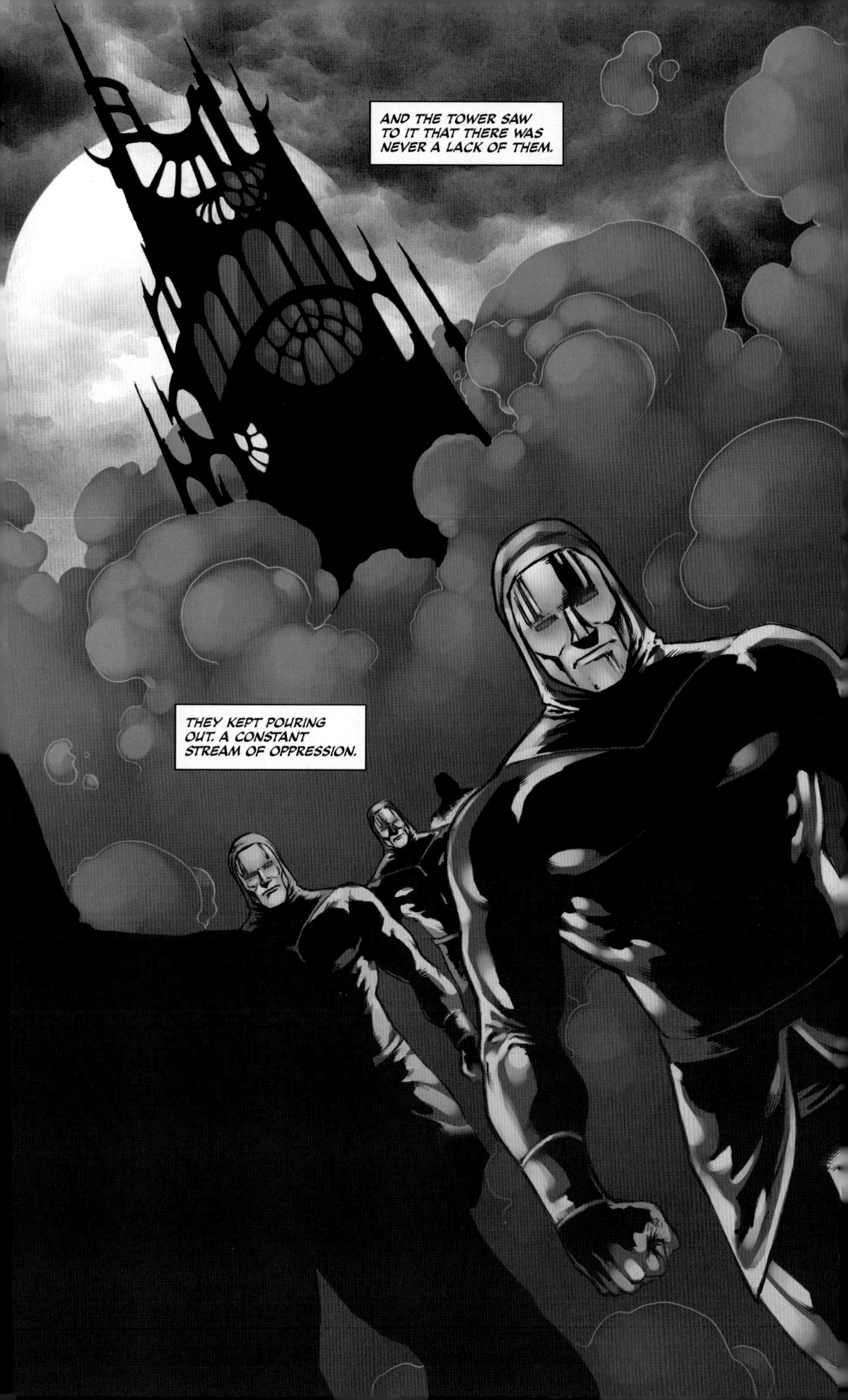
AND THE TOWER SAW TO IT THAT THERE WAS NEVER A LACK OF THEM.
THEY KEPT POURING OUT. A CONSTANT STREAM OF OPPRESSION.

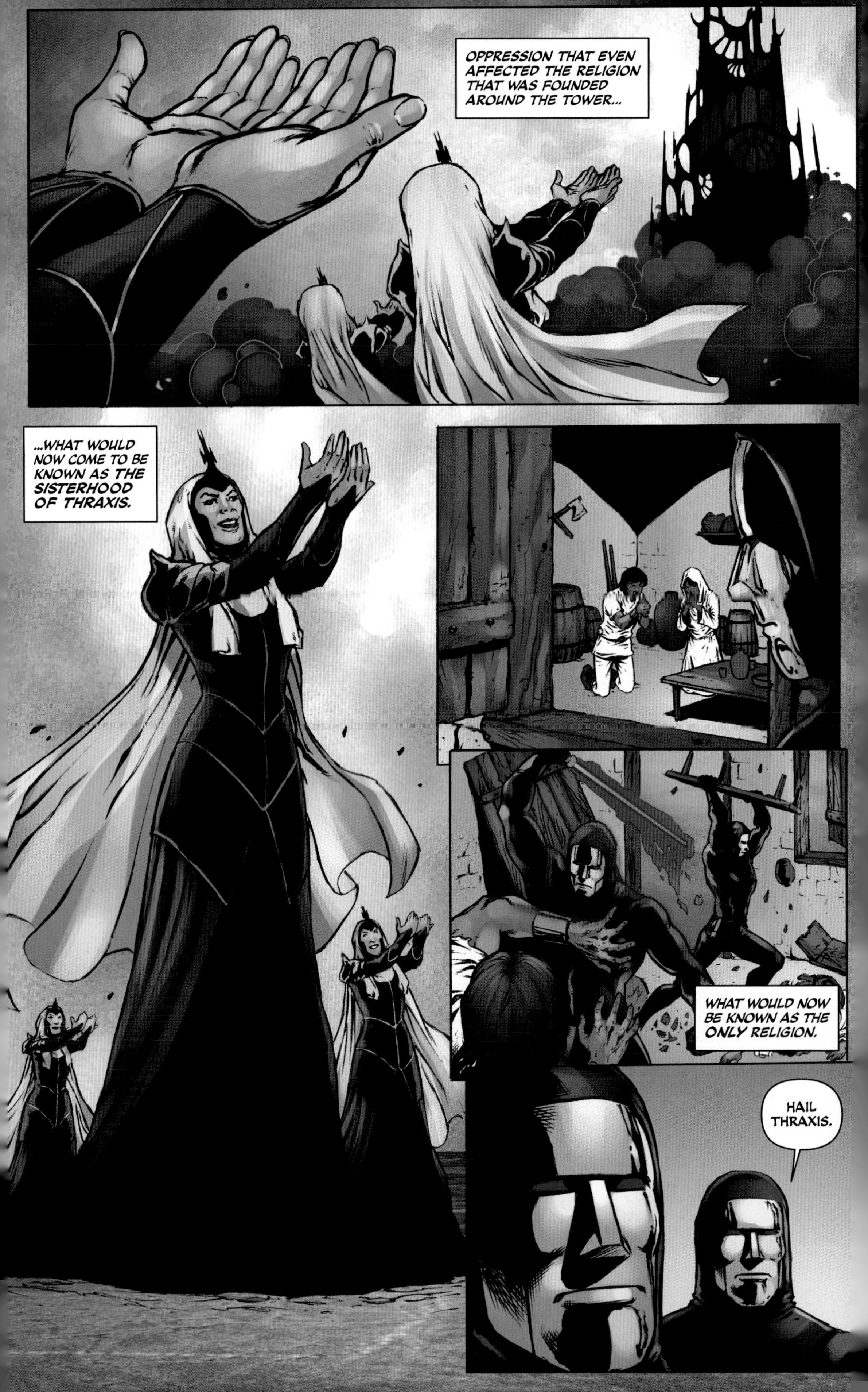
OPPRESSION THAT EVEN AFFECTED THE RELIGION THAT WAS FOUNDED AROUND THE TOWER...
...WHAT WOULD NOW COME TO BE KNOWN AS THE SISTERHOOD OF THRAXIS.
WHAT WOULD NOW BE KNOWN AS THE ONLY RELIGION.
HAIL THRAXIS.

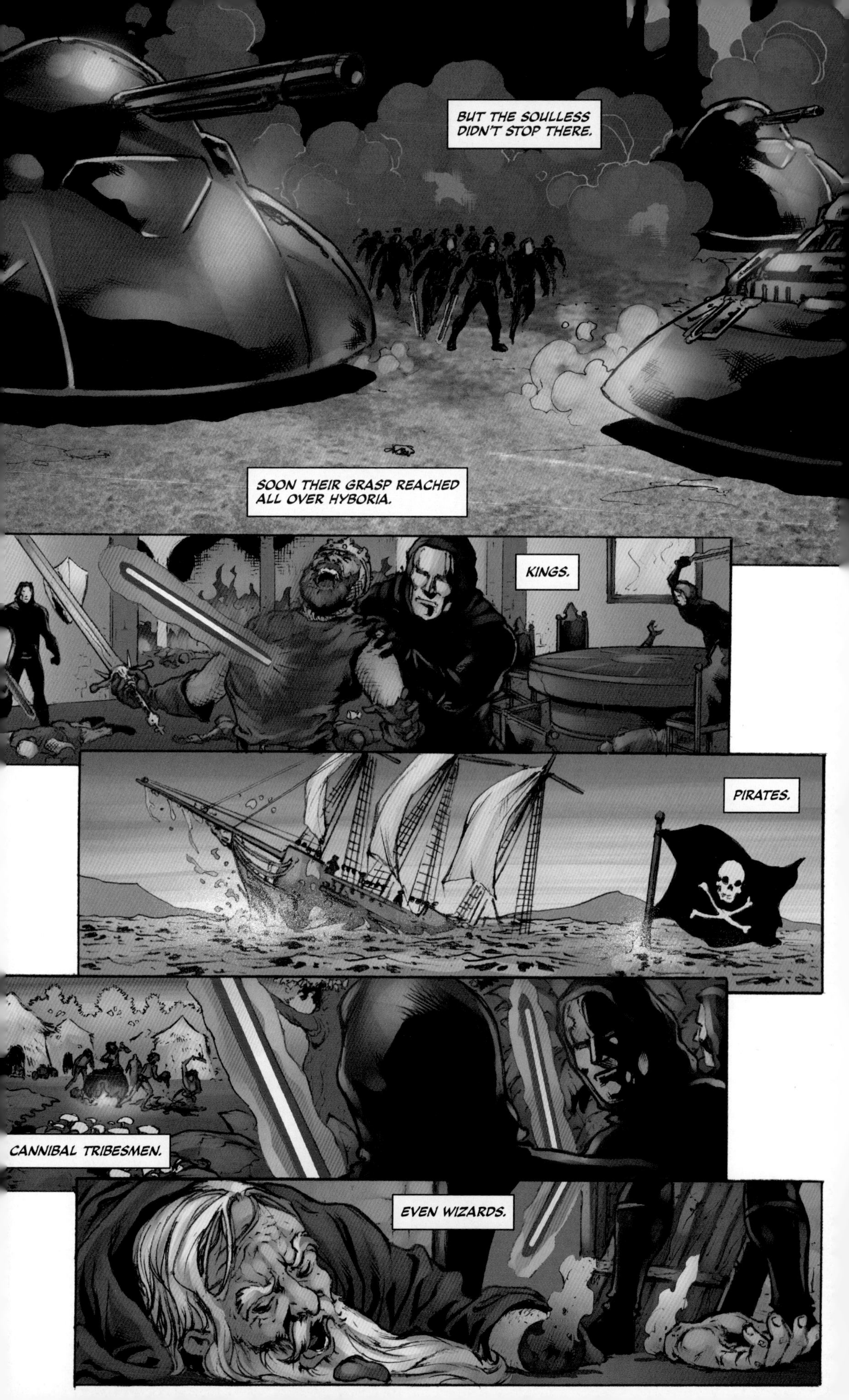
BUT THE SOULLESS DIDN'T STOP THERE.
SOON THEIR GRASP REACHED ALL OVER HYBORIA.
KINGS.
PIRATES.
CANNIBAL TRIBESMEN.
EVEN WIZARDS.

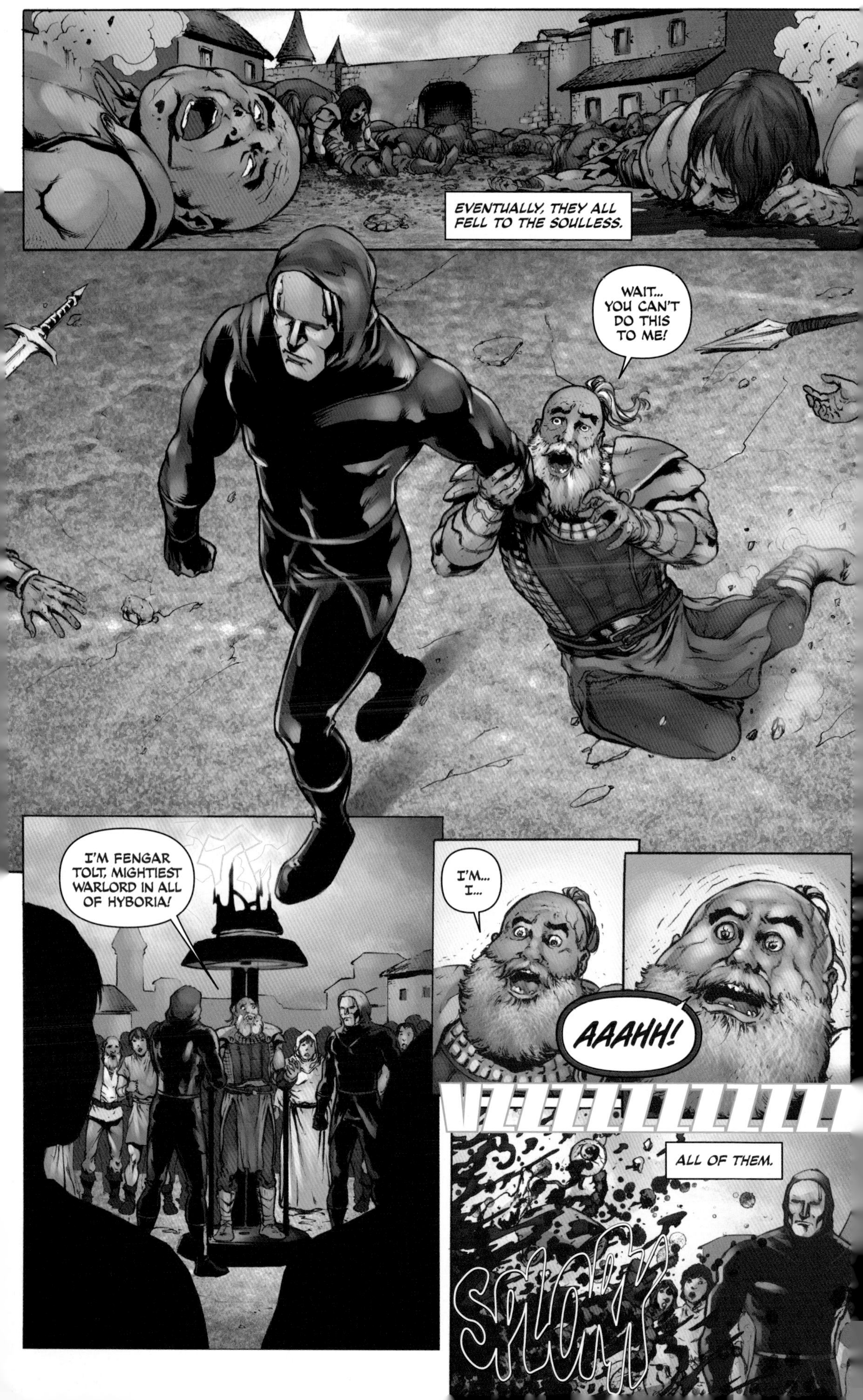
EVENTUALLY, THEY ALL FELL TO THE SOULLESS.
WAIT... YOU CAN'T DO THIS TO ME!
I'M FENGAR TOLT, MIGHTIEST WARLORD IN ALL OF HYBORIA!
I'M... I...
AAAHH!
VZZZZZZZZZZZ
ALL OF THEM.
SPLOOSH

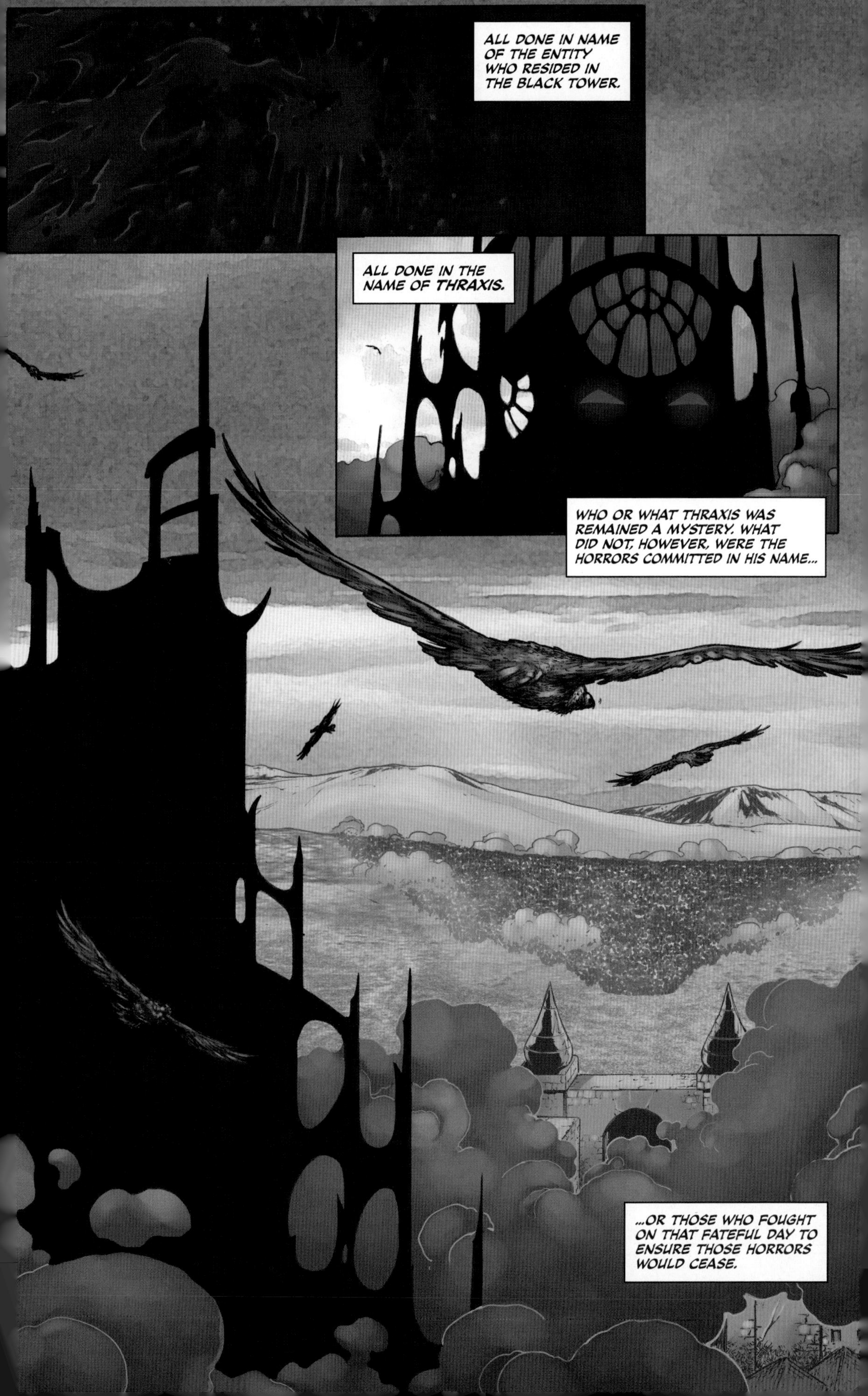
ALL DONE IN NAME OF THE ENTITY WHO RESIDED IN THE BLACK TOWER.
ALL DONE IN THE NAME OF THRAXIS.
WHO OR WHAT THRAXIS WAS REMAINED A MYSTERY. WHAT DID NOT, HOWEVER, WERE THE HORRORS COMMITTED IN HIS NAME...
...OR THOSE WHO FOUGHT ON THAT FATEFUL DAY TO ENSURE THOSE HORRORS WOULD CEASE.

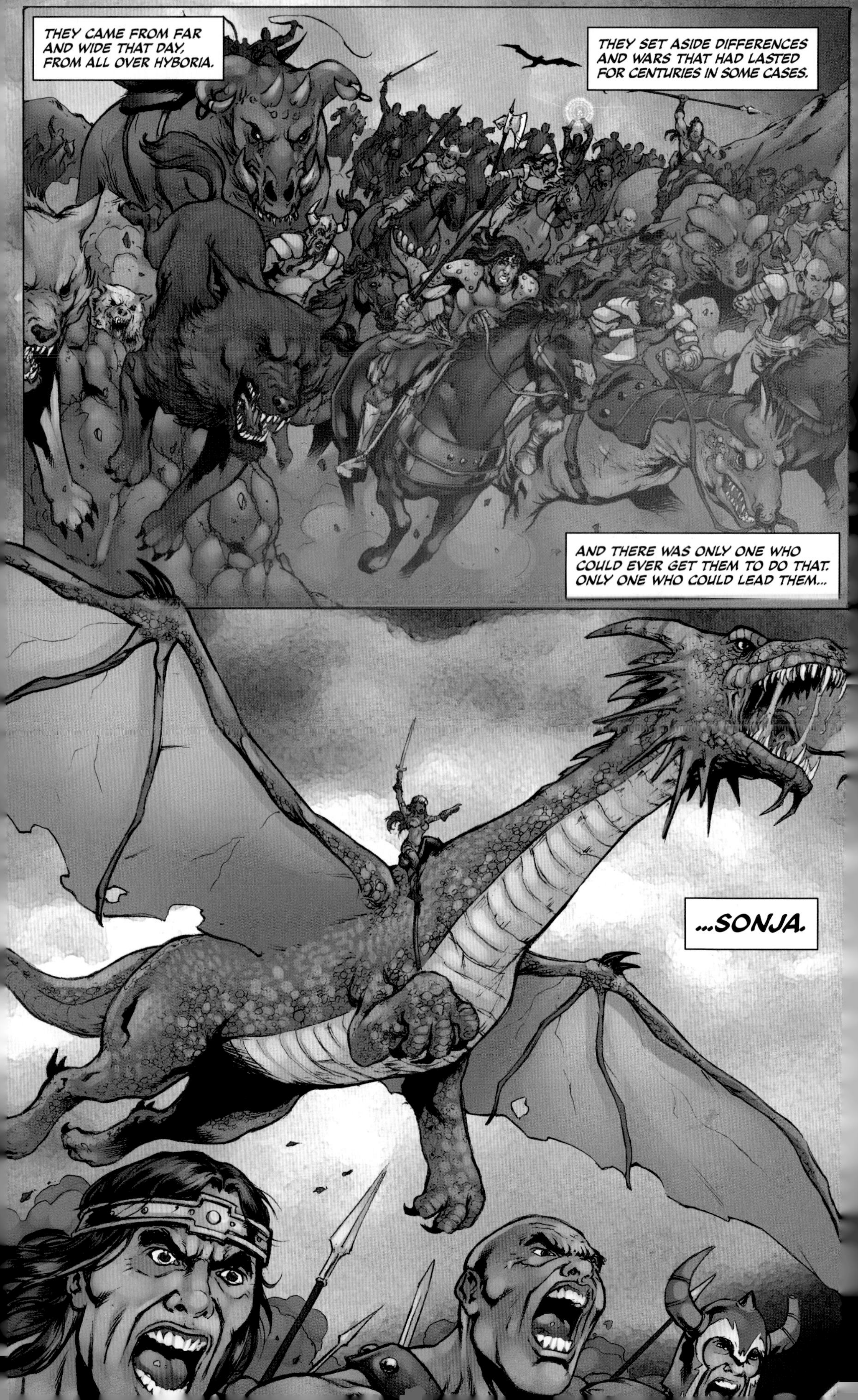
THEY CAME FROM FAR AND WIDE THAT DAY, FROM ALL OVER HYBORIA.
THEY SET ASIDE DIFFERENCES AND WARS THAT HAD LASTED FOR CENTURIES IN SOME CASES.
AND THERE WAS ONLY ONE WHO COULD EVER GET THEM TO DO THAT. ONLY ONE WHO COULD LEAD THEM...
...SONJA.

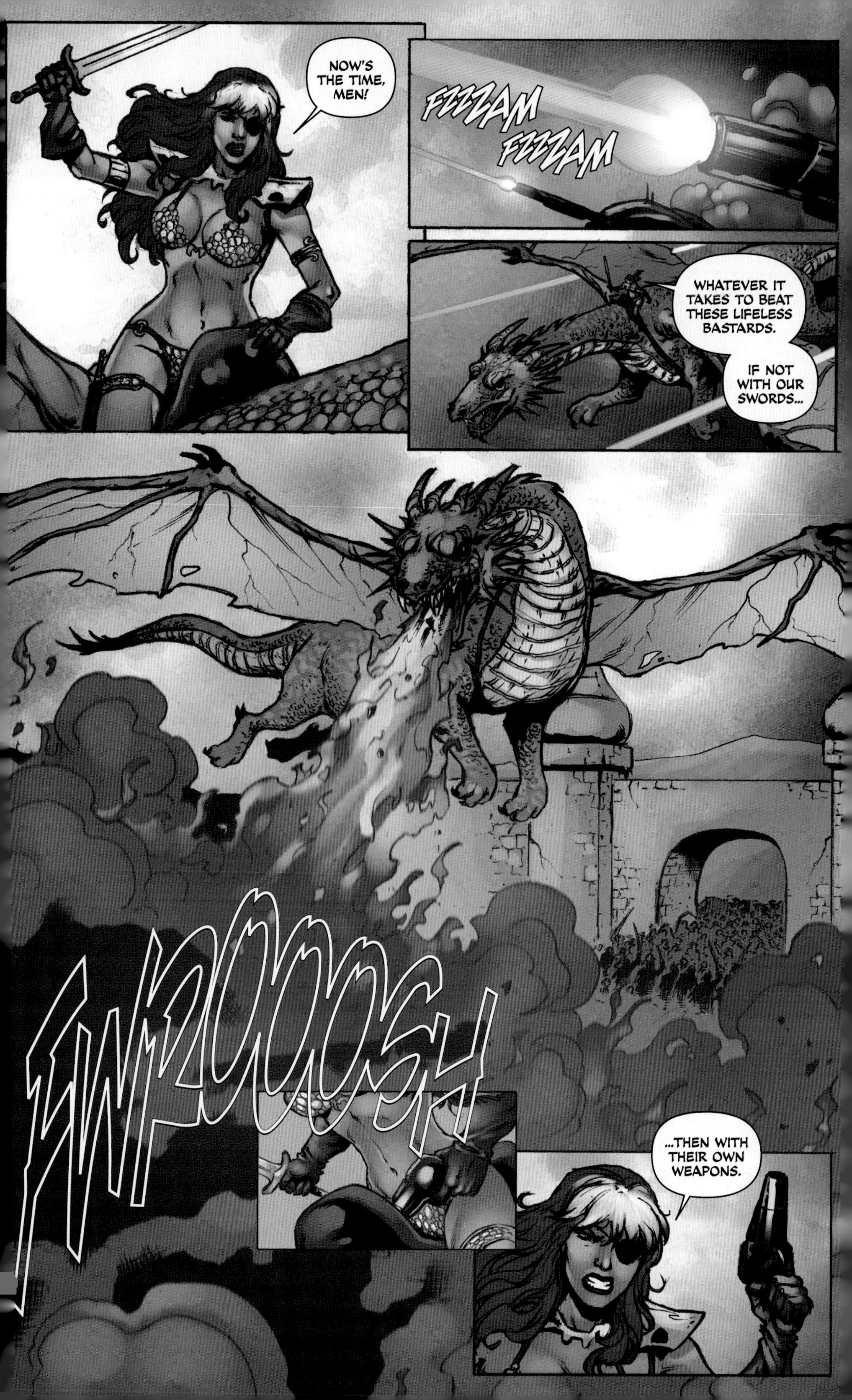
NOW'S THE TIME, MEN!
FZZZAM FZZZAM
WHATEVER IT TAKES TO BEAT THESE LIFELESS BASTARDS.
IF NOT WITH OUR SWORDS...
SWOOOOSH
...THEN WITH THEIR OWN WEAPONS.

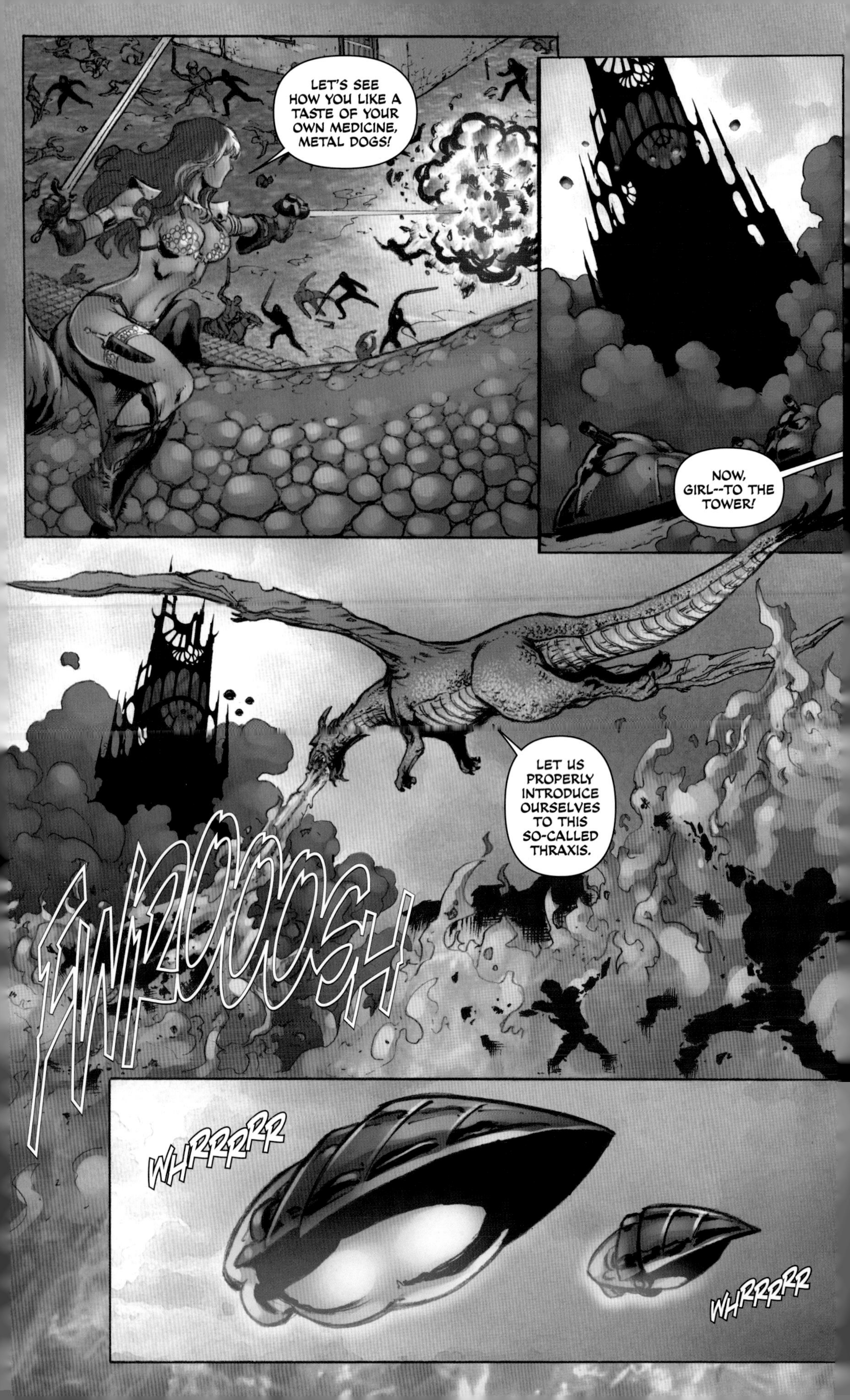
LET'S SEE HOW YOU LIKE A TASTE OF YOUR OWN MEDICINE, METAL DOGS!
NOW, GIRL--TO THE TOWER!
LET US PROPERLY INTRODUCE OURSELVES TO THIS SO-CALLED THRAXIS.
SWROOOOSH
WHRRRRR
WHRRRRR

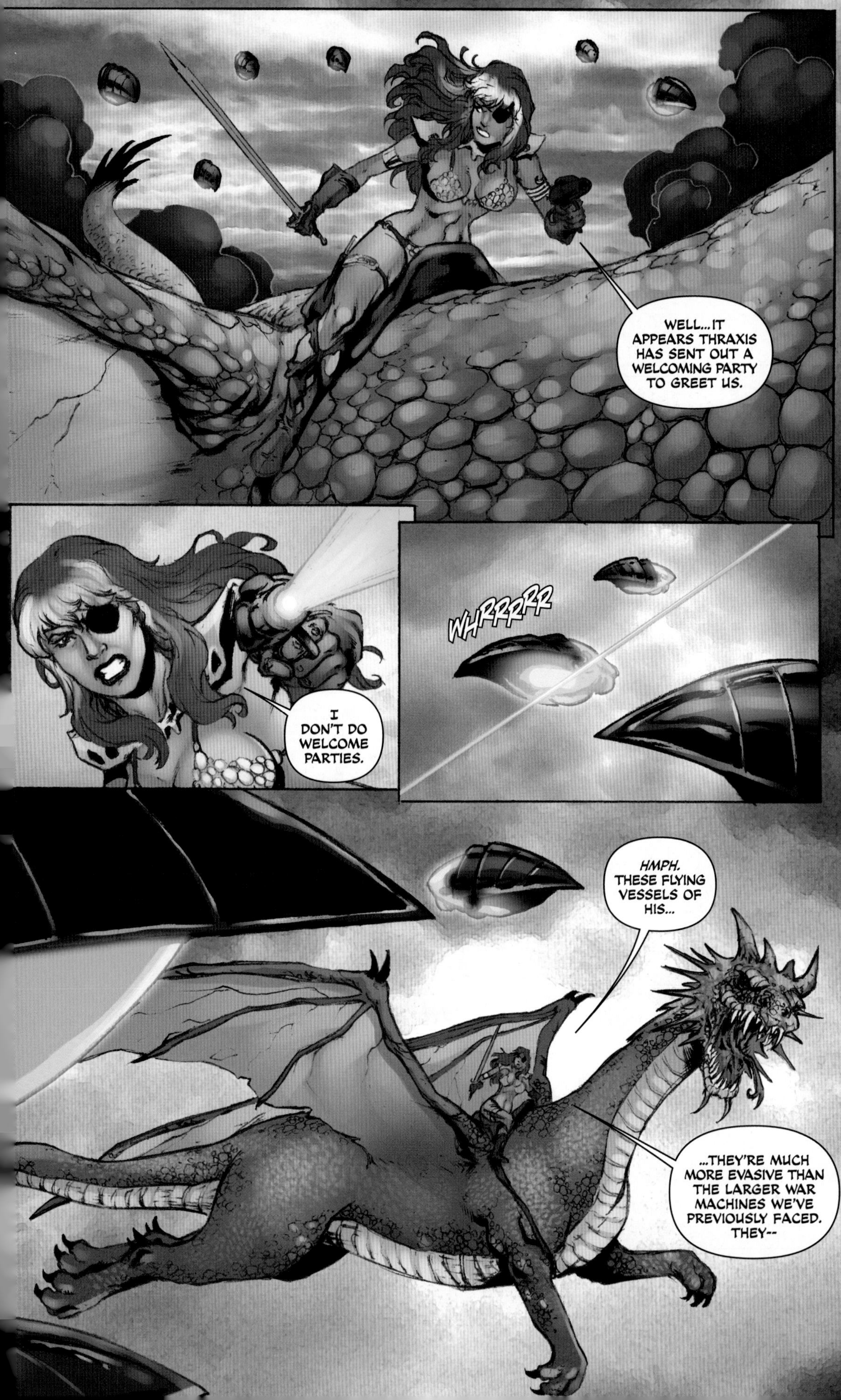
WELL...IT APPEARS THRAXIS HAS SENT OUT A WELCOMING PARTY TO GREET US.
I DON'T DO WELCOME PARTIES.
WHRRRRR
HMPH. THESE FLYING VESSELS OF HIS...
...THEY'RE MUCH MORE EVASIVE THAN THE LARGER WAR MACHINES WE'VE PREVIOUSLY FACED. THEY--

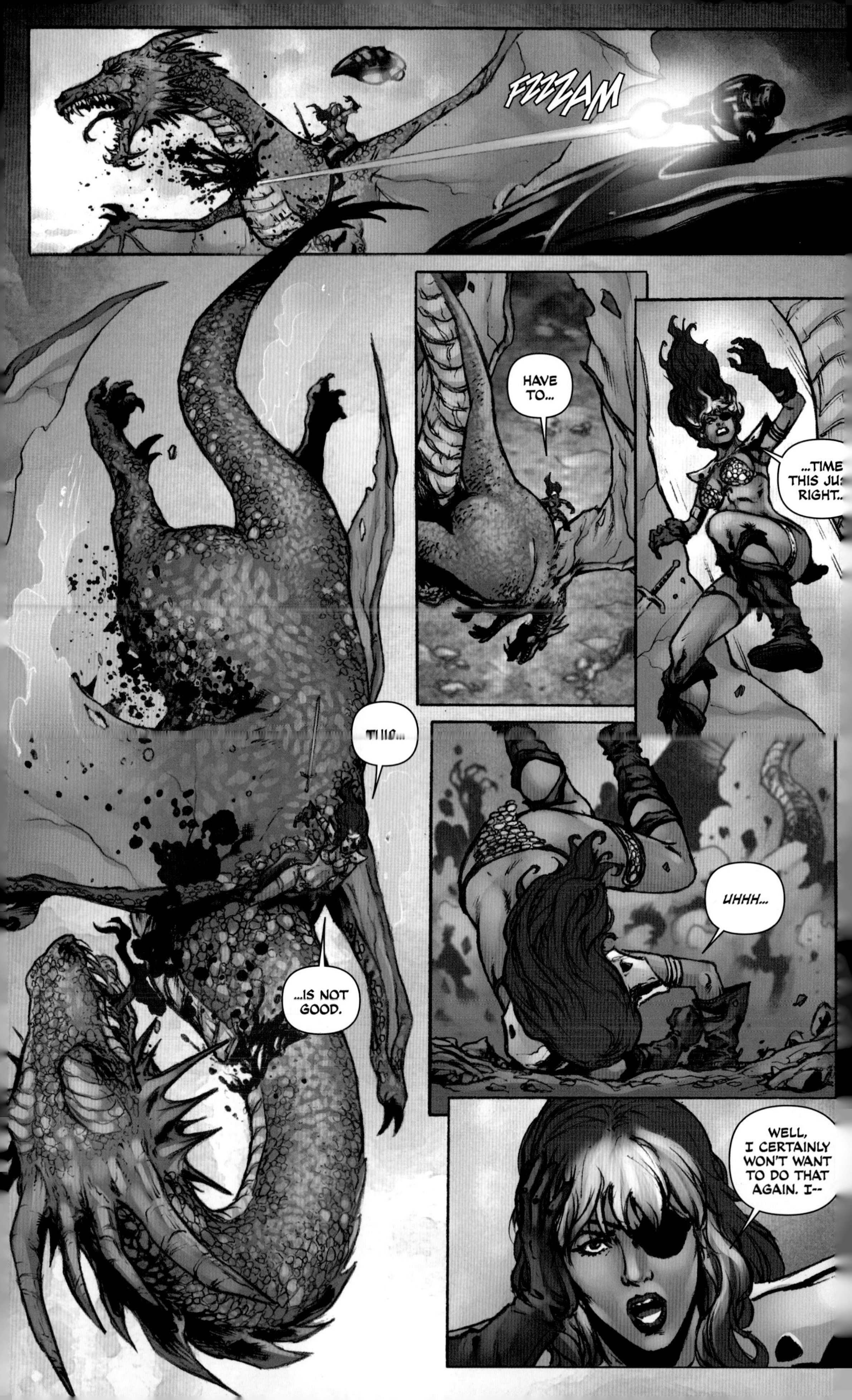
FZZZAM
HAVE TO...
...TIME THIS JU RIGHT..
...IS NOT GOOD.
UHHH...
WELL, I CERTAINLY WON'T WANT TO DO THAT AGAIN. I--

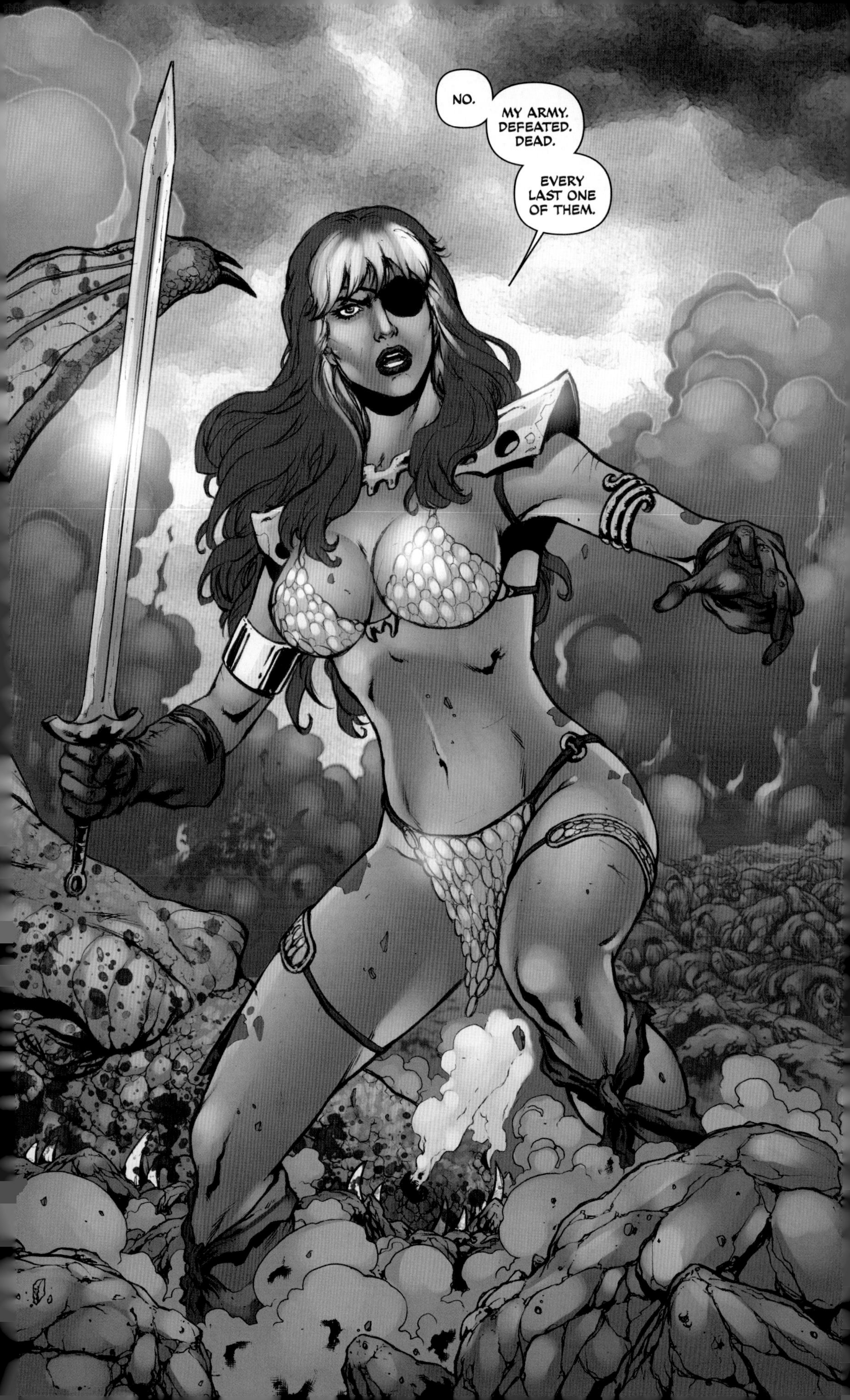
NO.
MY ARMY. DEFEATED. DEAD.
EVERY LAST ONE OF THEM.

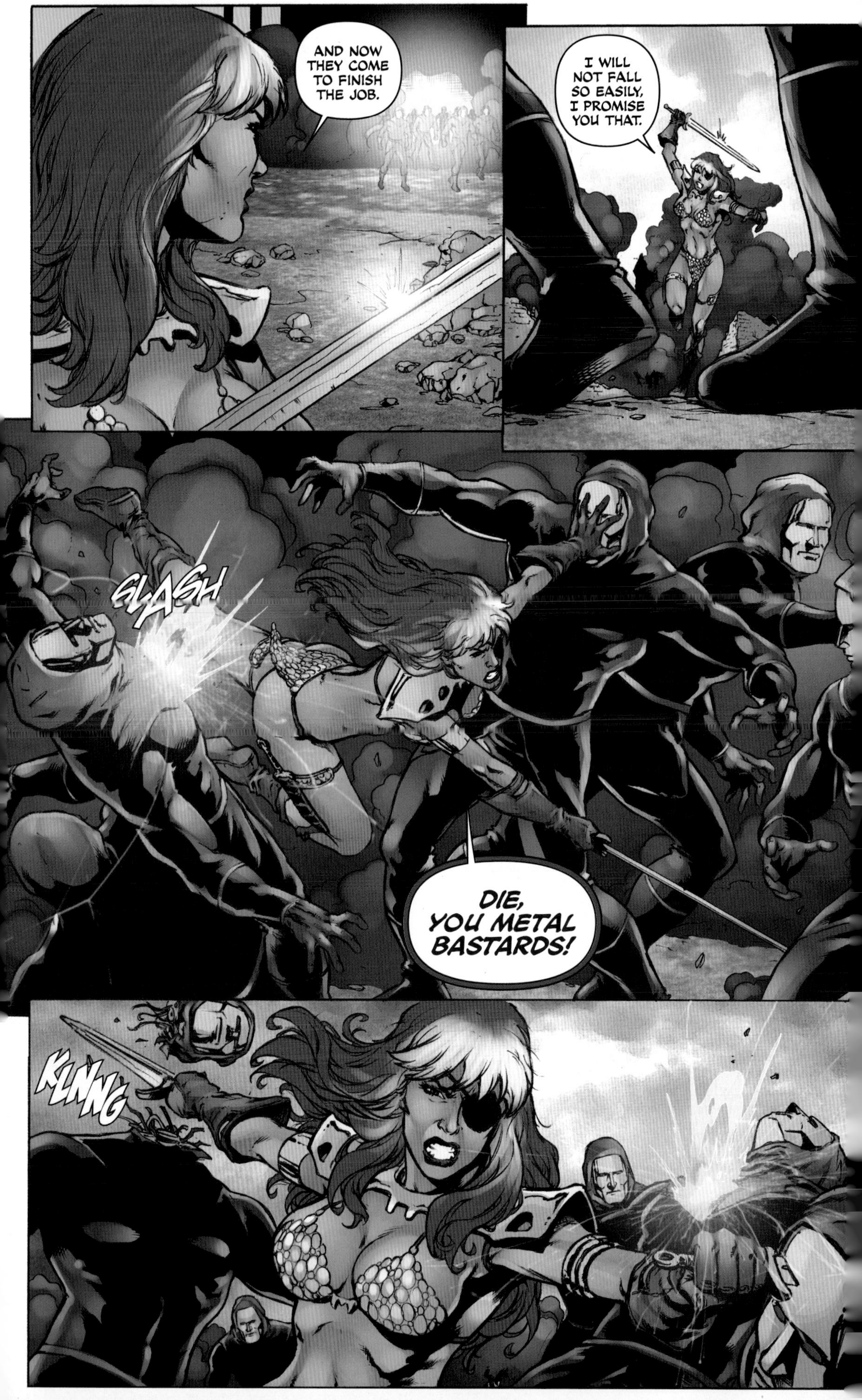
AND NOW THEY COME TO FINISH THE JOB.
I WILL NOT FALL SO EASILY, I PROMISE YOU THAT.
SLASH
DIE, YOU METAL BASTARDS!
KLNNG

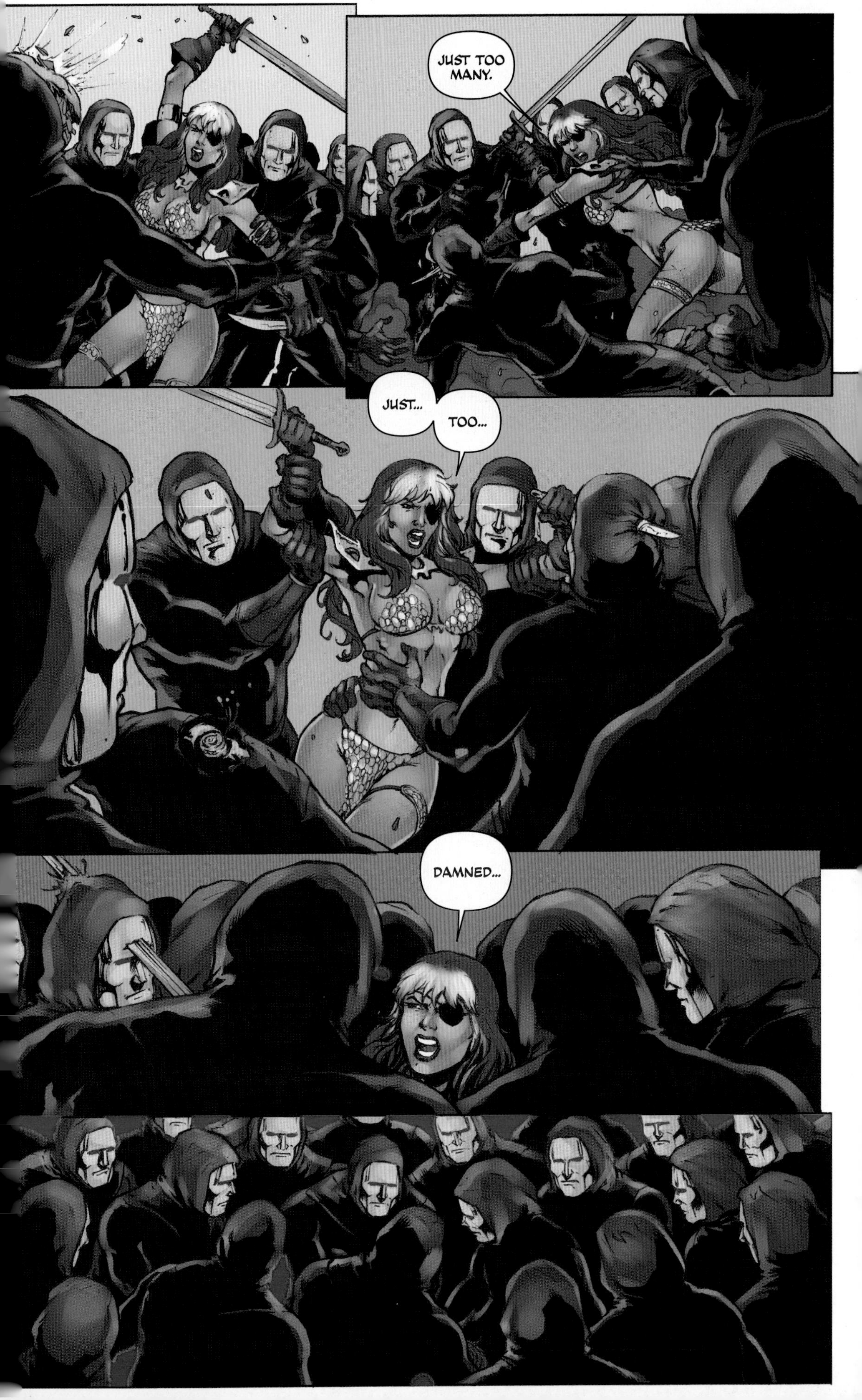
JUST TOO MANY.
JUST...
TOO...
DAMNED...

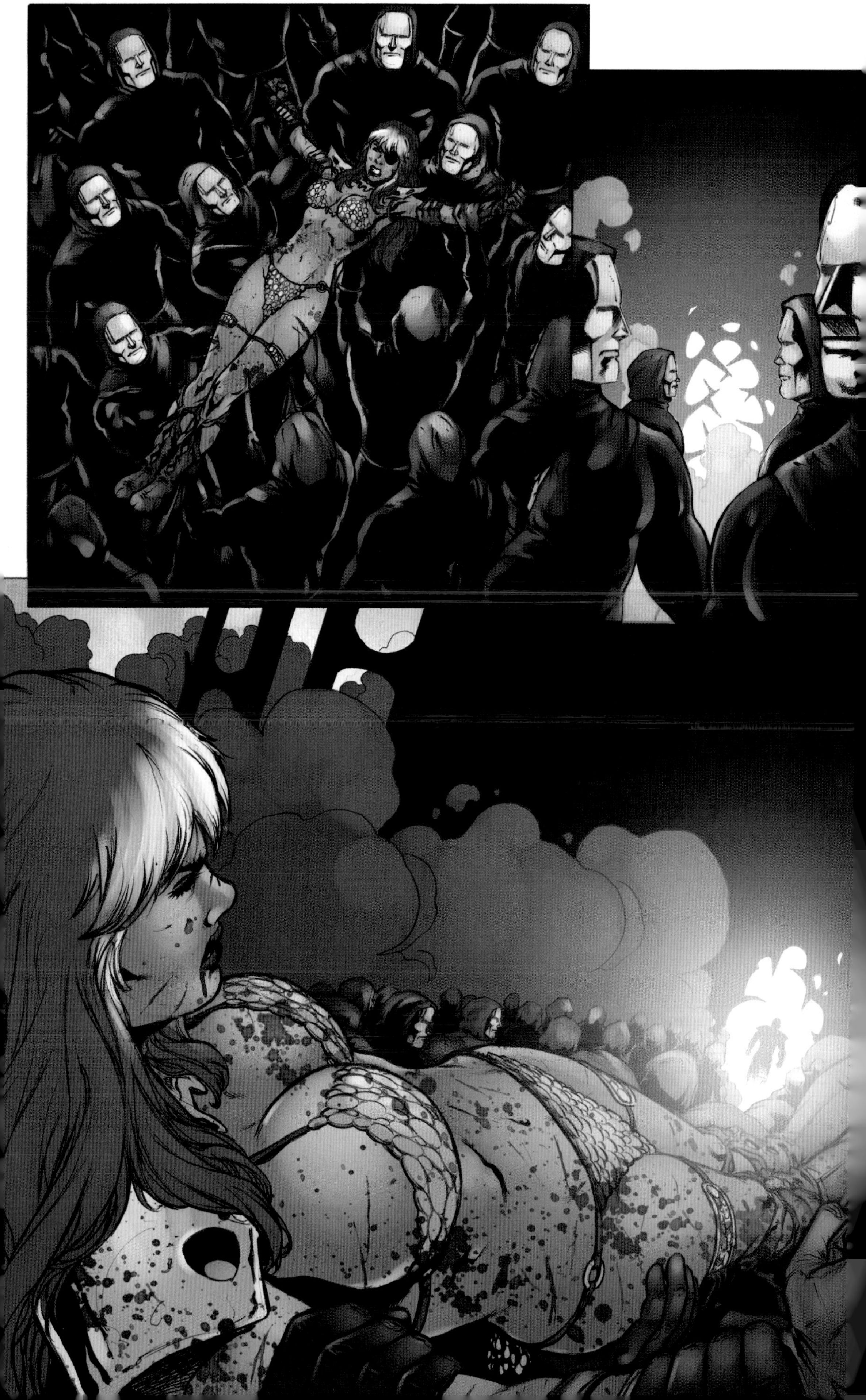

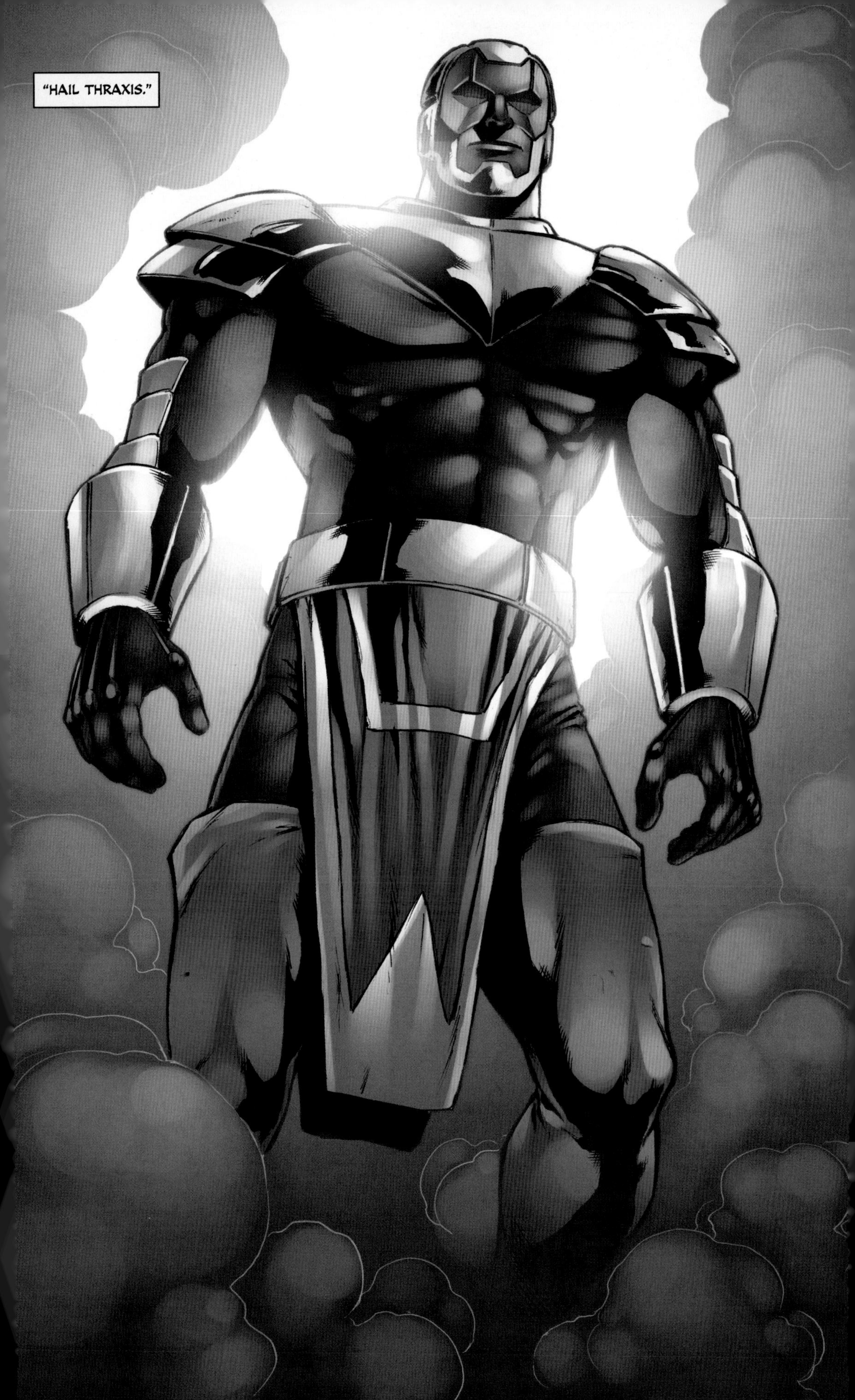
"HAIL THRAXIS."

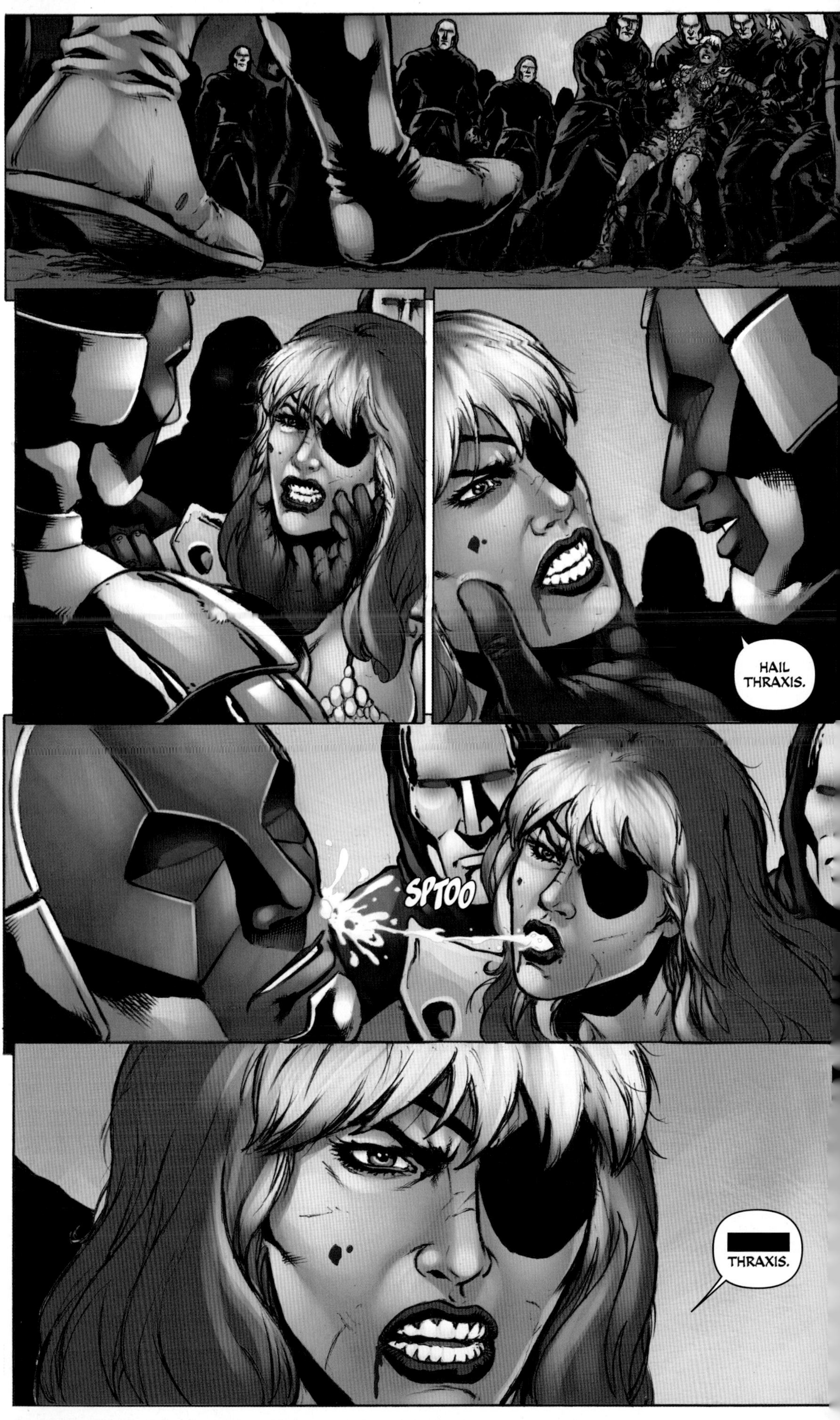
HAIL THRAXIS.
SPTOO
[redacted] THRAXIS.

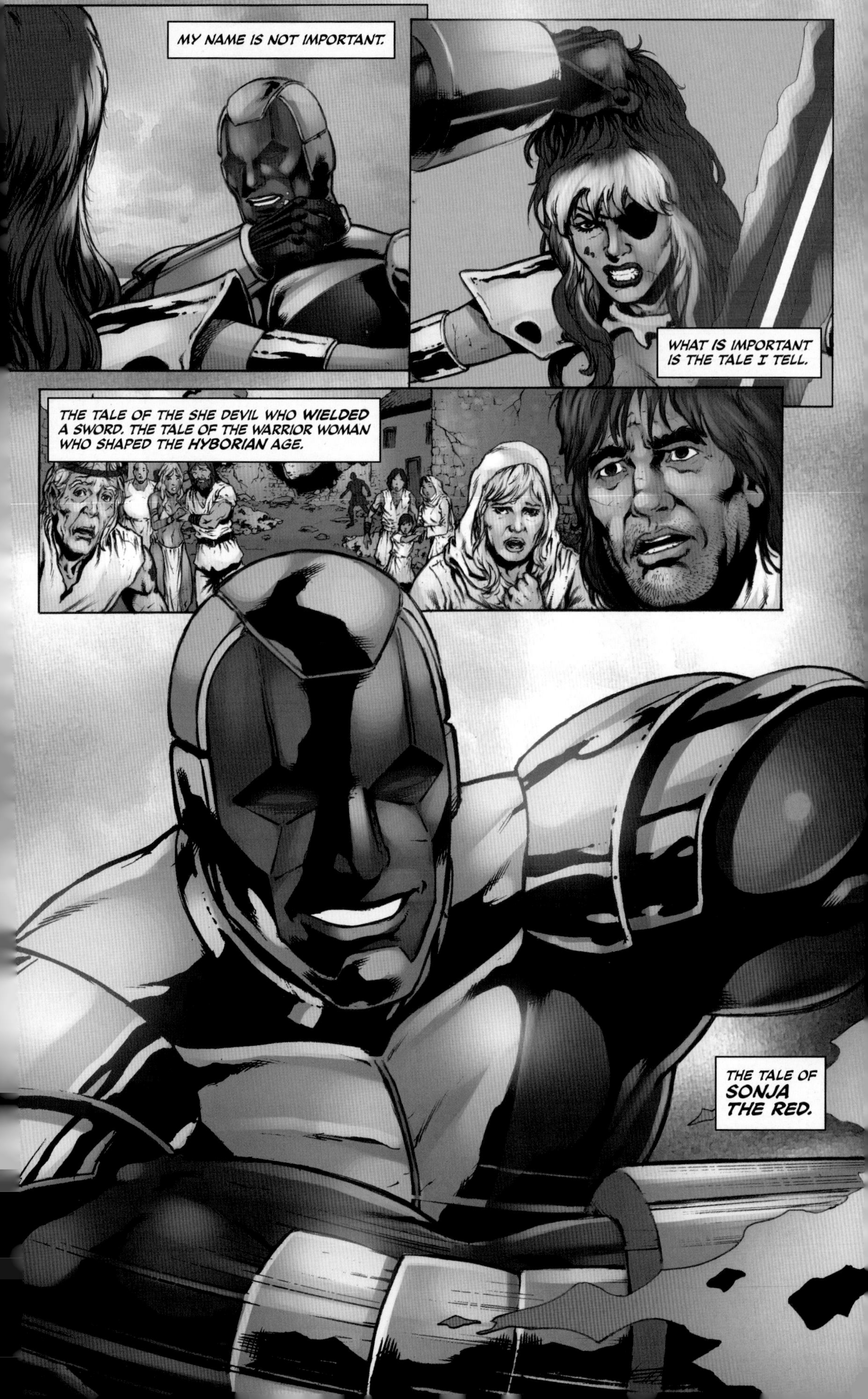
MY NAME IS NOT IMPORTANT.
WHAT IS IMPORTANT IS THE TALE I TELL.
THE TALE OF THE SHE DEVIL WHO WIELDED A SWORD. THE TALE OF THE WARRIOR WOMAN WHO SHAPED THE HYBORIAN AGE.
THE TALE OF SONJA THE RED.

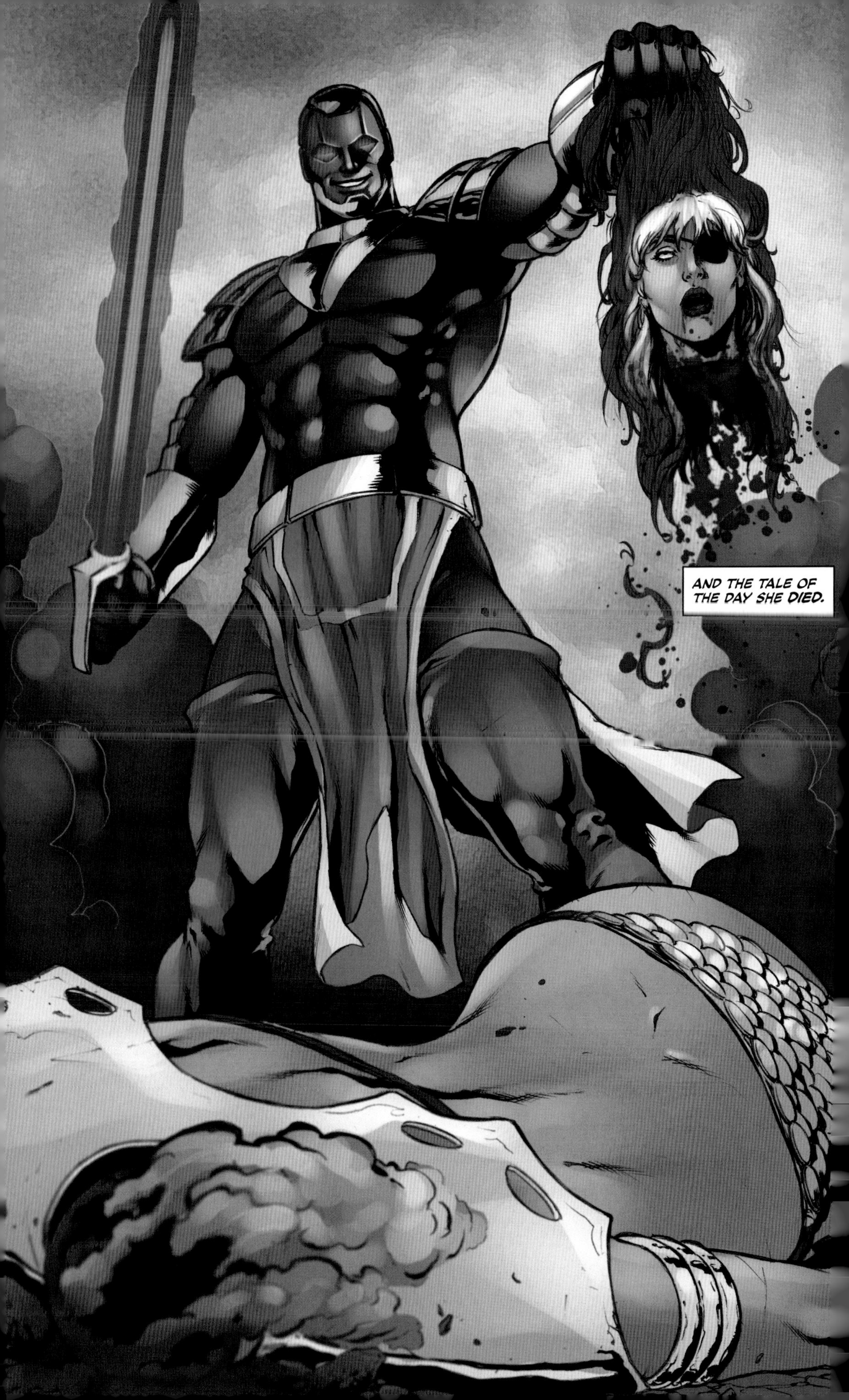
AND THE TALE OF THE DAY SHE DIED.

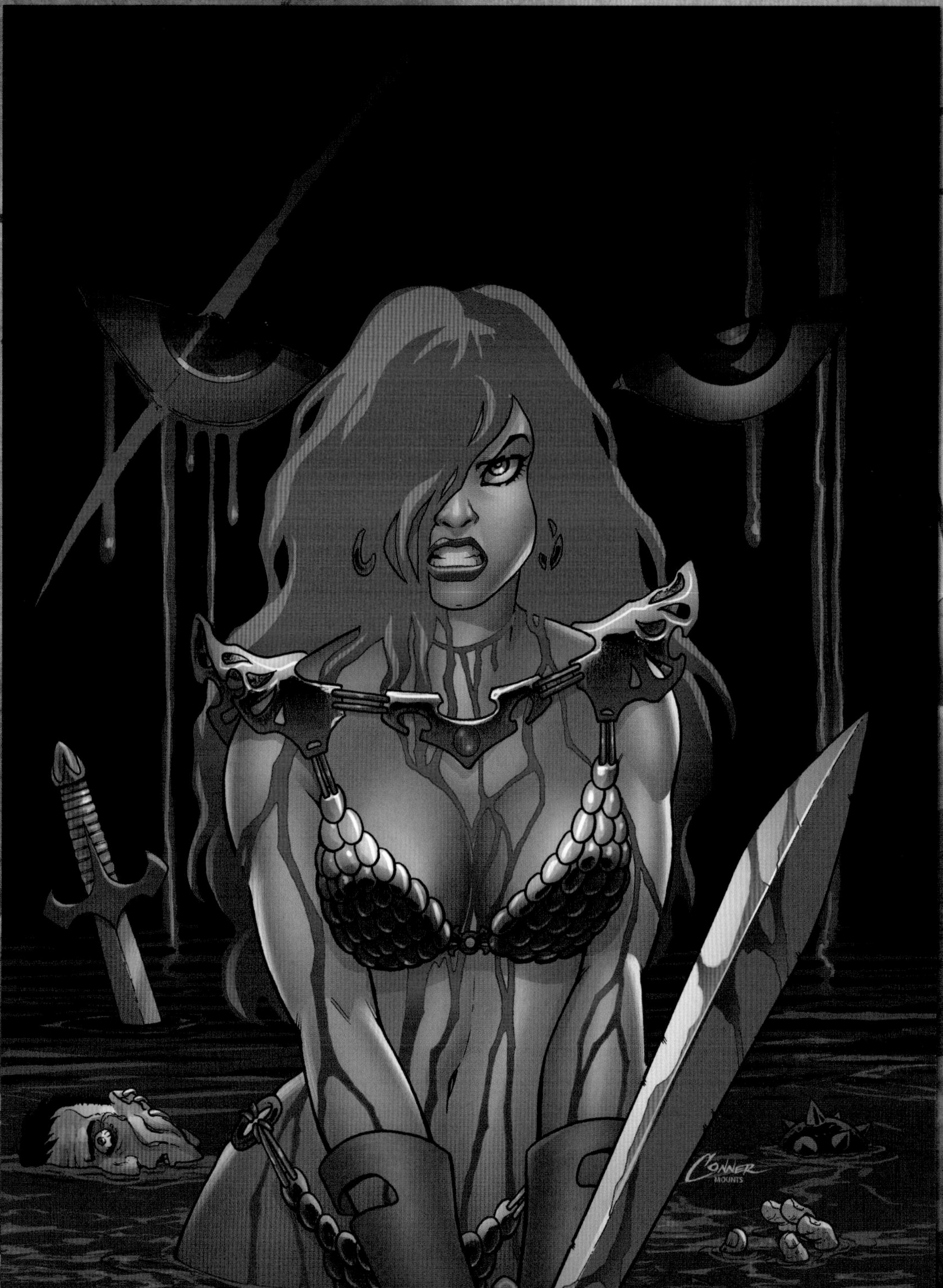
CONNER
MOUNTS

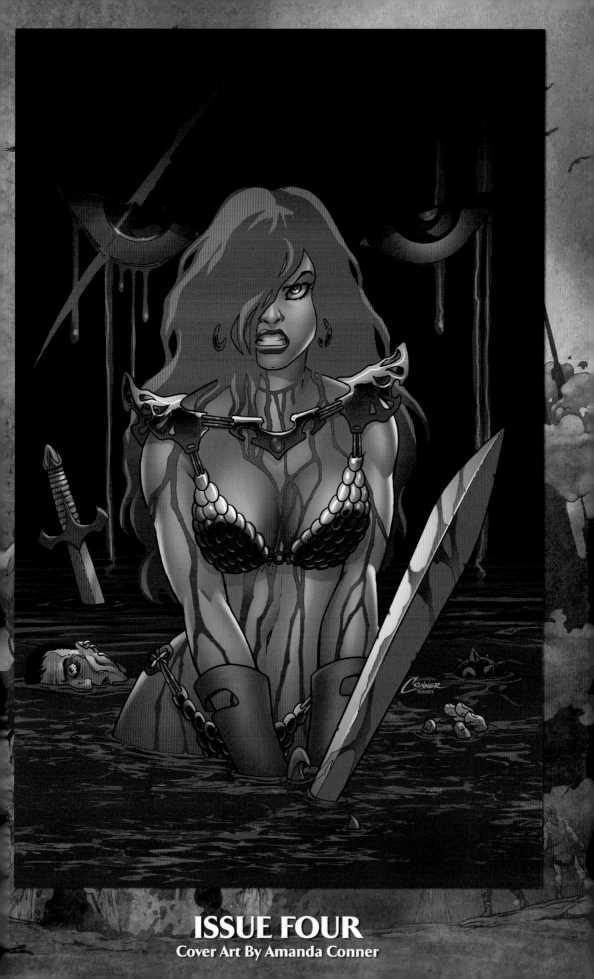

ISSUE FOUR
Cover Art By Amanda Conner

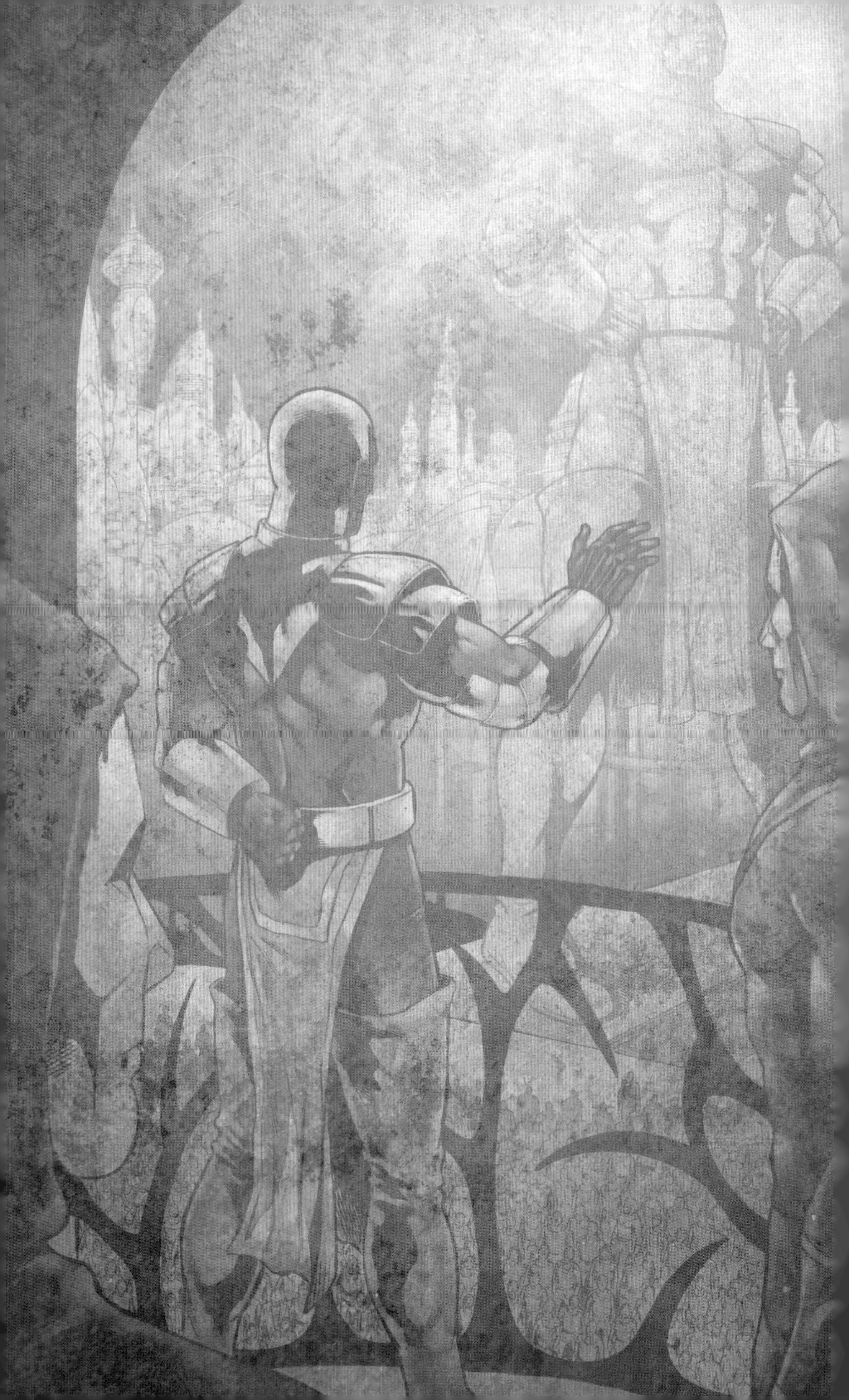

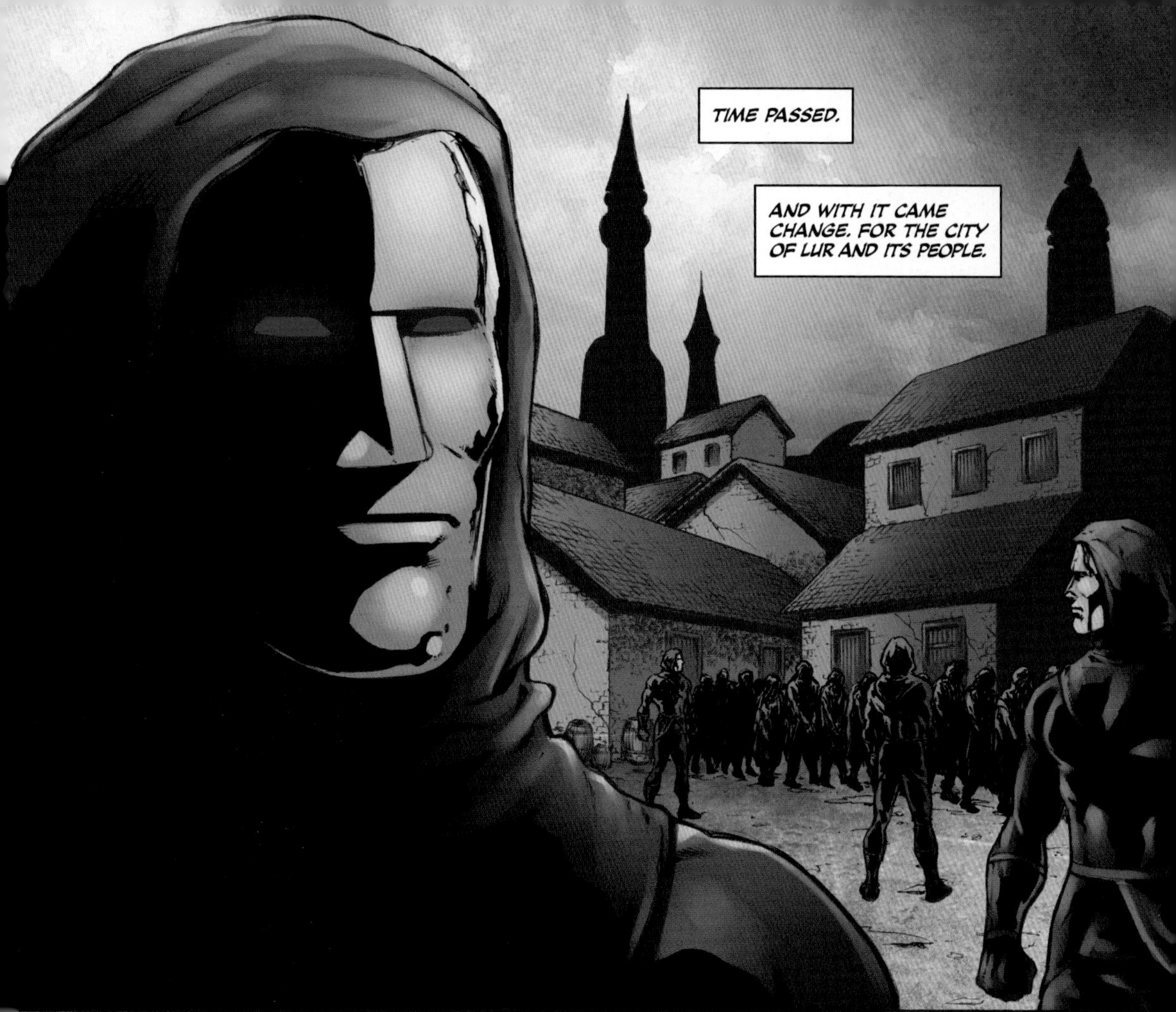
TIME PASSED.
AND WITH IT CAME CHANGE. FOR THE CITY OF LUR AND ITS PEOPLE.

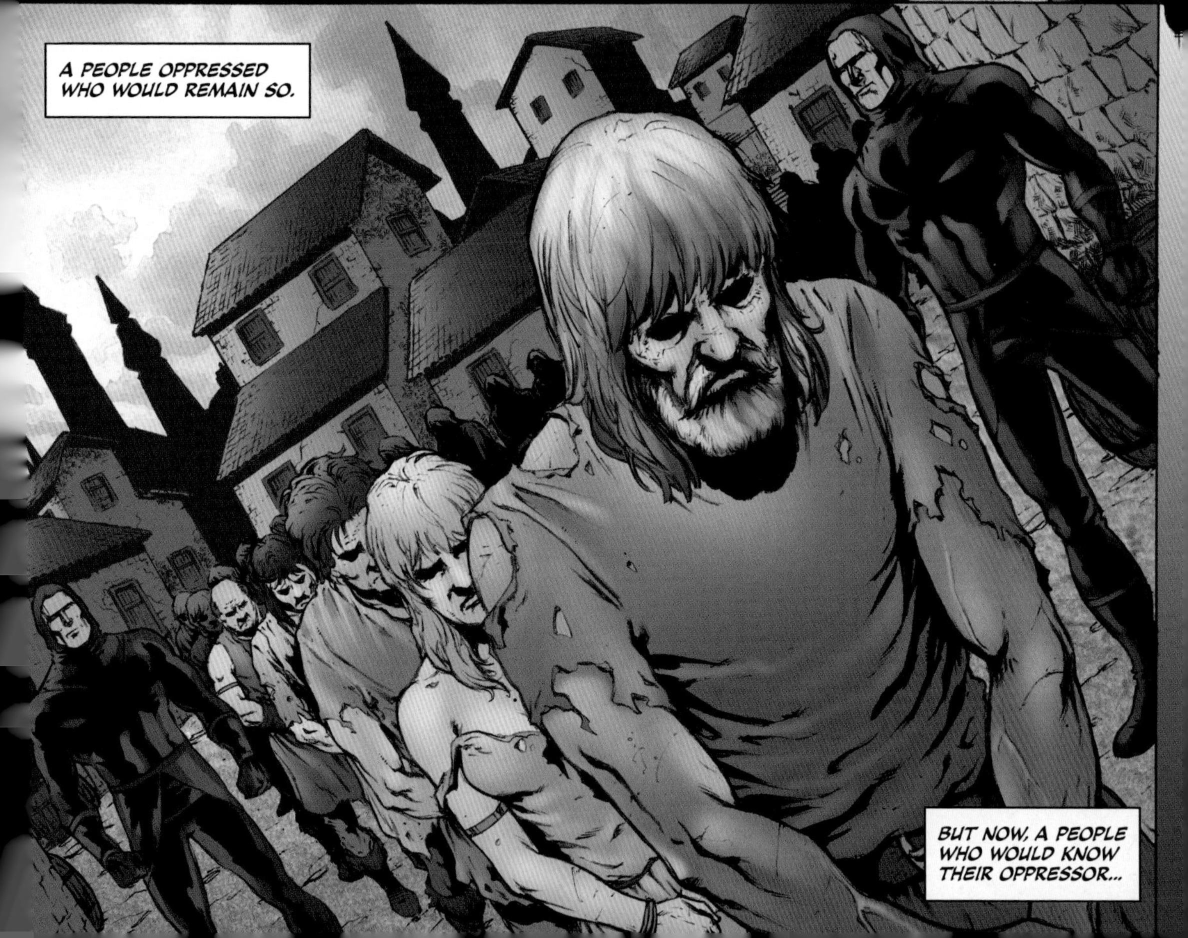
A PEOPLE OPPRESSED WHO WOULD REMAIN SO.
BUT NOW, A PEOPLE WHO WOULD KNOW THEIR OPPRESSOR...

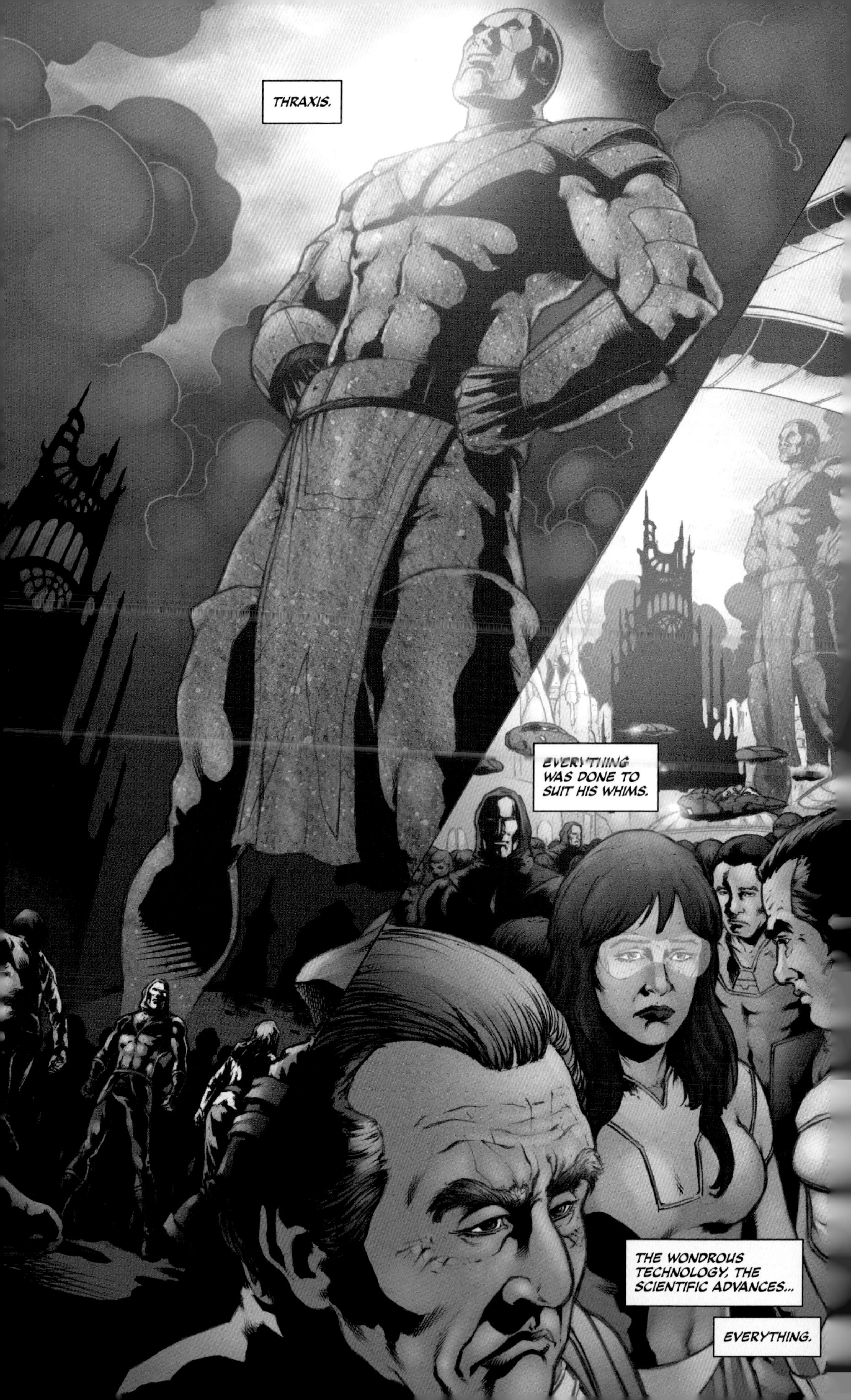
THRAXIS.
EVERYTHING WAS DONE TO SUIT HIS WHIMS.
THE WONDROUS TECHNOLOGY, THE SCIENTIFIC ADVANCES...
EVERYTHING.

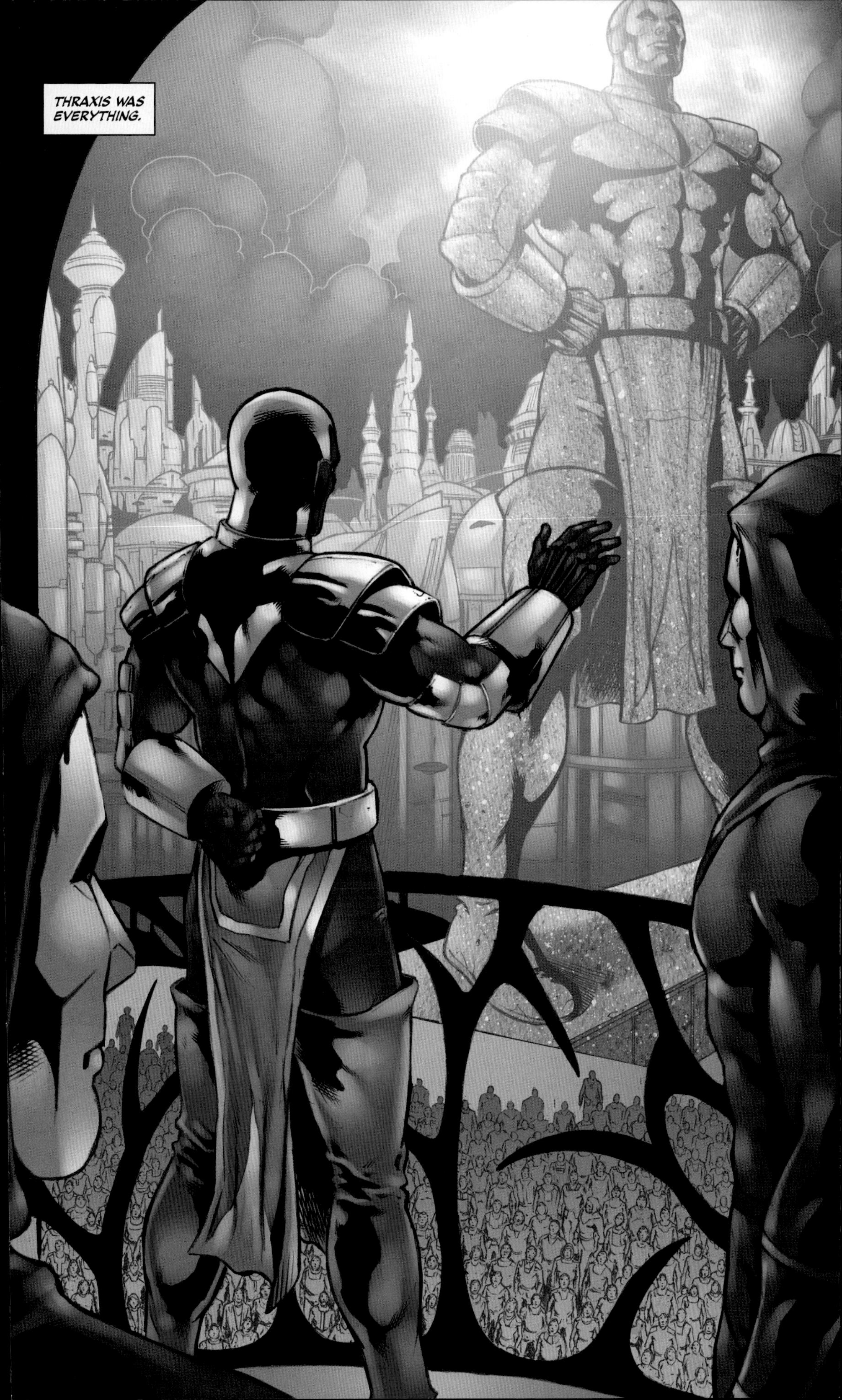
THRAXIS WAS EVERYTHING.

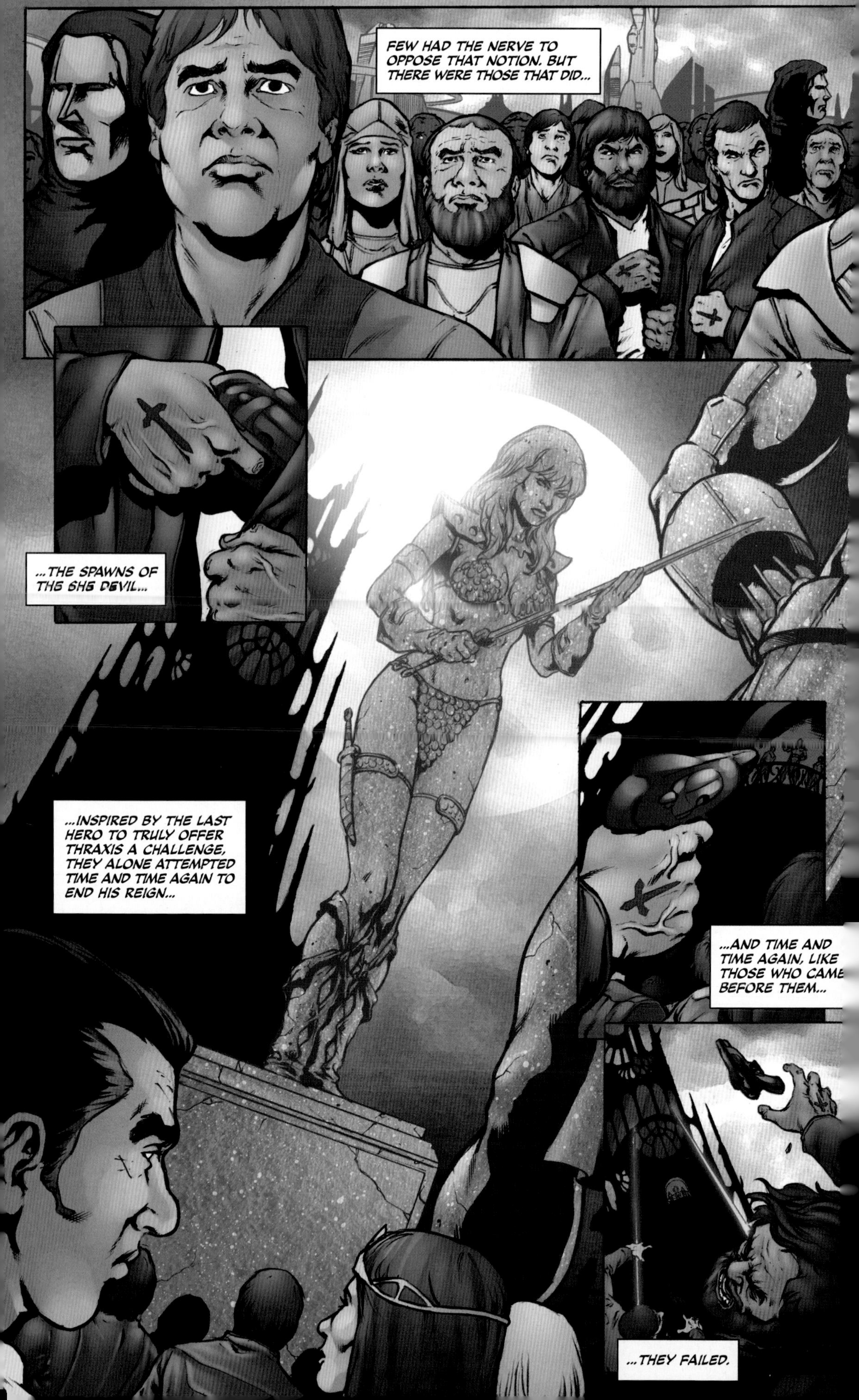
FEW HAD THE NERVE TO OPPOSE THAT NOTION. BUT THERE WERE THOSE THAT DID...
...THE SPAWNS OF THE SHE DEVIL...
...INSPIRED BY THE LAST HERO TO TRULY OFFER THRAXIS A CHALLENGE, THEY ALONE ATTEMPTED TIME AND TIME AGAIN TO END HIS REIGN...
...AND TIME AND TIME AGAIN, LIKE THOSE WHO CAME BEFORE THEM...
...THEY FAILED.

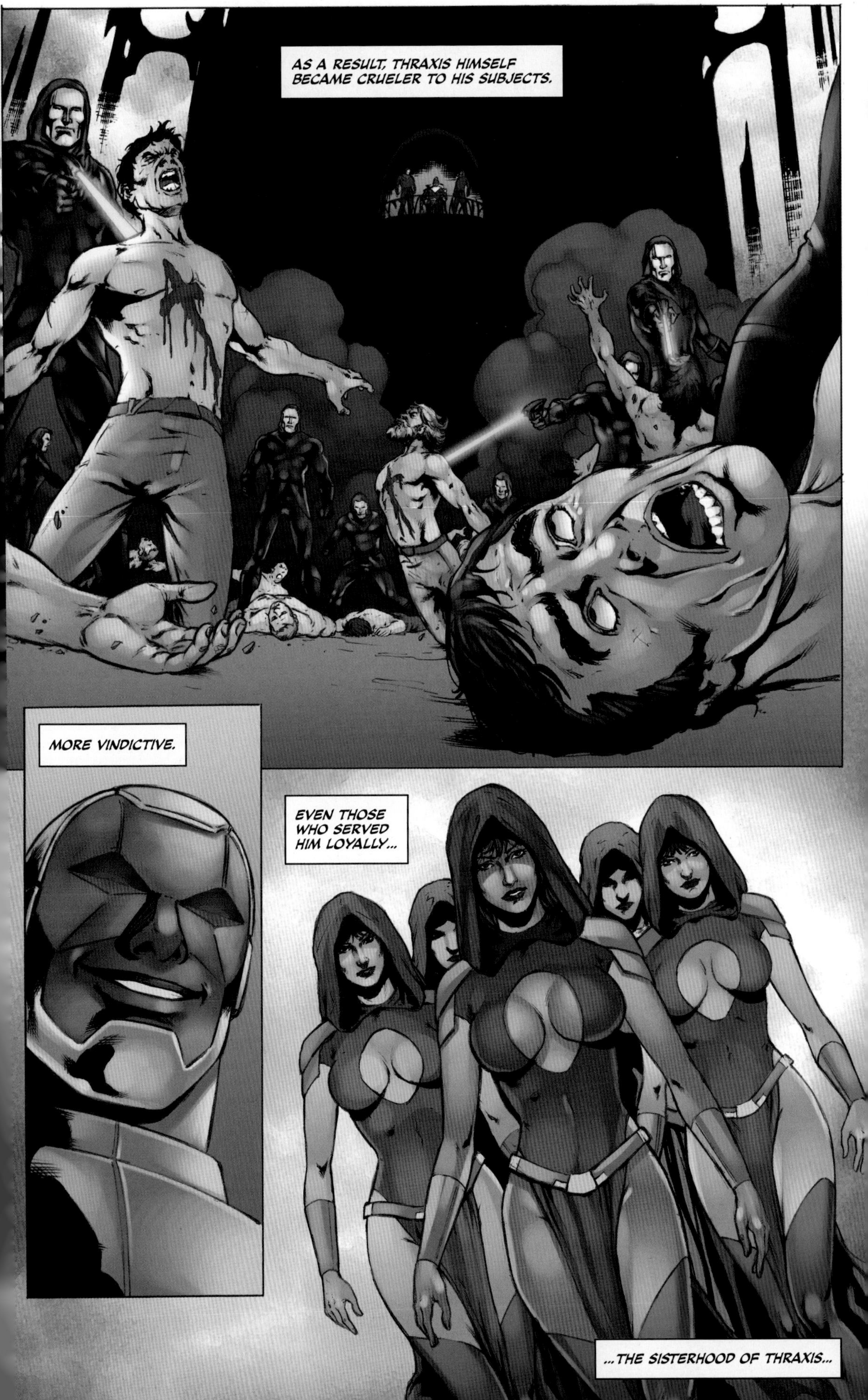
AS A RESULT, THRAXIS HIMSELF BECAME CRUELER TO HIS SUBJECTS.
MORE VINDICTIVE.
EVEN THOSE WHO SERVED HIM LOYALLY...
...THE SISTERHOOD OF THRAXIS...

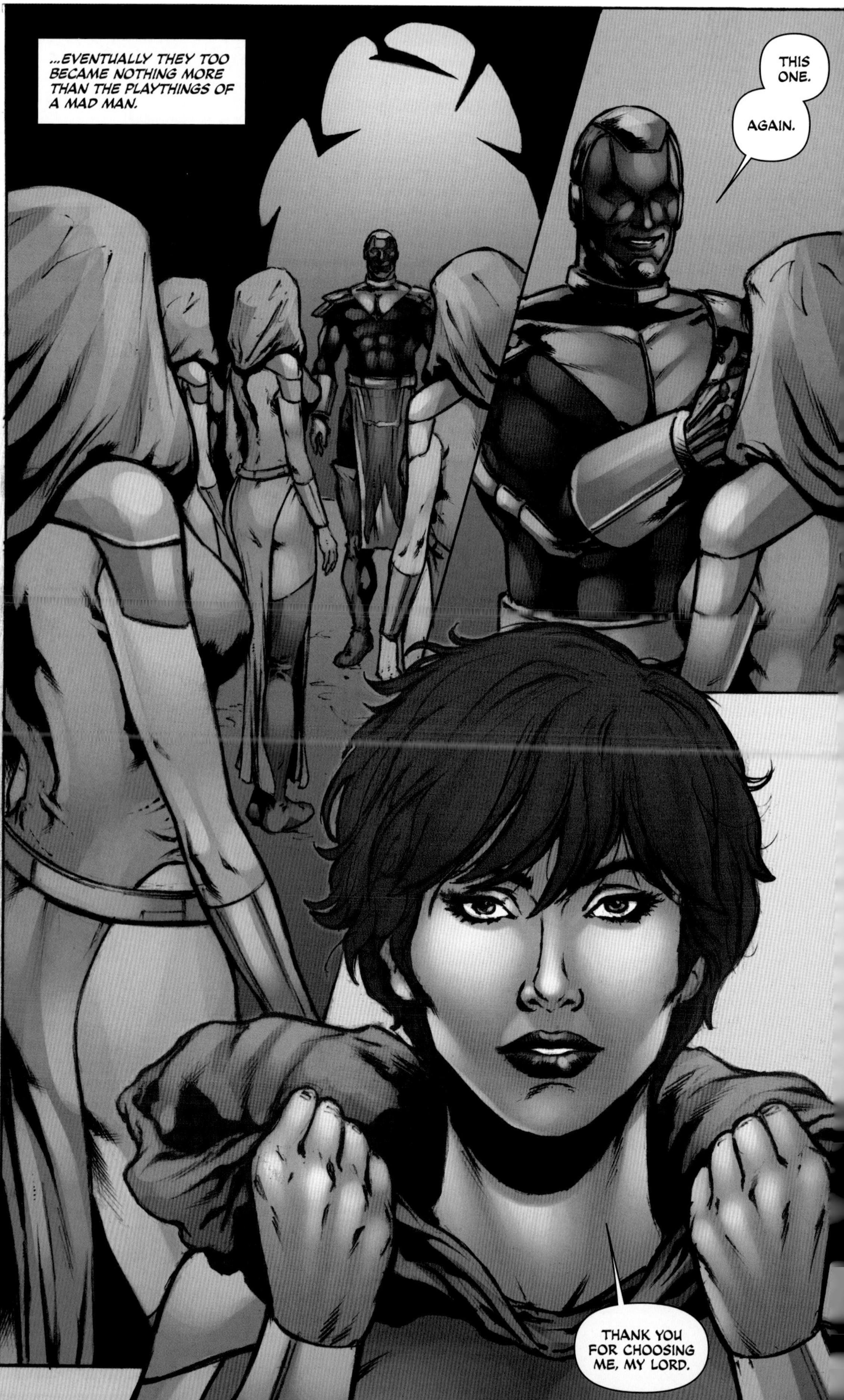
...EVENTUALLY THEY TOO BECAME NOTHING MORE THAN THE PLAYTHINGS OF A MAD MAN.
THIS ONE.
AGAIN.
THANK YOU FOR CHOOSING ME, MY LORD.

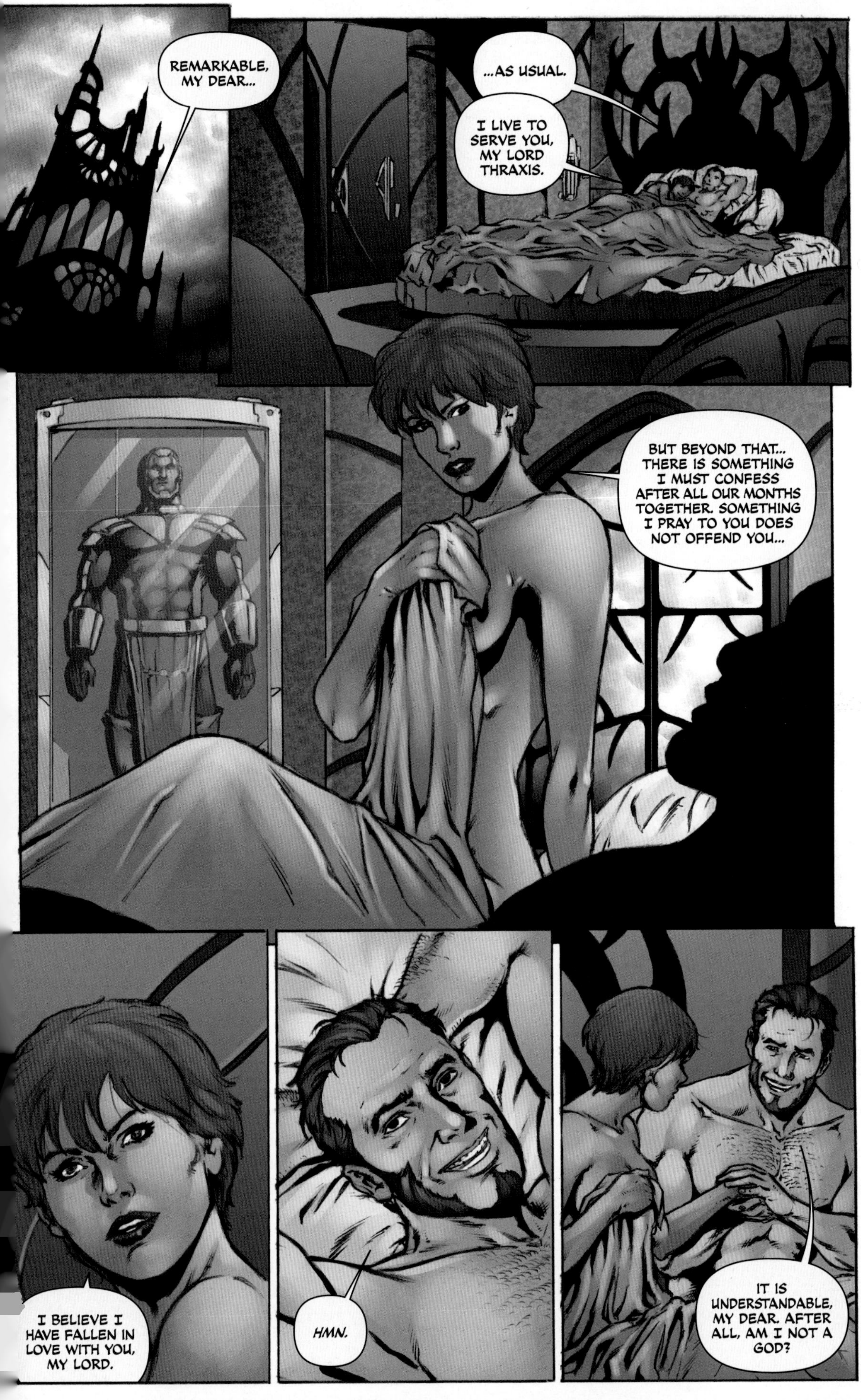
REMARKABLE, MY DEAR...
...AS USUAL.
I LIVE TO SERVE YOU, MY LORD THRAXIS.
BUT BEYOND THAT... THERE IS SOMETHING I MUST CONFESS AFTER ALL OUR MONTHS TOGETHER. SOMETHING I PRAY TO YOU DOES NOT OFFEND YOU...
I BELIEVE I HAVE FALLEN IN LOVE WITH YOU, MY LORD.
HMN.
IT IS UNDERSTANDABLE, MY DEAR. AFTER ALL, AM I NOT A GOD?

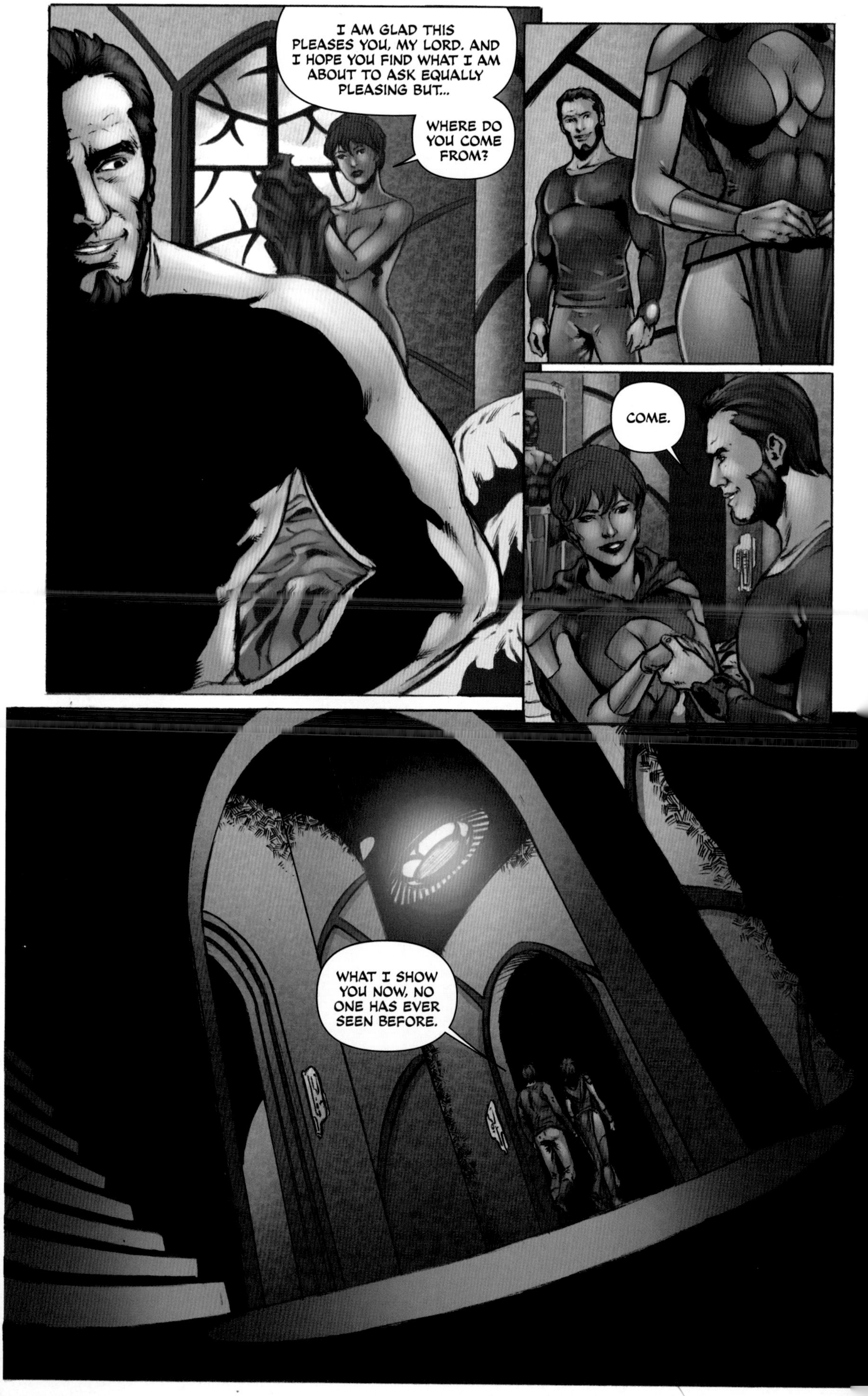
I AM GLAD THIS PLEASES YOU, MY LORD. AND I HOPE YOU FIND WHAT I AM ABOUT TO ASK EQUALLY PLEASING BUT...
WHERE DO YOU COME FROM?
COME.
WHAT I SHOW YOU NOW, NO ONE HAS EVER SEEN BEFORE.

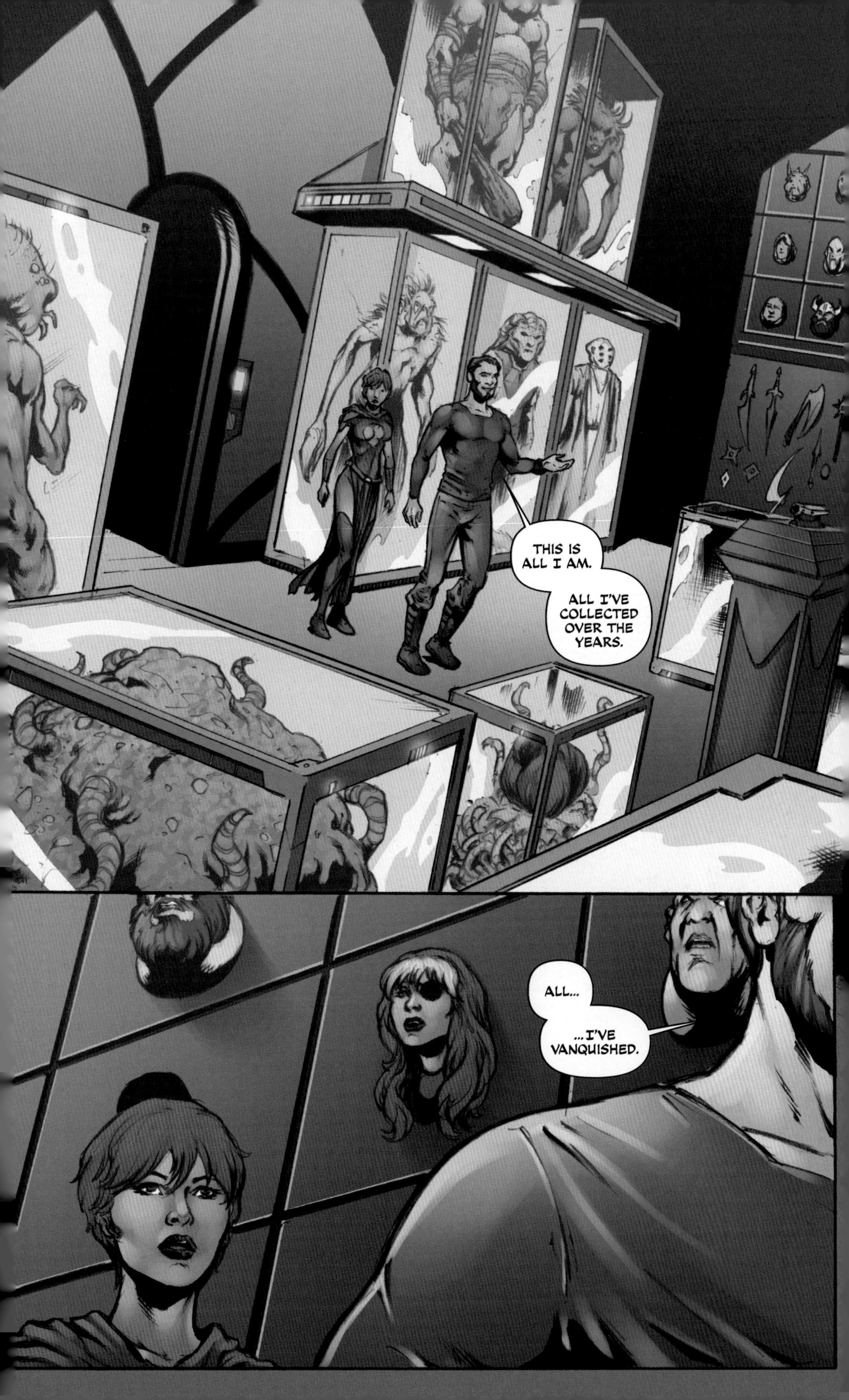
THIS IS ALL I AM.
ALL I'VE COLLECTED OVER THE YEARS.
ALL...
...I'VE VANQUISHED.

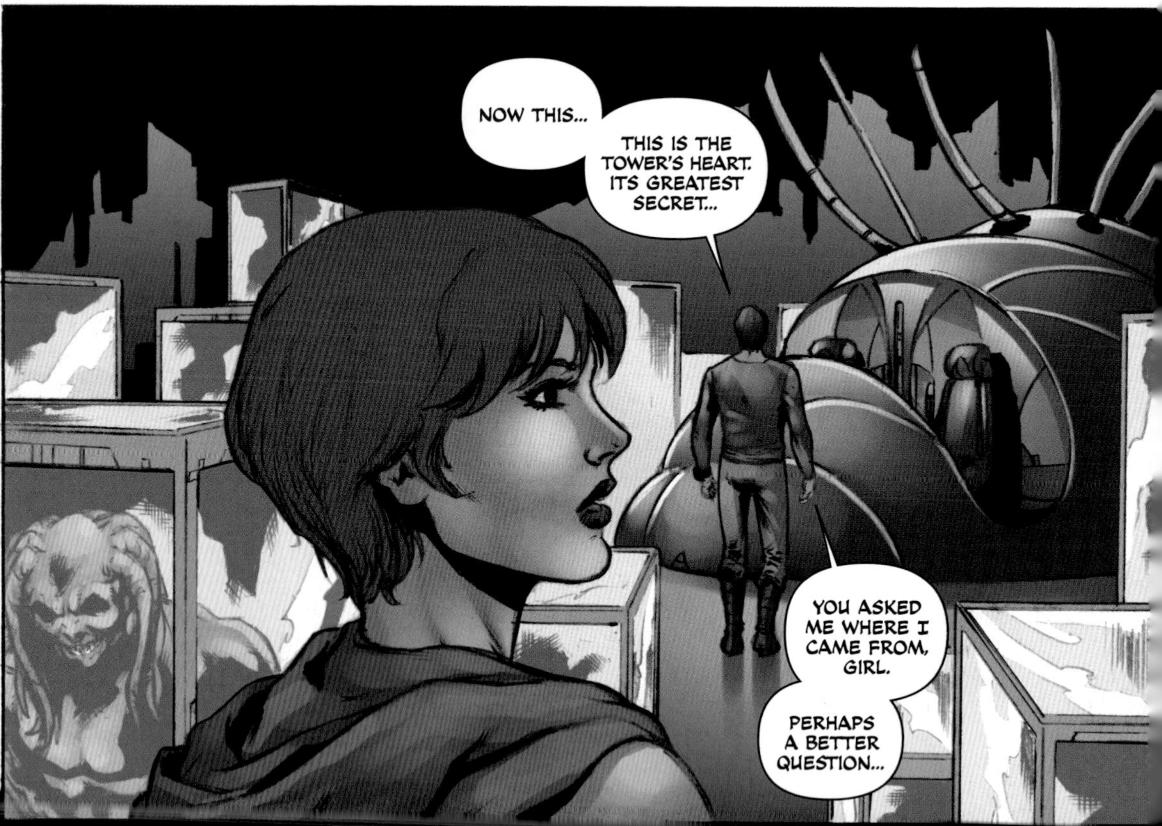
NOW THIS...
THIS IS THE TOWER'S HEART. ITS GREATEST SECRET...
YOU ASKED ME WHERE I CAME FROM, GIRL.
PERHAPS A BETTER QUESTION...

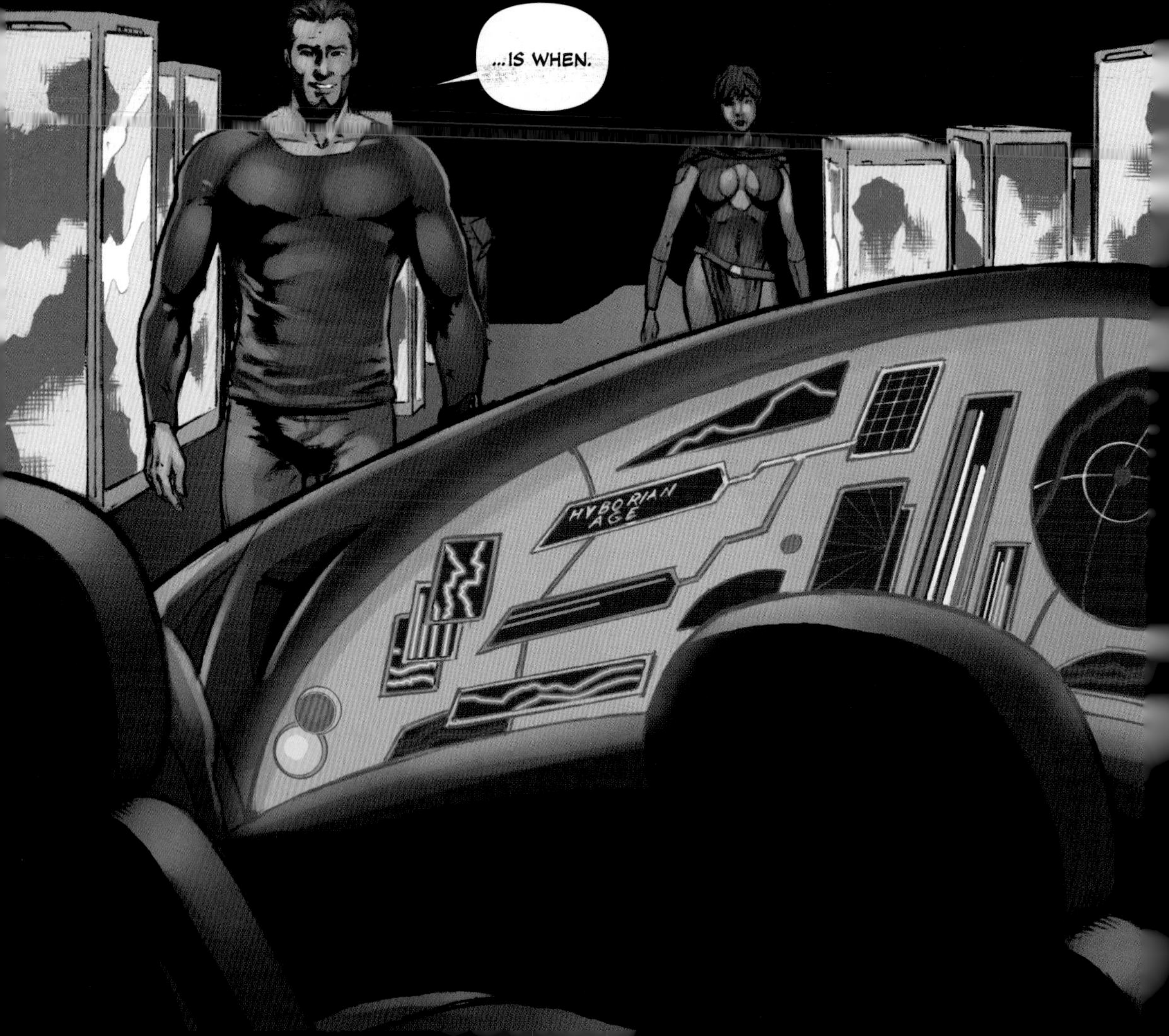
...IS WHEN.
HYBORIAN AGE

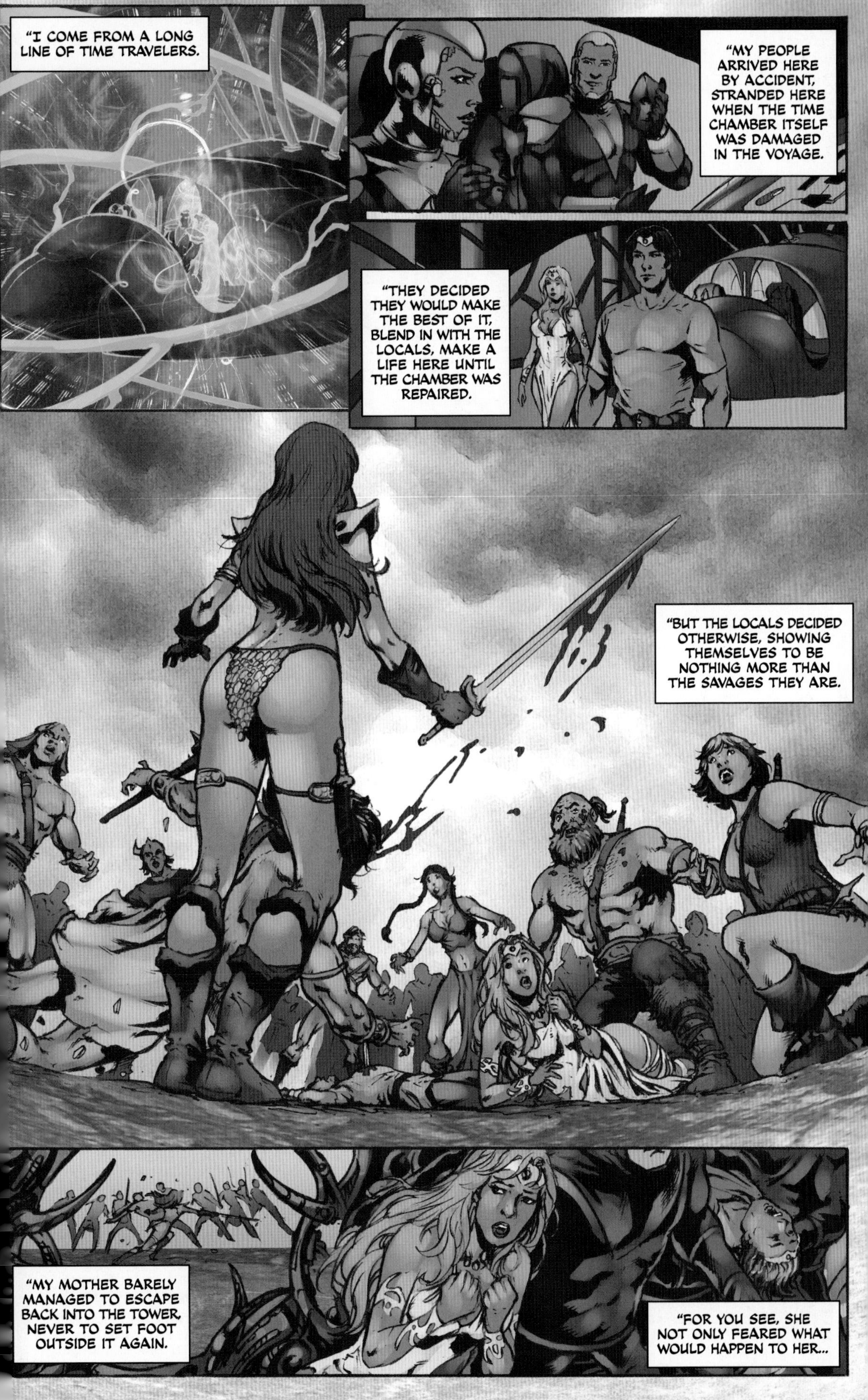
"I COME FROM A LONG LINE OF TIME TRAVELERS.
"MY PEOPLE ARRIVED HERE BY ACCIDENT, STRANDED HERE WHEN THE TIME CHAMBER ITSELF WAS DAMAGED IN THE VOYAGE.
"THEY DECIDED THEY WOULD MAKE THE BEST OF IT, BLEND IN WITH THE LOCALS, MAKE A LIFE HERE UNTIL THE CHAMBER WAS REPAIRED.
"BUT THE LOCALS DECIDED OTHERWISE, SHOWING THEMSELVES TO BE NOTHING MORE THAN THE SAVAGES THEY ARE.
"MY MOTHER BARELY MANAGED TO ESCAPE BACK INTO THE TOWER, NEVER TO SET FOOT OUTSIDE IT AGAIN.
"FOR YOU SEE, SHE NOT ONLY FEARED WHAT WOULD HAPPEN TO HER...

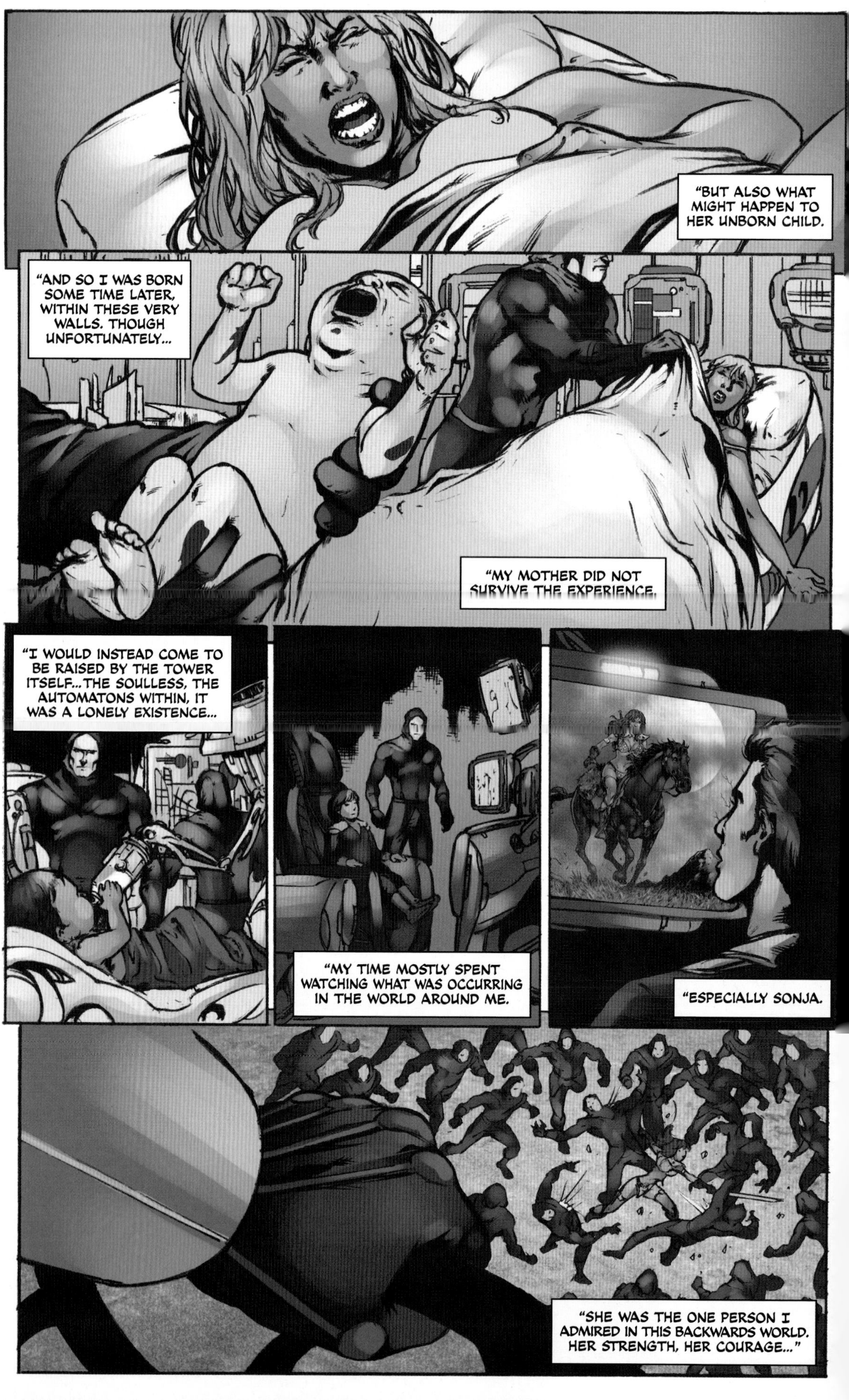
"BUT ALSO WHAT MIGHT HAPPEN TO HER UNBORN CHILD.
"AND SO I WAS BORN SOME TIME LATER, WITHIN THESE VERY WALLS. THOUGH UNFORTUNATELY...
"MY MOTHER DID NOT SURVIVE THE EXPERIENCE.
"I WOULD INSTEAD COME TO BE RAISED BY THE TOWER ITSELF...THE SOULLESS, THE AUTOMATONS WITHIN. IT WAS A LONELY EXISTENCE...
"MY TIME MOSTLY SPENT WATCHING WHAT WAS OCCURRING IN THE WORLD AROUND ME.
"ESPECIALLY SONJA.
"SHE WAS THE ONE PERSON I ADMIRED IN THIS BACKWARDS WORLD. HER STRENGTH, HER COURAGE..."

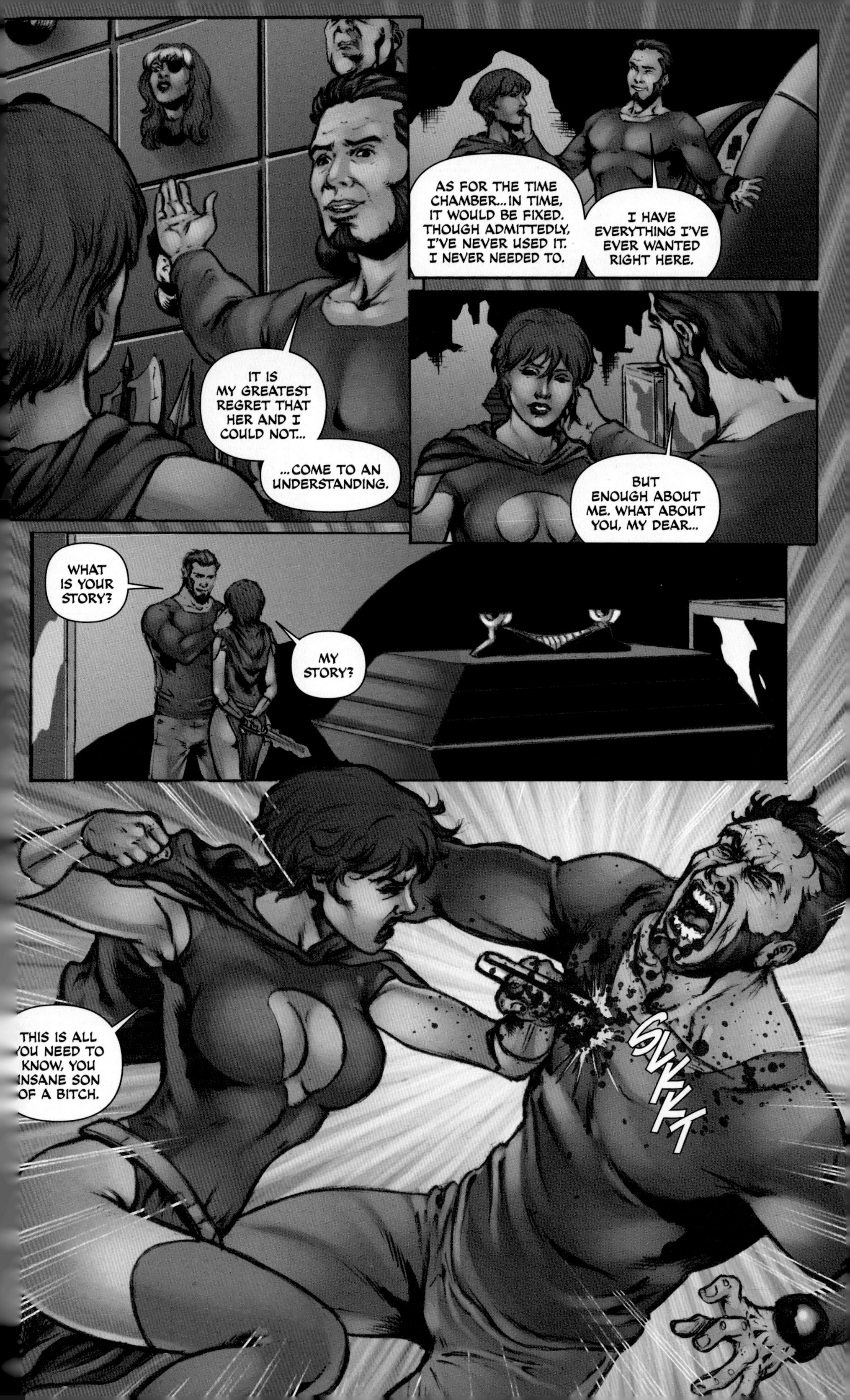
IT IS MY GREATEST REGRET THAT HER AND I COULD NOT...
...COME TO AN UNDERSTANDING.
AS FOR THE TIME CHAMBER...IN TIME, IT WOULD BE FIXED. THOUGH ADMITTEDLY, I'VE NEVER USED IT. I NEVER NEEDED TO.
I HAVE EVERYTHING I'VE EVER WANTED RIGHT HERE.
BUT ENOUGH ABOUT ME. WHAT ABOUT YOU, MY DEAR...
WHAT IS YOUR STORY?
MY STORY?
THIS IS ALL YOU NEED TO KNOW, YOU INSANE SON OF A BITCH.
SLKKT

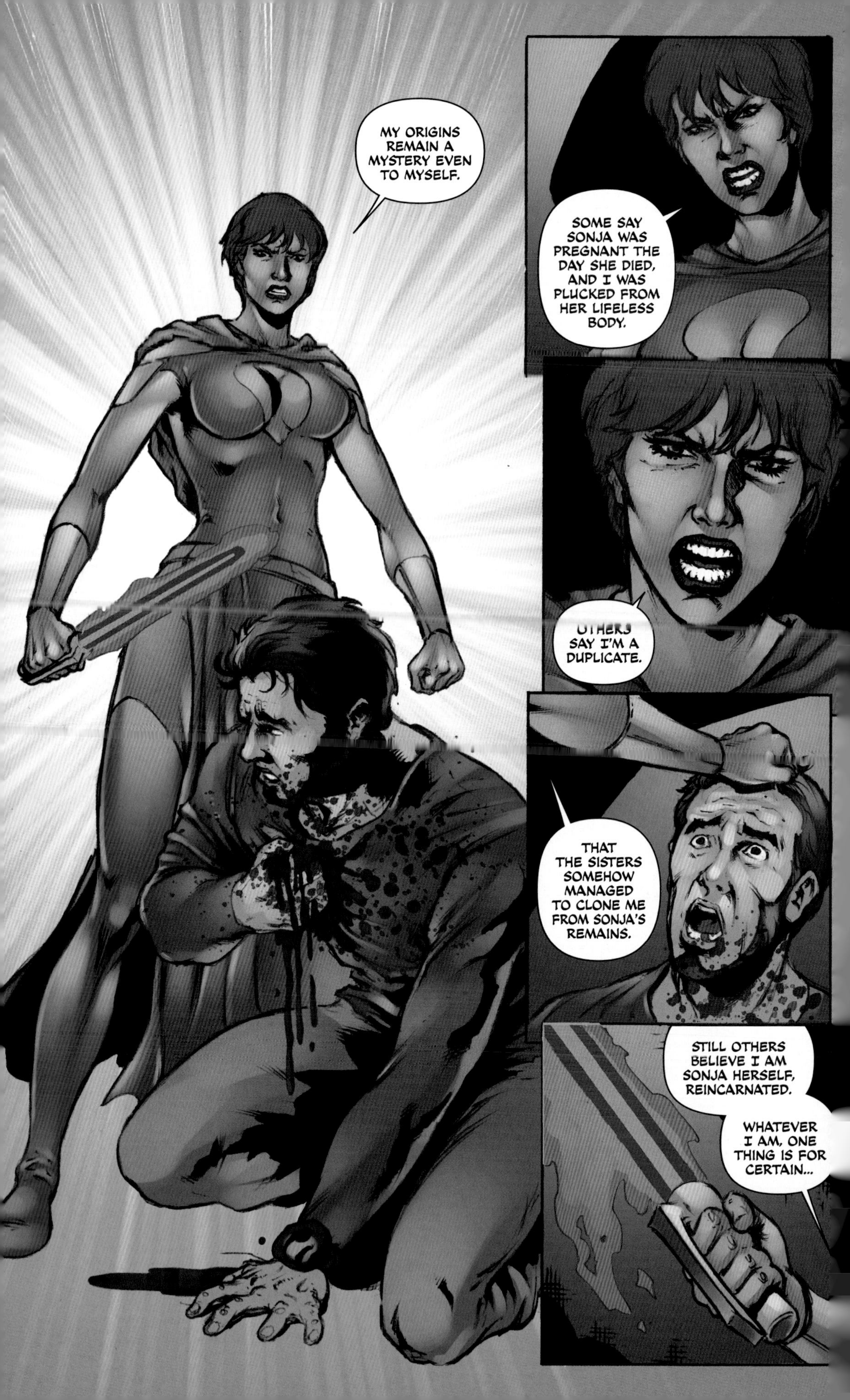
MY ORIGINS REMAIN A MYSTERY EVEN TO MYSELF.
SOME SAY SONJA WAS PREGNANT THE DAY SHE DIED, AND I WAS PLUCKED FROM HER LIFELESS BODY.
OTHERS SAY I'M A DUPLICATE.
THAT THE SISTERS SOMEHOW MANAGED TO CLONE ME FROM SONJA'S REMAINS.
STILL OTHERS BELIEVE I AM SONJA HERSELF, REINCARNATED.
WHATEVER I AM, ONE THING IS FOR CERTAIN...

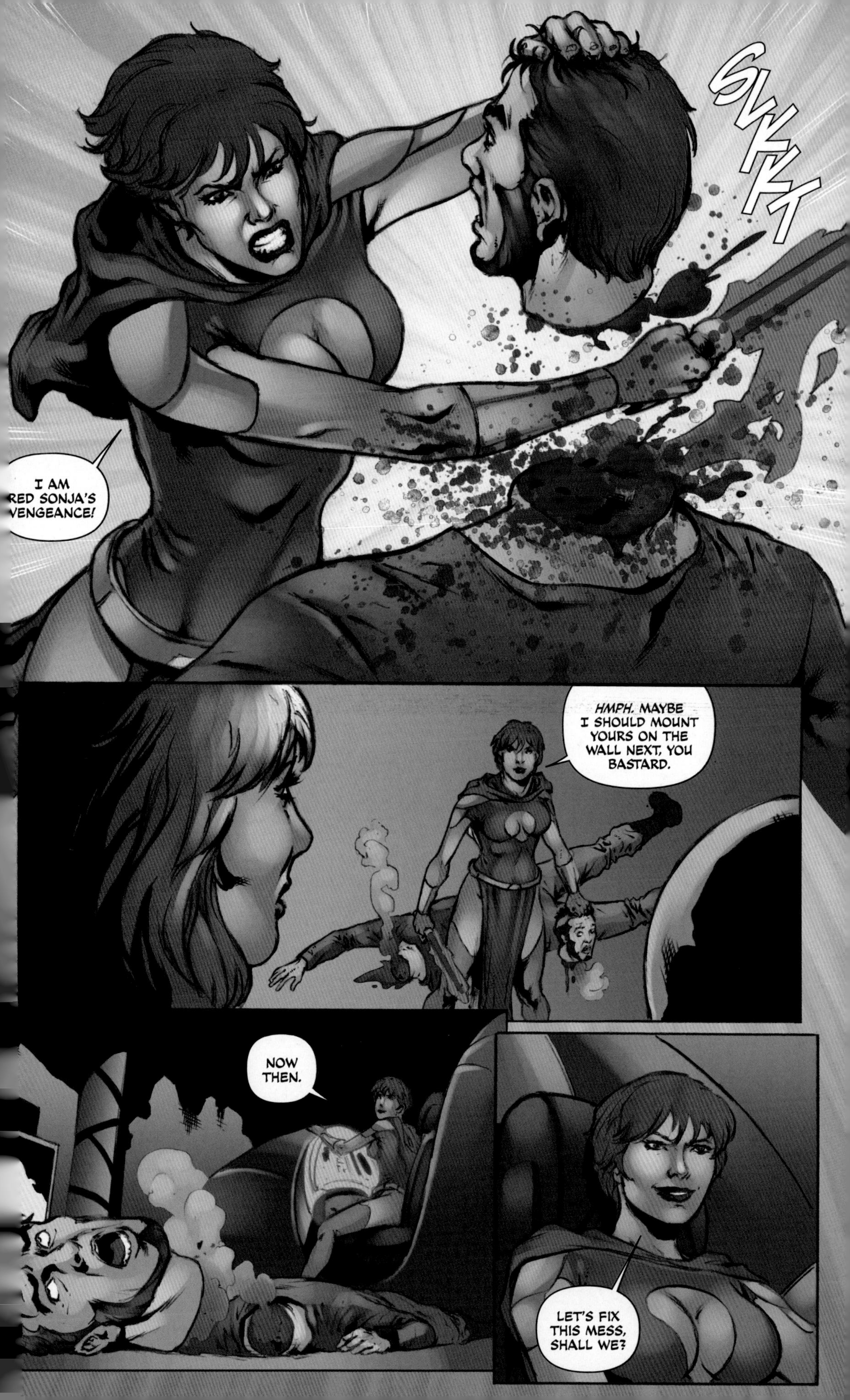
SVKKT
I AM RED SONJA'S VENGEANCE!
HMPH. MAYBE I SHOULD MOUNT YOURS ON THE WALL NEXT, YOU BASTARD.
NOW THEN.
LET'S FIX THIS MESS, SHALL WE?

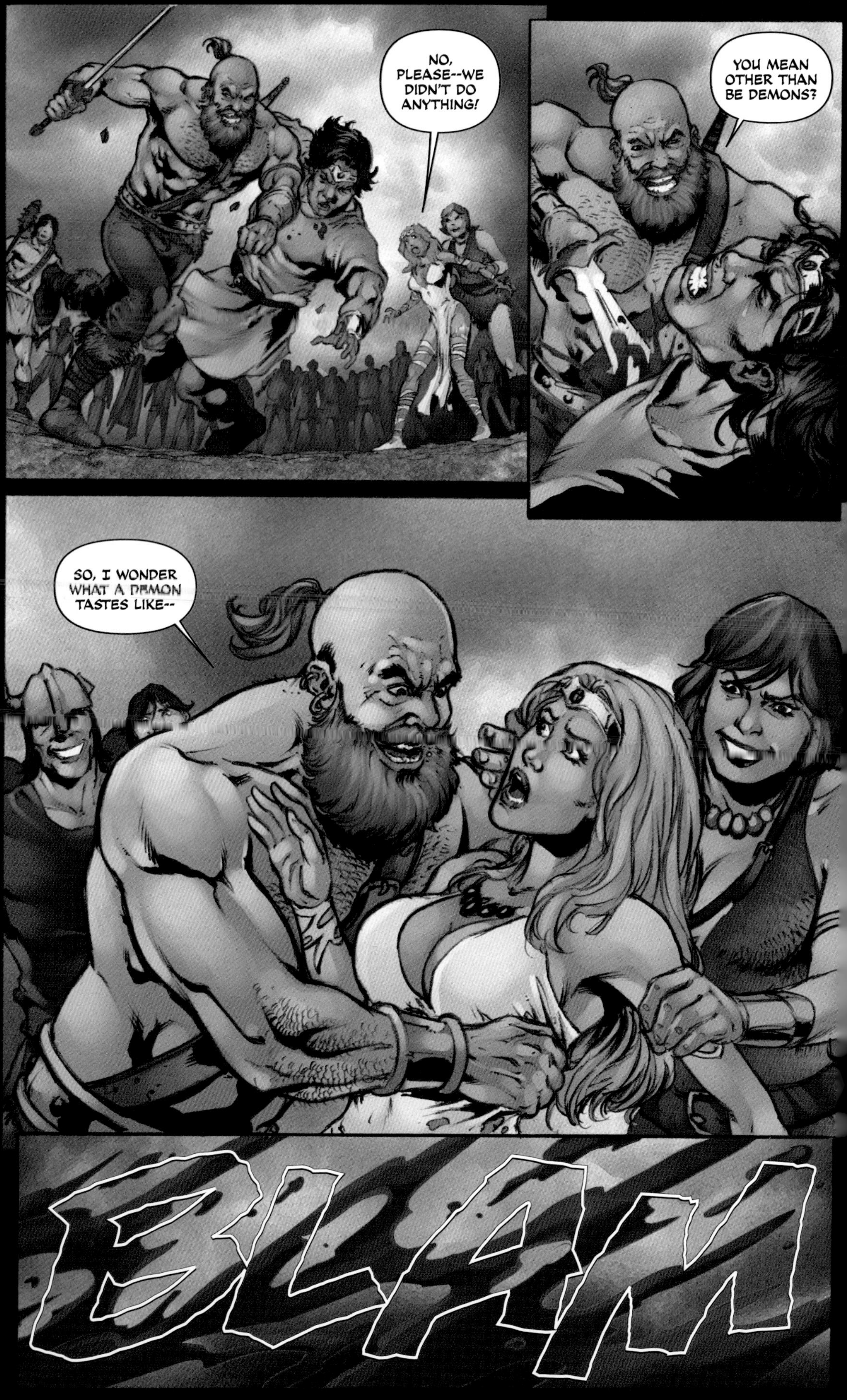
NO, PLEASE--WE DIDN'T DO ANYTHING!
YOU MEAN OTHER THAN BE DEMONS?
SO, I WONDER WHAT A DEMON TASTES LIKE--
BLAM

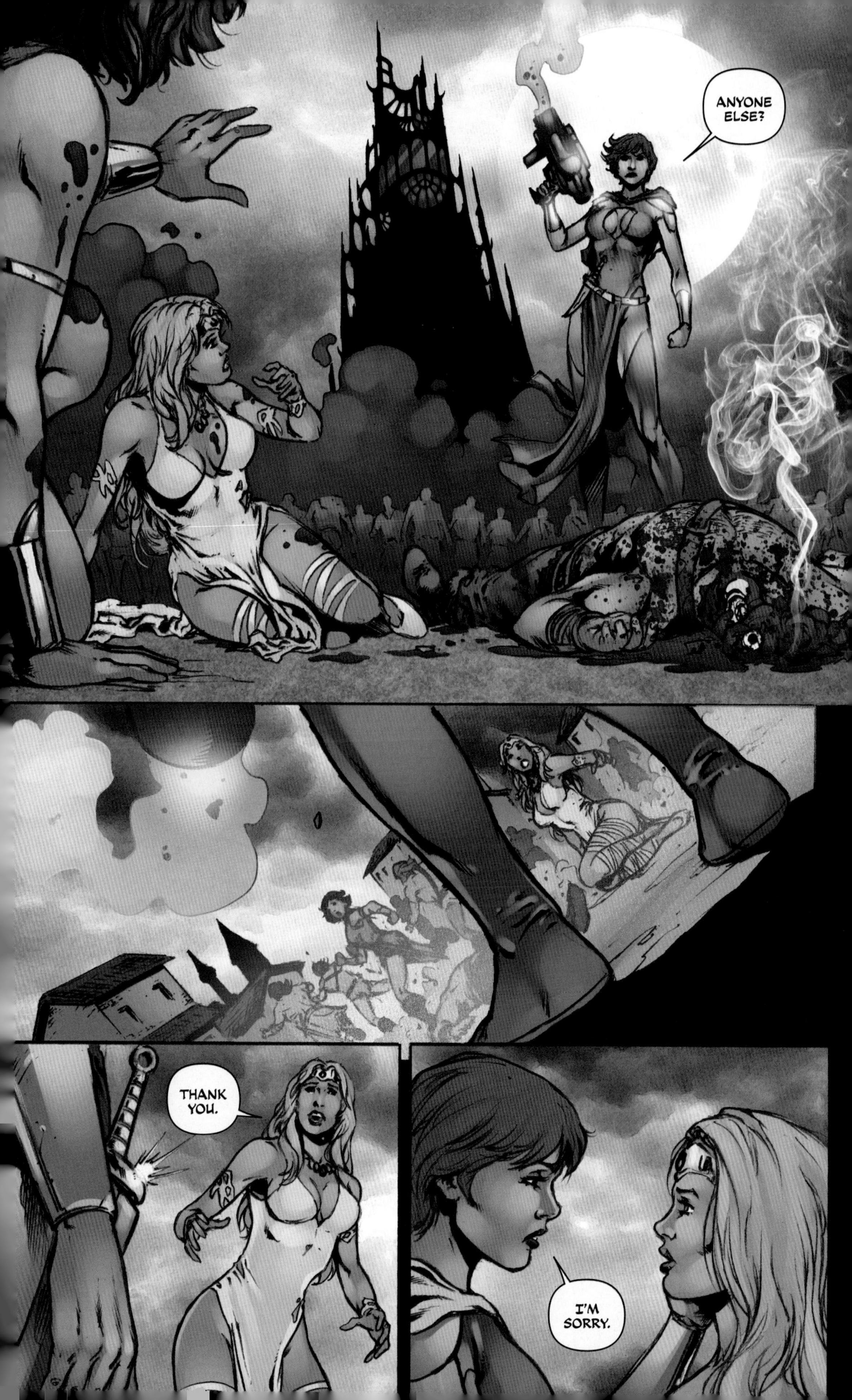
ANYONE ELSE?
THANK YOU.
I'M SORRY.

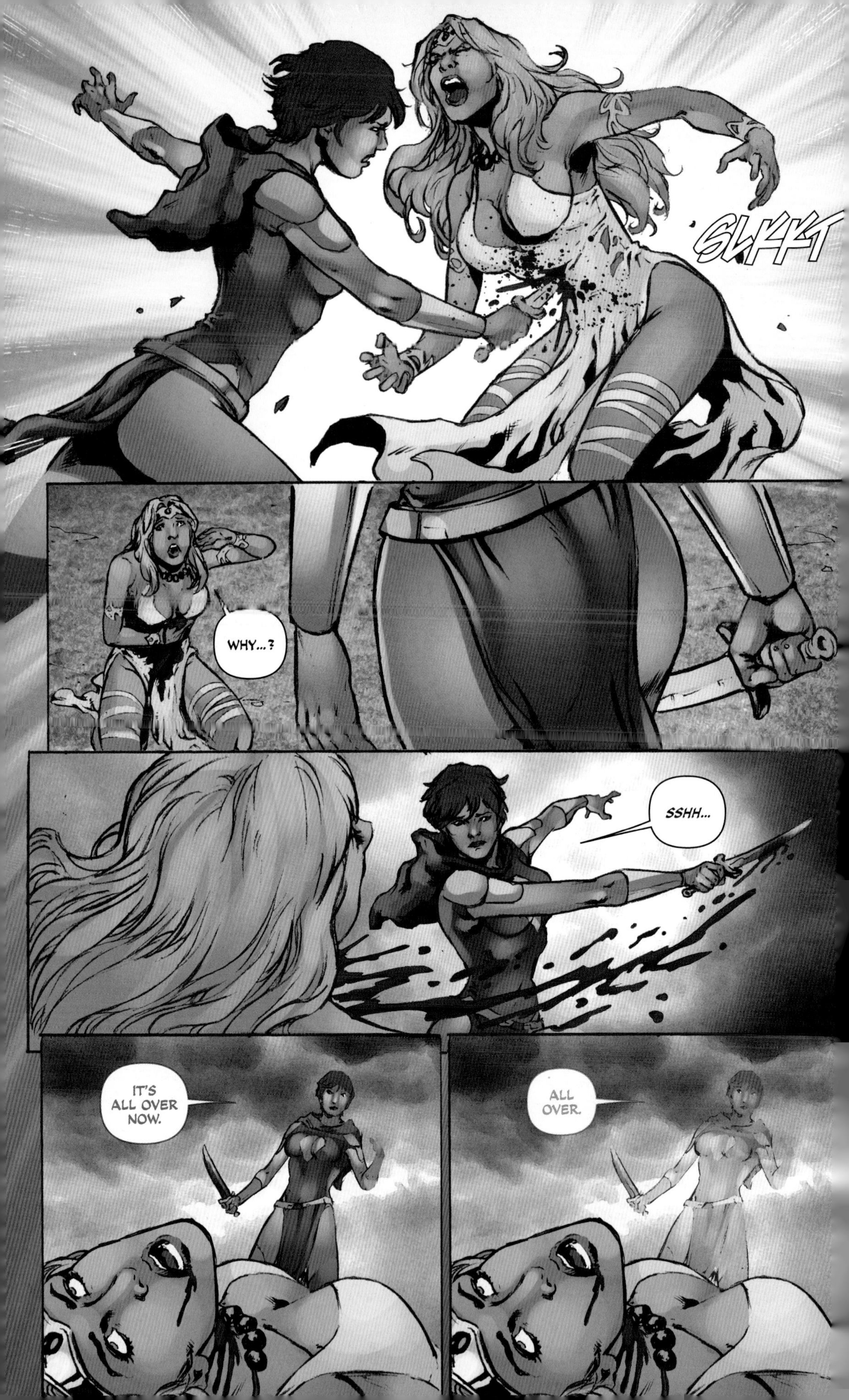
SLKKT
WHY...?
SSHH...
IT'S ALL OVER NOW.
ALL OVER.

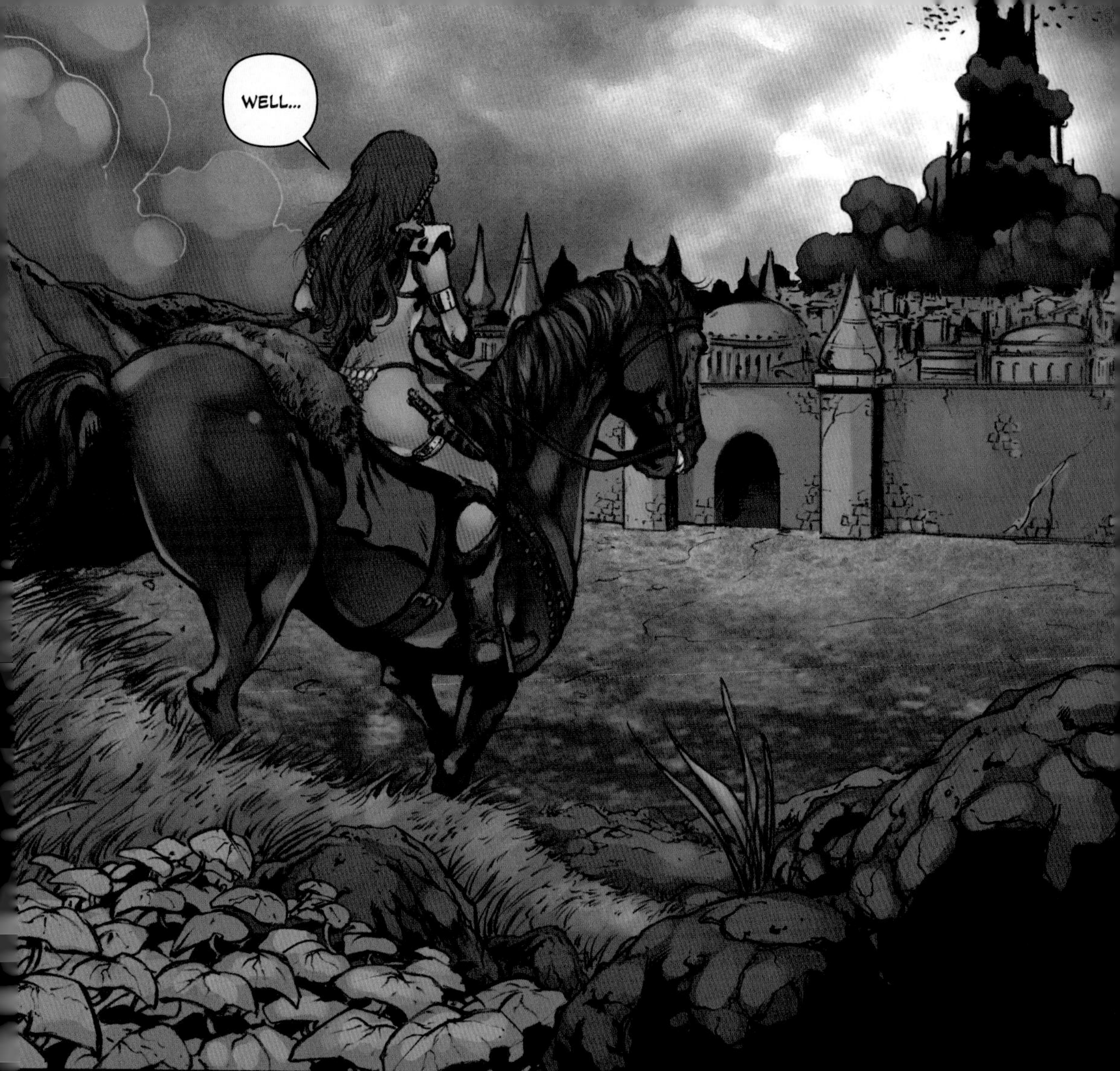
WELL...

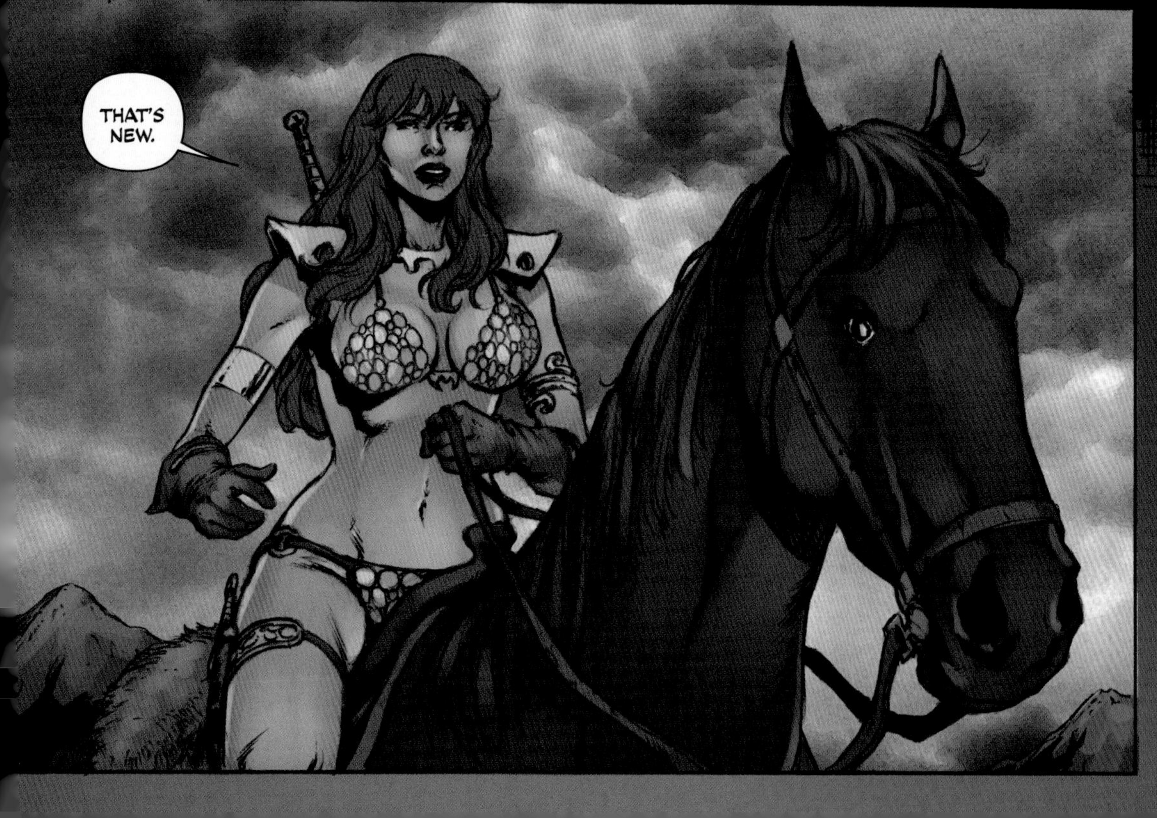
THAT'S NEW.

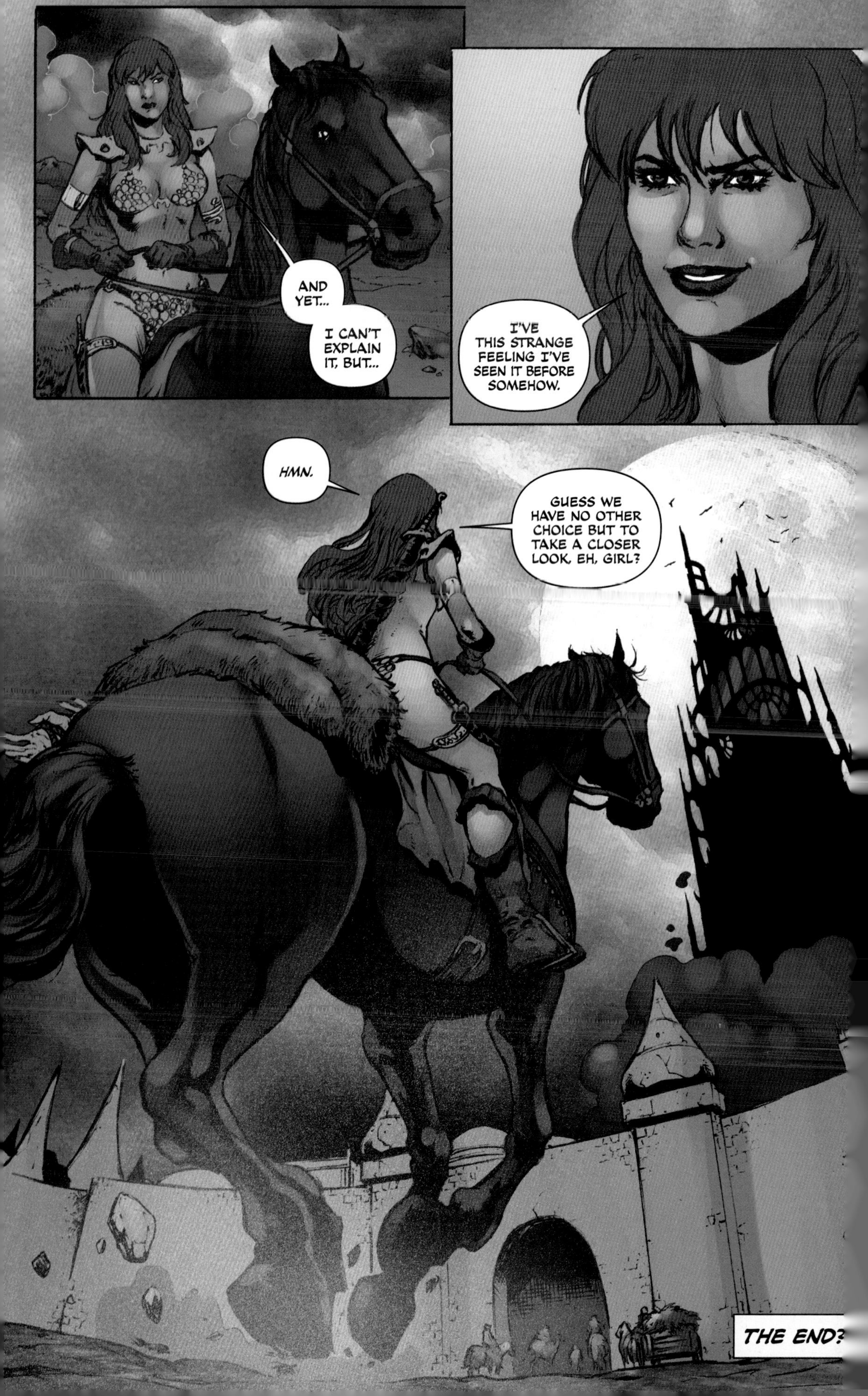
AND YET...
I CAN'T EXPLAIN IT, BUT...
I'VE THIS STRANGE FEELING I'VE SEEN IT BEFORE SOMEHOW.
HMN.
GUESS WE HAVE NO OTHER CHOICE BUT TO TAKE A CLOSER LOOK, EH, GIRL?
THE END?

Interview with the Author: Frank Tieri

Dynamite has been very tight-lipped about the events of THE BLACK TOWER. What can you tell us about this top-secret comic project, without giving away its spoilers?

I think I can safely say the Black Tower—and what lies inside it-- is a threat unlike any other RED SONA has ever faced before. And I'm not just saying that. Trust me.

When Nick Barrucci approached me to do something for Dynamite there was really always just one character that I was interested in… Sonja. And I knew I wanted to do something different with her. Something special. And we believe that when fans read our series, when they find out what's in the Black Tower, they'll agree.

Oh… and by the way? What IS actually in the Tower… it kills her. Yes, you heard right. We actually kill Red Sonja in this series. Just thought I should mention that.

Um… so is that giving away a spoiler?

Red Sonja is a character with over 40 years of comic book history. What are your thoughts on contributing to the legacy of such a powerful and enduring character?

I've always been a sucker for sword and sorcery stuff but especially CONAN THE BARBARIAN. I used to gobble those books up as a kid—but to me, his adventures with Sonja were the best. Those were the ones you waited for. Sonja was really the only character in that world that could go toe to toe with Conan, who was arguably his equal. And I always thought that was bad ass. So to answer your question, to be able to contribute to the Sonja legacy, to hopefully leave my mark with her… it's an honor. You know, I've been pretty fortunate to work with some of the industry's biggest icons over my career like WOLVERINE, BATMAN, IRON MAN, PUNISHER, etc…and to add Sonja to that list is a really cool feather to be able to put in my cap.

What do you personally enjoy most about the Red Sonja character?

I like that she's this total bad ass—that she's the WOLVERINE of her world, that she's The Man With No Name-- but she's also a woman. Because you don't often see that. You don't often see it being a woman that walks into a bar and everybody tenses up, everybody pees their pants. And in Sonja's case, if you underestimate her, if you just dismiss her as "just a woman"—she's going to make you pay for it. And then some.

You've worked on a ton of high-profile projects for Marvel and DC Comics. When you look at your body of comics work, are there particular themes that you see revisited in RED SONJA: THE BLACK TOWER?

If you look at my career, I've always tended to be involved with darker characters—"tough guy" heroes like Wolverine, Deadpool and the Punisher or even out and out villains. Those are the characters I like to explore and have fun with. So Sonja definitely fits the bill here.

How I treat her in this series… it's like this force of nature. She rolls into town and the scumbag portion of the population gets significantly reduced by the time she leaves. So in that way, she's really not all that different than some of the characters I've written in the past at all.

Why will RED SONJA fans new and old love THE BLACK TOWER?

Simply put, THE BLACK TOWER is an old fashioned mystery—and as we all know, everybody loves a mystery. In fact, I'd say at times, this story is more in line with a Stephen King story than your typical Sonja tale.

The Tower just appears out of nowhere one day—nobody knows why, nobody knows how. People are scared, they're confused—and they start turning on each other. That's when Sonja enters the picture. And what she finds is mystery that will span decades, that will pit people against each other, that will cost many lives… including her own.

Now… I think that's a story fans will want to see how it turns out, don't you?

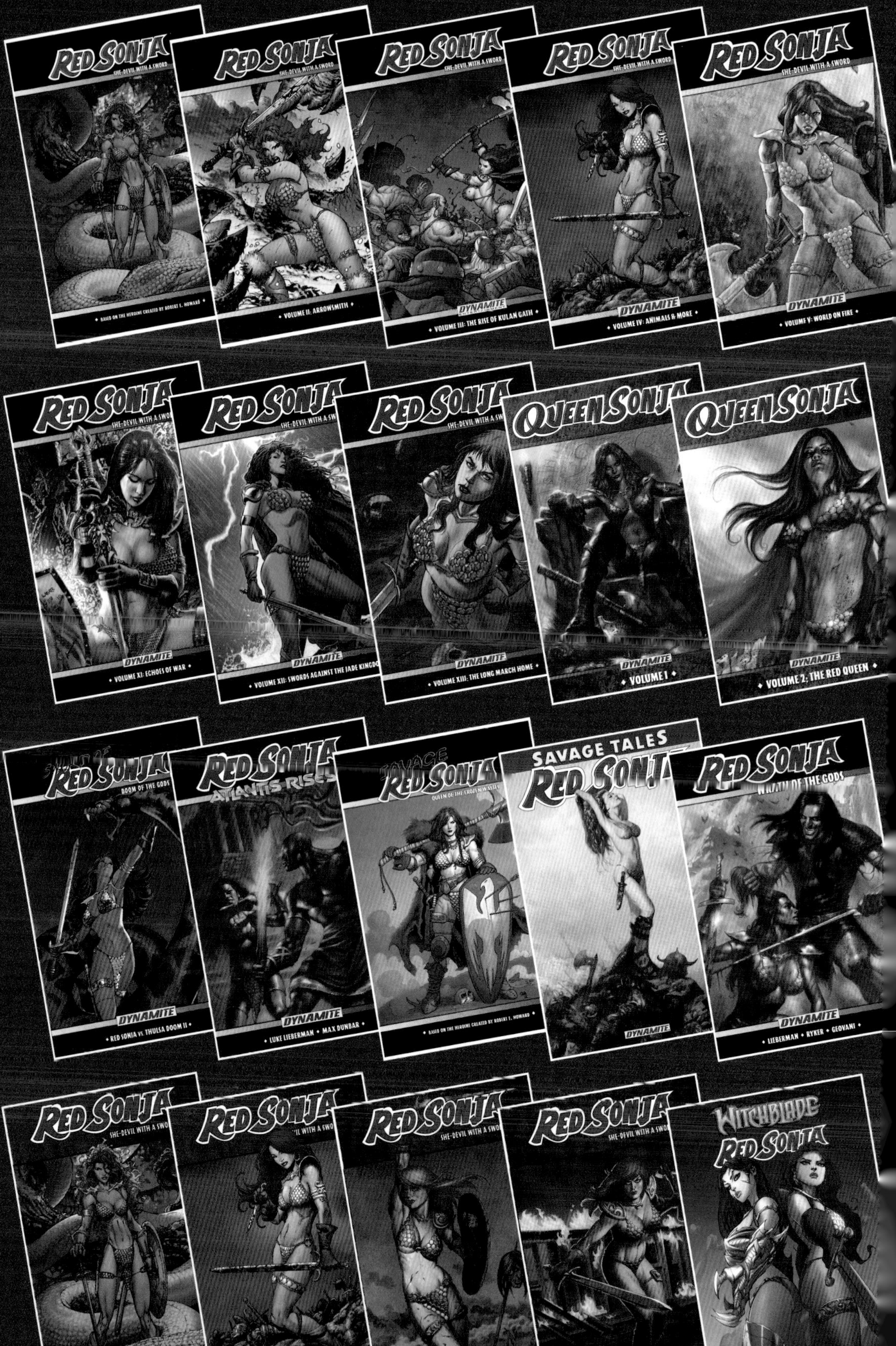
RED SONJA
SHE-DEVIL WITH A SWORD
BASED ON THE HEROINE CREATED BY ROBERT E. HOWARD
VOLUME II: ARROWSMITH
VOLUME III: THE RISE OF KULAN GATH
DYNAMITE
VOLUME IV: ANIMALS & MORE
VOLUME V: WORLD ON FIRE
VOLUME XI: ECHOES OF WAR
VOLUME XII: SWORDS AGAINST THE JADE KINGDO
VOLUME XIII: THE LONG MARCH HOME
QUEEN SONJA
VOLUME 1
VOLUME 2: THE RED QUEEN
DOOM OF THE GODS
RED SONJA vs. THULSA DOOM II
ATLANTIS RISES
LUKE LIEBERMAN • MAX DUNBAR
QUEEN OF THE FROZEN WASTES
SAVAGE TALES
WRATH OF THE GODS
LIEBERMAN • RYKER • GEOVANI
OMNIBUS VOLUME 1
OMNIBUS VOLUME 2
OMNIBUS VOLUME 3
OMNIBUS VOLUME 4
WITCHBLADE
RED SONJA

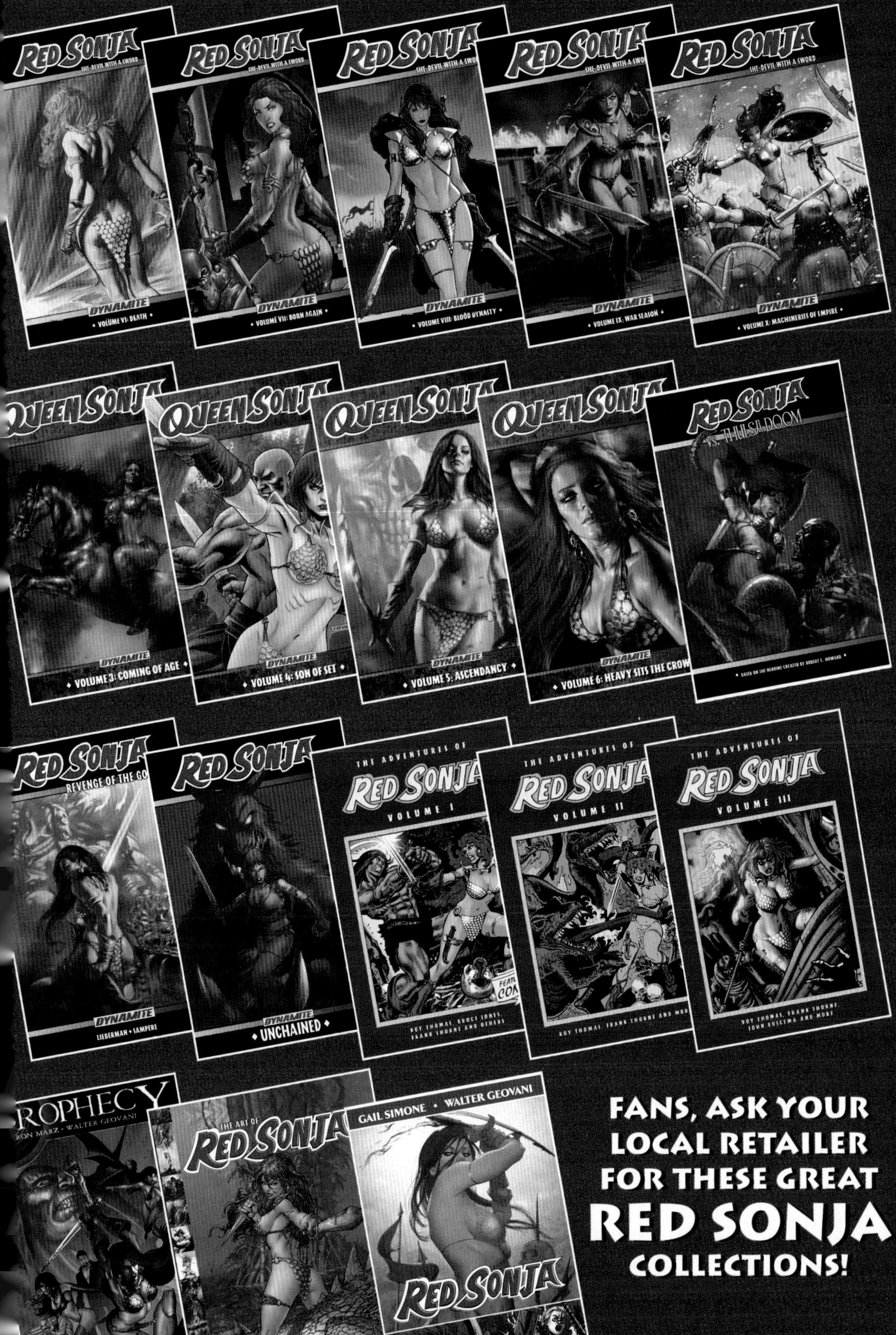
RED SONJA
SHE-DEVIL WITH A SWORD
DYNAMITE
VOLUME VI: DEATH
VOLUME VII: BORN AGAIN
VOLUME VIII: BLOOD DYNASTY
VOLUME IX: WAR SEASON
VOLUME X: MACHINERIES OF EMPIRE
QUEEN SONJA
VOLUME 3: COMING OF AGE
VOLUME 4: SON OF SET
VOLUME 5: ASCENDANCY
VOLUME 6: HEAVY SITS THE CROW
RED SONJA VS. THULSA DOOM
RED SONJA
LIEBERMAN • SAMPERE
UNCHAINED
THE ADVENTURES OF RED SONJA
VOLUME I
ROY THOMAS, BRUCE JONES, FRANK THORNE AND OTHERS
VOLUME II
ROY THOMAS, FRANK THORNE AND MORE
VOLUME III
ROY THOMAS, FRANK THORNE, JOHN BUSCEMA AND MORE
THE ART OF RED SONJA
GAIL SIMONE • WALTER GEOVANI
RED SONJA

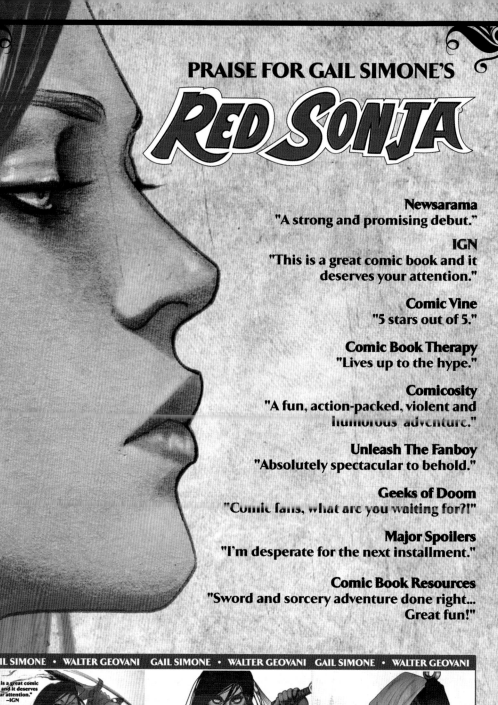

PRAISE FOR GAIL SIMONE'S

RED SONJA

Newsarama
"A strong and promising debut."

IGN
"This is a great comic book and it deserves your attention."

Comic Vine
"5 stars out of 5."

Comic Book Therapy
"Lives up to the hype."

Comicosity
"A fun, action-packed, violent and humorous adventure."

Unleash The Fanboy
"Absolutely spectacular to behold."

Geeks of Doom
"Comic fans, what are you waiting for?!"

Major Spoilers
"I'm desperate for the next installment."

Comic Book Resources
"Sword and sorcery adventure done right... Great fun!"